MW01635824

BROKEN BUTTERFLY

WANDA GRAY

One Printers Way
Altona, MB R0G 0B0
Canada

www.friesenpress.com

First Edition — 2025

Illustrated by Erin Gray

Front Cover Design Credit: Artist: pixiecoldart.
Image of original supplied by Michelle M. Warner.

Author photo credit: Cindy Middleton Photography

A portion of the proceeds from sales of this book will be donated to The Healing Hearts program, a free grief support service offered and facilitated by *Moms Stop The Harm* volunteers. Additional donations will be made to organisations sponsoring fund raising events where the author has been requested to speak on book-related subject matter.

ISBN
978-1-03-833205-9 (Hardcover)
978-1-03-833204-2 (Paperback)
978-1-03-833206-6 (eBook)

1. *FAMILY & RELATIONSHIPS, DEATH, GRIEF, BEREAVEMENT*

Distributed to the trade by The Ingram Book Company

BROKEN BUTTERFLY

REVIEWS

This book is an amazing story of undying love; of despicable, merciless cruelty; and of the complexities of addiction, which is shown to be far more than a simple brain disease caused by using addictive drugs. The author writes both in her own voice as a bereaved mother, and in the voice of her deceased daughter. Both voices speak of the dynamics of a mother-daughter relationship full both of steadfast love and of painful ambivalence and misunderstanding.

—Bruce K. Alexander, Professor of Psychology Emeritus, author of *The Globalization of Addiction: A Study in Poverty of the Spirit*, Oxford University Press, 2008.

On reading *Broken Butterfly*, I was indeed filled with a sense of understanding that the author's account of the tragic months in this story was replete with Aristotle's ingredients of a writer of tragedy. There are large measures of pity and fear for the reader, and even more so for the characters who bore the burden of carrying the action which ended in such a disastrous manner. The author's writing showed clearly the deep love between mother and daughter. One is left to be consoled by the thought that there is life after death and yet, as written in the old Latin tag, "Dum spiro, spero" [While I breathe, I hope]. Indeterminate origin, (Wikipedia, 2025).

—D.S. Myall, English Teacher Extraordinaire

Broken Butterfly is a powerful and emotionally charged memoir that offers a compelling and insightful look into the lives of Wanda and Erin Gray. It is a testament to the strength of the human spirit and the enduring power of love, even in the face of overwhelming adversity. This book is a must-read for anyone seeking to understand the complexities of addiction, mental health, and the unbreakable bond between a mother and daughter.

—Jacqueline R. Armour, Ph.D.

Erin adored animals—and then she met a beast. How can anyone understand a mother's pain from watching helplessly as a monster slowly pulls the wings from a butterfly? In this chilling recollection of anguish and perseverance, Wanda Gray recounts what she felt—and with excerpts of Erin's diary—how her daughter felt, at the hands of a brute. *Broken Butterfly* is both a heartbreaking story of a mother's unstoppable love for her daughter and the gripping tale of two tremendously courageous women.

—Mark Brennae, Capital Daily

A story of captivity, trauma, addiction, loss, grief, and the chaotic and unbreakable bond of a mother and daughter.

This is a memoir and cautionary tale by two writers: one in the physical realm, one in the spirit realm. They are connected by a spiritual thread of love only a mother and daughter can share. And a set of wind chimes. Together they tell their story.

AUTHOR'S NOTE

This is a true story. Even though the events are factual, I've changed a few names in the story to protect other victims, my daughter's memory, and, in some elements, the privacy of our family. I use the initials of the offender, not to protect his identity, but so I don't have to keep saying his name. His name still hurts my heart. I have not forgiven him and, at this point in time, I cannot see that happening. It's true that many major crime offenders crave attention. The sick minds of sociopaths and psychopaths thrive on others knowing and being horrified by their dark deeds. I don't intend for my daughter's memory in this book to be a tool for him to achieve infamy and notoriety.

This story is interspersed with Erin's poetry, some of which she wrote while in captivity and during recovery. What she could not say out loud, or could not describe, came out in her writing. It can paint a horrible picture, but it's the truth. Her drawings and paintings are also interspersed to help tell the story and show her true nature—the child-like essence of fun-loving, funny Erin. These works of art are the other side of the darkness she experienced, illustrations of her love of life.

TABLE OF CONTENTS

PREFACE

This dual re-telling of our story has been my most challenging, rewarding, painful, and joyful undertaking, but learning to live with the deepest grief has been made easier through this work of love. It took three years to write and as re-traumatizing as it often was during the process, it has been cathartic.

I am writing about the greatest young woman who ever lived. She never spoke a harsh word to anyone, even in the worst of times when her body and mind were at war. This is my daughter Erin. You might say to yourself, "Yeah, so what? All mothers think their kids are the greatest people ever born." And you'd be right. For the most part. Let's face it, not all mothers are the greatest. And not all kids are the greatest, perhaps because of that.

But in this case, I'm going to tell you the story about someone who truly reached that point of greatness in her short life. She showed incredible bravery that resulted in the capture and conviction of a monster, saving countless women from his torture and terror. But it cost her life. This is her story, and this is my story. She has been my cheerleader from beyond the veil and I have been her voice. Together we constructed the memories and events with two goals: to preserve the memory of Erin and to together tell her story with the hope that it reaches even just one person with the impact to save a life. Partway through this story, you will read where Erin set the goal for herself to travel and speak to other young girls and women and make them aware of potentially life-altering or life-ending situations. As she is no longer able to do this herself, I am attempting to finish this love-filled task for her. But not without her help.

My hand has been guided by Erin's from conception to completion, and I have cherished every moment spent with her—even the moments that have left me crying, exhausted, and back in those first full stages of raw grief. To bring her story to life, I've had to navigate those rough waters over and over again, but I've also shed tears of joy on this journey through memories. Erin's pure light has brought me peace and joy, and I hope I've shared those in a positive way with you as well.

Erin's story is sometimes written from her perspective and sometimes from mine, so that I could provide a clear, first-person recounting of events from both sides. I'm hoping this will be helpful for other families currently experiencing or who have experienced similarly traumatic events. If you feel, by the time you come to the end of this story, that it is a script for a tragic movie, you aren't alone. Sometimes, terrible things happen to good people and you hear yourself saying, "I can't imagine…"

Please know that trauma can affect the sharpness of good and bad memories. I have done my best to be accurate with details and I'll tell you shortly how Erin and I worked together on these memories. But there are times I've had to expand the story to fit what I remember best. Some may call it "creative licence." I call it hauling a heavy emotional load uphill and using words as tools to help me carry it. I hope the reader can see this story as not only a way for a mother to honor her daughter's short life and share her incredible artistic talent but as a teaching tool for other young women and girls to raise awareness and use their intuition to recognize when they are being lured by a predator.

And then there is the *big* topic of substance use and addiction. A major component of this story is drug addiction, the trauma that precedes it, and the chaos that follows it, never letting go. Perhaps you are reading this and something triggers you into a better state of understanding and awareness of people you love who are suffering. Hopefully you will reach out to them with love, compassion, and a newfound willingness to help rather than floundering in hopelessness and ignorance—like I did at the beginning. I hope the lessons are helpful in becoming aware and listening to your own keen intuition. Your life and the life of a loved one may depend on it.

To help clarify how Erin helped me write this book, I'll tell you about the wind chimes. A dear friend had given me a beautiful set of "grieving chimes" when Erin died. I felt a sense of peace when I first heard their melodious ring. But they were incredibly beautiful, and I didn't want them to be outside. I set them up where I could see them and give them a light little push when I needed to hear the angelic chiming. When I first started writing our story, I got stuck on some of the events. I'd write, rewrite, and repeat, struggling with the timeline and the details. The first time this happened, and I was getting frustrated and a bit teary, I was suddenly startled by the wind chime, only two or three feet from my writing desk as it gently sounded a very soft note. Just one soft ding. And I knew I'd reached accuracy in the story details. Erin was reaching out from the spirit world. That soft melodic ring was her way of giving me the spiritual thumbs up. "Yup, Mom. That's correct." There was no plausible reason for what else could have made that wind chime ring. It didn't happen every time I got stuck, but often enough to give me confidence to forge ahead. What a gift that little push from her was. It was later that I learned just how much incredible energy it takes for loved ones to reach out to us from the spirit world.

A WORD OF CAUTION

This may be a "hard read," with roller coaster moments ranging from gut-wrenching horror (graphic-content warning for a range of violent actions and sexual traumas) to warm feelings of amusement and joy. The explicit horror comes from court records and also from my heartbreaking conversations with Erin when she was freed. My goal is to present my daughter's life in such a way that, despite her painful experiences in this dimension, you are left with the joy of this young woman's impact on others and her beautiful artistic legacy. Out of tragedy can come knowledge, love, acceptance, and peace. Please sit back, read, and learn about Erin. I think you'll come to love her almost as much as we do. Always and forever, our angel in heaven.

AN ANGEL OPENED HER EYES,
AND A BUTTERFLY TOOK WING.

PROLOGUE: ERIN

I'm not sure what day it is. I only know it's night by the lack of light coming in past the edges of the heavy curtains that are always closed. I'm curled on the floor next to Harley, my German shepherd. He never leaves me and becomes extremely frantic, scratching, whining, and howling at the door when he's shut out during those times I try not to remember. This time I'm alone, no unknown faces leering greedily over me before my mind shuts down for the duration. I'm so grateful to have this time alone with Harley, just me and him being quiet with each other and understanding how badly we both need the silence.

I'm twenty years old and I know I've missed another birthday with my family. I feel my dry, pale skin stretching tightly against my bones, so unhealthy and unlike my past self. My hair is thin with bald spots randomly coming through. I miss my naturally blonde hair. He made me dye it black to make me more exotic for his "clientele." I knew I was being sex trafficked, but I don't know when I lost the fight to survive because the drugs have stolen any sense of time. Clarity is a thing of the past.

I know I'm not the first young woman he's taken as he often calls me by the wrong name and there's evidence of others being in this house. He once said I was his "favorite" and I wondered how he could say that when I last looked in the mirror. That was weeks ago. I no longer look in the mirror. I think I will start to scream and never stop.

As I lie on the floor with Harley, I wonder how long my jailor has been gone this time. He trusts me now, enough to not lock me in like he used to, but it's my fear of what might happen that keeps me from running away down the street. Fear for my dog's life, my life, and now his latest threat that he will burn my mother's house while she sleeps. I know he'll do it if I escape. He is the devil.

It's been months now, I think. Every day is a fog of strangers coming and going, of intense physical pain, and of the disgust and hate I feel for him and the drugs he forces into me. Those drugs have now become my friend because they protect me from the pain. And from this horror that has become my life … and from the fear when I hear his truck pull into the driveway.

THE DEVIL CAME IN A DIESEL by Erin Gray

I can still remember wanting to die
dissolve, disappear
cease to exist
I can still remember crawling
on the devil's cold tile
Dirty bathroom floor
Staring at someone I don't know
In a broken mirror

I can still remember the colors
Of 4 a.m. turning into 5 a.m., eyes wide
Heart pounding out of my chest
As the birds began to softly wake
In the safe serenity of outside

Crawling up the wall
I reach for my Harley Davidson Zippo tin
And numbed myself again
With the devil's white powder

Packing, rushing, pushing myself for days
I laid on oil spots on the garage floor
Crying wailing, sobbing

Into my shepherd's soft, sun-smelling fur
As the devil was fishing
Tormented, tortured, totally lifeless
I laid there until the stars came out
And for once I was unafraid
To hear the diesel coming

Seven grams go by that day
The day I couldn't die
I was so sure of horses and fire
blackmail, bones and broken dreams

I wasn't taught in Sunday School
The devil came in a diesel

PART ONE:
INTRODUCING ERIN

CHAPTER ONE:
MOM

BABY TO BUTTERFLY (1987)

Every mother who has given birth to a daughter believes she has produced an angel. That's just the way it is—the love is deep, intense, and perhaps so profound because daughters are a projection of their mother. As soon as we hear "it's a girl," a plan begins to unfold. She will be everything we wanted to be. She will change the world and not make the same mistakes we did. The mantras are endless and the excitement is barely contained at the chance to remake ourselves in this little pink bundle of beauty and innocence. Innocence.

The doctor delivering our angel was wearing a tux under his scrubs. Odd that I should remember that so clearly and he explained a little later that he had been accepting some kind of "Doctor of the Year" award when the hospital called. Due to complications with the birth of our son two years earlier, his attendance was imperative. Our baby girl came fast and furious into the world—maybe because she was two weeks overdue or maybe it had to do with the inducement that was supposed to take several hours but only took one. Whatever the reason behind her swift arrival, it was clear she was in a hurry to get her life started. Labor was intense and quick, and then our beautiful girl was placed on my chest. We looked into ice-blue eyes so much like her father's. We gently touched the silky blonde tufts of hair so much like mine. We pulled her blanket back and counted her fingers and toes—yup, right number. But not everything was textbook. Due to a broken, badly healed tailbone from a fall off a horse when I was fourteen, our little girl had navigated a very bumpy road on her way through the birth canal.

We were devastated to see that each of her vertebrae was an angry purple from bumping against my misshapen bone. I hoped this was not the beginning of a painful life for her. The bruising faded eventually while her beauty, warm heart, and loving personality grew.

Here she was: Erin, an Irish name meaning peace, and in the beginning her life was filled with nothing but peace, happiness, and love.

CHAPTER TWO:
ERIN AND MOM

SAVING THE CRITTERS (1991)

ERIN

There was a birthday party for me on the deck at our farm and I was so excited to open my presents. I was four years old today and the whole family was there. Mom, Dad, my brother Ryan, Grandma, Grandpa, aunts, uncles, and all of my cousins. Mom said I had ten cousins, and I felt so lucky because it was so much fun! Everyone was busy getting their food and I was excited to see the special cake Mom always made for our birthdays. But there was somewhere else I needed to be first.

The barn was my favorite place in the world. It was full of cats! The horses were out in the field and the doors to all the stalls were open so I could crawl under the hay mangers and look for new kittens. As I listened to the telltale sound of tiny meows, I noticed one of the moms, Calico Cat, sitting by one of the stall doors with her paw planted firmly on something bigger than a mouse. I recognized the light, yellowy-brown color of a gopher. And it was such a tiny one—she had caught a baby. No! I had to save it! The big cats were hunters, and I didn't like them to catch the gophers because they were really cute and deserved to live. I had saved lots of gophers and, even though I wasn't supposed to, I made it up to the cats by dumping more kibble into their pans in the barn. I guess I thought that if I kept the big cats full, they'd stop hunting.

This little gopher was so small, and I could see it was still alive, panting and terrified of course. I chased the mom cat away and bent over the little guy (or maybe it was a girl?) to pick it up. I had thoughts of showing off my saved critter to the family. I don't even know how it happened because the movement was so quick, and I didn't feel any pain at first. I could see tiny teeth firmly embedded in the finger of my right hand—my pointer finger, Mom called it. Oh, it hurt! Tears welled up in my eyes. I wasn't going to cry, though. The gopher was only really scared, and I still wanted to save it. But it had to let go of my finger!

MOM

Where is Erin? I was just about to send her brother to look for her in the barn (where she could always be found) when I saw her climbing the three steps up to the deck. She had her hand behind her back, she was so pale, and I could see the tears in those big beautiful blue eyes.

"What's wrong, birthday girl?" her dad asked.

I was horrified when she pulled her arm from around her back and we could all see a half-grown gopher hanging from her hand. Blood was seeping down her arm and dripping onto the deck floor.

"It's not his fault" she cried. "He's scared but I saved him from Calico Cat!"

Grandpa came to the rescue as we gently pried open the gopher's mouth and it reluctantly released its hold on Erin's tiny finger.

"I'll take him back out to the field, sweetie, where he can find his mom again," said my dad as he gave me a meaningful look over the top of her head.

Bandages, antibiotic ointment, a kiss, and a big hug for the birthday girl. Then a loud rendition of the "Happy Birthday" song and all was forgotten.

I think about that day a lot—especially over the past few years. That was my girl. All love, forgiveness, patience, and determination. A natural-born rescuer of anyone or anything that needed help. I didn't know then that those qualities would result in so much vulnerability. But, if I had paid attention, maybe I could have prepared her for life better.

My mother was a fiercely devoted grandma to her grandkids, and she was known for her keen intuition and wise advice. When Erin was three years old, I went to pick her and her brother up from Grandma's house where they were staying while I ran some errands. Mom met me at the door, quite agitated, and said she'd had a premonition about Erin. She told me that I had to keep an extra close eye on her because Erin had something special about her. Mom had received a strong feeling that someone would try to take her—someone foreign—not from here.

Everyone knew Mom was very intuitive from past experiences, but I chose to brush her warning off that day. It was ominous but I didn't have a clue what she meant, and I wasn't going to worry about something that couldn't possibly happen in our safe little world. But perhaps I was operating from a sense of disbelief, or maybe even outright denial. Her words haunt me to this day.

CHAPTER THREE: MOM

DOLPHIN DAYS AND HORSES (1992)

Where could my two kids have gotten their love of water from? Personally, I love being *on* the water but have never liked being *under* the water and these two lively kids seemed to prefer the opposite! I stood nervously at the side of the swimming pool in our small town on the prairies. It was the most popular place to be during hot summer months and the squeals and splashes of excited, happy kids echoed off the tall white water tower a few yards away from the chain-link fencing.

Erin, who had just turned five years old, took her turn to jump into the water at the shallow end.

"Watch this," her swimming teacher said in my ear.

Erin immediately dove down to the bottom and as I kept my eyes peeled on her, I was flabbergasted, the only word to describe the mixed feelings of amazement and terror I experienced watching her. She never came off the bottom or up for air once, swimming extraordinarily fast from the shallow to deep end, doing an expert kick off the wall and swimming all the way back. It seemed seconds had passed when she came up where I was standing a few feet from the shallow end. Her blonde head surfaced, her big blue eyes were slightly red from the chlorine in the water, and she had a huge grin on her face.

"Hi Mom!" she shouted at the top of her lungs, then she did a little back flip and swam back to the edge of the shallow end, popping up onto the deck like a cork out of a bottle. She was surrounded by the happy little voices and wrapped in the skinny little arms of her pool friends as they giggled on their way to the bleachers.

I turned my attention to her swimming teacher, who was grinning from ear to ear. "She's been practising this all week so she could show you what she's learned," she said proudly. "Honestly, she seemed to take to the water so naturally and she's been the easiest of all the kids to learn the ropes. Although her attention could use a little work as she's always chatting or offering to help other kids learn. She's doing my job!" she laughed good naturedly.

Erin's love for swimming was only superseded by her love for all creatures—particularly horses. Living on a farm and trying to diversify our income let me indulge my own passion for all things equine. We had a few mares and had acquired a breeding stud. He had a long registered name, but we called him Dude, his nickname. He was like a giant pitbull in build but had the personality of Bambi—if he took a liking to you. He was not fond of men, only a select one or two could get near him, and I suspected it was because he had been abused before coming to us. I thought he was perfect because he let me handle him with a halter, brush, and patience. Most importantly, he was kind to the female horses (some studs can be far too aggressive).

Under no circumstances was anyone allowed in his paddock without me or a male friend of mine who had been instrumental in bringing Dude to our farm. Dude trusted my friend and me, but both of us were schooled enough in horse rearing to always keep a watchful eye on where he was and what he was doing. He was a powerhouse on very quick hooves!

As time went by and Dude became a fixture on the farm, I started allowing him to hang out in different grazing areas. One of those places was a fenced area right beside our huge vegetable garden. And this is where Erin comes into the picture. She was an outdoorsy, horsey, tomboy-type of little girl, despite the pink clothes and glorious blonde hair. If I was going to the garden, she was right beside me, digging in the dirt and singing softly to the plants, birds, cats, dogs, and whatever else was in the vicinity. One day, I heard a vehicle pull in the driveway, so with strict instructions to Erin to stay put in the garden, I went to see who was popping in. If memory serves me correctly, it was a close neighbor and we only chatted a few minutes when I said I needed to get back to the garden before Erin picked all the raspberries, green or red!

There was a path through the woods that led to the garden behind the house and as I came through the opening, I didn't spot Erin right away. But I did look to my left over the fence dividing the garden and the pasture to admire, once again, my faithful horse Dude, who I'd left contentedly munching on the grass. Can a heart instantly stop beating? Just for a second or two? My world went still when I saw that Erin had crawled under the fence and was standing right under Dude's nose, holding up a dandelion as an offering to the horse she had only been allowed to worship from a place of safety on the other side. I could tell at once from Dude's relaxed musculature that he was completely at ease with her. He was gently taking the dandelion from her outstretched hand, and I could hear her softly chatting to him without a care, worry, or fear in the world. It was only sheer luck that I had my camera sitting on the top of a post that day. I think I had planned on snapping a picture of the sunset, the colors of the prairie sky just too beautiful to remember. I slowly retrieved it from the post and climbed through the fence to move around to the other side of Erin and Dude, holding my breath but feeling much less trepidation that anything awful was going to happen. Neither of them paid any attention to me as they were completely engrossed in each other's company. I'm so grateful to have a photo of that beautiful moment, capturing the soul-sharing experience between my daughter and the horse.

Following that day, Erin constantly asked if she could go visit Dude and take him a treat. I never did let her go by herself, as the unpredictable can always happen, but witnessing their exchange in the garden as the sun was beginning to set is forever a soul-stirring memory for me. Now, all these years later, I know that my girl started life with trust, love, and an open heart. She had no guile and animals can sense that quality more than humans.

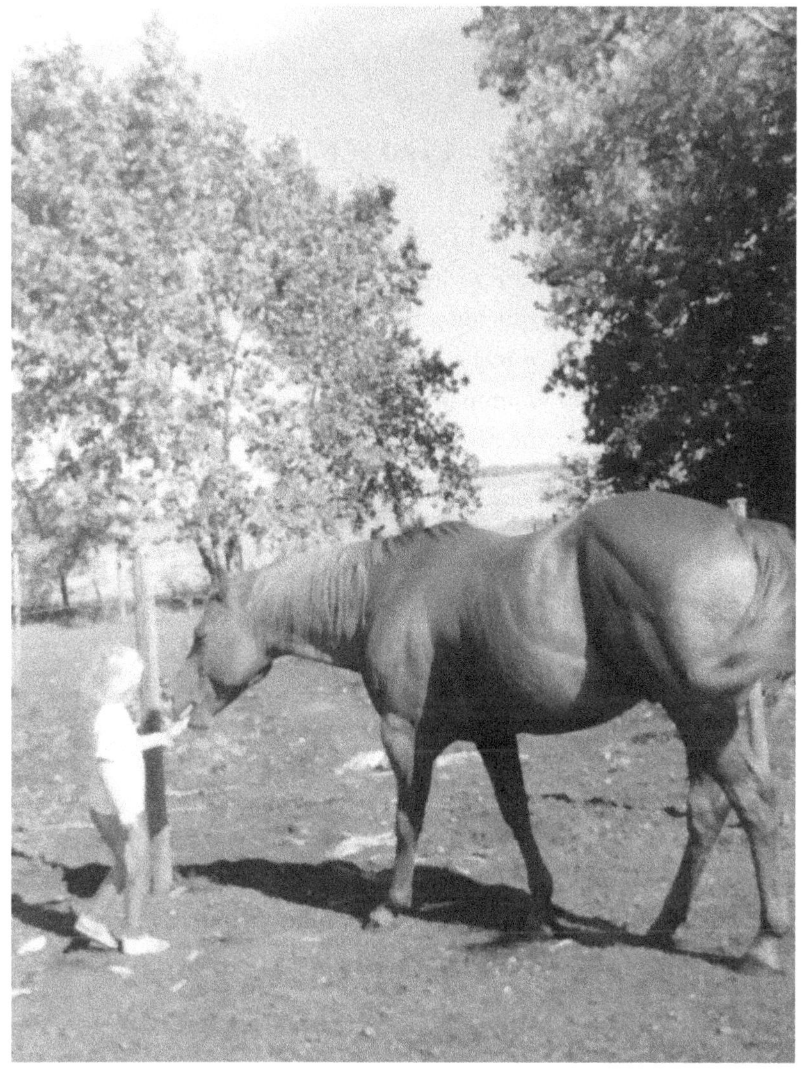

CHAPTER FOUR:
MOM

UNKNOWN (1993)

The years were flying by and six-year-old Erin was now the center of attention at school and a favorite of her teachers. We were so blessed. Two amazing children, our son a bit shy and his sister always finishing his sentences for him. But she worshiped him, following him around and trying to get him to jump off the hay bales with her or hang out in the barn, still her favorite place to spend time. Life excited her, everything was an adventure, and she lit up a room with no expectations of anything but love in return—easy to do, especially when she was such a joyful child to have around!

It was about this time that we discovered she had a talent for art and poetry. Her outdoors exploring had slowed down a bit and we would find her at the kitchen table or in her room, happily drawing pictures of animals and people and using her extensive vocabulary to piece together simple bits of prose. She spoke early, walked early, and read early. I used to think it was because we spent a lot of time reading to our kids, right from birth. We are a family of readers and writers, and it seemed natural that sitting with our children and a giant kid's book was the best time of the day. It took twenty years for me to understand that it was trauma that triggered this creativity in our little girl.

CHAPTER FIVE:
ERIN

MY SECRET (1996)

I'm about to turn nine years old. I have lots of school friends and every birthday has been a pretty big deal around our house. I'm feeling the weight of my secret though. Sometimes I feel like I'm choking because I'm trying so hard to keep it in. I get called Chatty Cathy lots because I like to talk, but the happiness I used to feel is somewhere else now. I wish I could get it back. The past three years have been different for me, and I can't wait to grow up, because then maybe I will feel better about what makes me sad. I feel icky and maybe I did something bad, but I don't understand what happened to me.

I want to tell Mom, but I'm scared to. She and Dad have been really quiet lately, and sometimes I hear them arguing outside where they think we can't hear them. I don't want to make things worse. Dad has been so grumpy and sad. Mom is always stressed about work, and I don't even know what's happening, but I think I have to stay quiet. I can't say anything. I don't understand why our family isn't happy anymore; something is going on and maybe it's my fault. Mom and Dad don't have a clue, and I certainly can't talk to my brother about it because I think he is hurting too. He used to be my best friend but now everything feels so wrong.

I'm someone else when I'm drawing. Someone who doesn't feel like they are choking. I'm into anime now, and there is always a boy and a girl who have names that I've made up but sometimes they don't have faces. I don't know why I can't seem to imagine what they look like.

CHAPTER SIX: MOM

THE DIVORCE (1997)

If we knew then what we know now. We've all said this at some point in our lives, and on more than one occasion. Divorce is torture. The couple tries to keep the pain and anger out of their children's lives, but despite their best efforts the stress seeps into all family members' hearts and souls and jades them. "They'll be okay, kids adjust," I was told by friends who had experienced this same life-altering, painful process. I accepted that, thinking it must be true. This is denial. But this is also just the tip of the iceberg.

When Erin was fourteen, she began writing poetry earnestly and, at the same time, became more interested in boys. I was expecting this, the normal progression of being a teenage girl, but I had also hoped horses and poetry would kind of keep a lid on the frenetic energy that comes with awakening this stage of life.

We had recently moved halfway across the country to Vancouver Island for my work, and I had been worried about the kids settling in to a strange place. Erin had a natural ability to attract friends as she was so outgoing and seemed to have such confidence, which I later understood to be more of a well-practiced coverup for her internal loneliness. My son, Ryan, who was two years older and much more reserved, struggled more openly to fit into the new environment.

Erin met her first boyfriend when she joined the local air cadet unit in the community and I watched her like a hawk, as mothers do when their daughters start down the confusing path of dating. Sadly, it did not last, he broke her heart, and I recall glibly telling her that he wasn't worthy of her anyway and she shouldn't take it too seriously. I didn't know at that time, but Erin wasn't able to process these natural life occurrences as "normal" and instead withdrew into her creative world. I should have seen the signs that something more painful was lurking beneath the surface of my golden-haired girl. She was losing her way early on and I thought it was just teenage growing pains. Finding this poem in a school notebook, written when she was just barely fifteen years old, told me that her pain was not typical. Something dark had moved into her psyche, more deeply than teenage, young-love-lost angst.

SWEET LIAR by Erin Gray

The hurt… the heartache, do I not deserve better
than the painful days which we've had together?
Your betrayal and deceit just ripped my heart in two.
How could you do this to me, when I gave all my love to you?
Was she worth it? Was she worth all this pain you've caused me?
And you made it worse with your honey-coated words which at first caused me not to see.
But I saw through your facade, eventually, your barrier of lies.
And with each little lie adding to your long list, the more of you I despised.
Your excuses burned deep and to know you could have told me the truth, but deliberately lied, and for what reason?
To spare me the pain of knowing you were going behind my back?
Because with each little lie you told, you pricked my heart like the fiercest attack.
Slowly and thoroughly chipping away at my emotional state.
For when the truth finally did come,
it came far too late.
But eventually I will overcome this empty bitterness you've left.
And I will conquer it little by little as I move with each step.
And I will remember you, sweet liar.
Because like you, I will never become.
With your sugar sweet promises which will never be kept.
And I regret every tear, every moment I've wept.
Love and happiness again I will find.
And I will put you out of my life, my heart, and my mind.

CHAPTER SEVEN: ERIN AND MOM

THE PAGEANT (2001)

ERIN

I don't know what really made me do it. Recognition? Defiance? A desire to belong in the echelons of the beautiful people? I saw an ad for applications for the Miss Teen Canada competition and I found myself filling in the blanks, with not much hope of actually being short-listed, never mind being selected. I did not have the confidence for that, but I did have the determination to at least try. There was no local live competition in my area, so I submitted my photo, an essay, and completed the super-long application form. The decision would be based on the best mailed-in submission.

I didn't expect a response, except for perhaps a rejection letter, but to my incredible surprise, my application was accepted! I would be representing the entire island where I lived. My elation quickly turned to concern. How was I going to tell Mom? She had no idea I had even applied. Mom had bought a hair salon from a friend who was having some personal struggles, and she was juggling working and running the shop. I had been helping by manning the front desk and I think that's where I got my fascination with beauty. Hair, makeup, and clothes became a much higher priority when I was surrounded by it. I hoped what I was learning in the salon would give me a leg up in the competition.

Mom was dead set against beauty pageants. She felt they were "fluff" and exploited young women by promising fame and fortune. And they were money-makers for the organizers. Anxious, I approached her.

"Mom don't be mad and hear me out. I'm really lucky, I've been selected to represent the Miss Teen Canada pageant for the whole island!"

The look on her face was incredulous. "How in the world did that happen?" she asked. "I didn't know about any contest, and you know I would have said no way are you entering it."

I was defiant and, I must admit, manipulative. Mom had a soft heart, and she had been worrying about what was going on with me, especially after my first-ever-boyfriend breakup. The mood changed and very quickly we were in the throes of planning for our trip out east to the pageant and all the prep work that had to be done before we left. It was expensive and I know she made sacrifices to ensure we could go. Off we went to what turned out to be a very life-altering experience for me. And for her, I think.

MOM

Once I got used to the idea of my daughter subjecting herself to the pomp and circumstance of a beauty pageant (that was a hard one for me to accept), I decided to try and make it a positive, fun trip and, hopefully, a good experience as well. I knew most of these girls were polished pageant contenders with experience and likely a bit of attitude as well. Erin was still our gorgeous but naive little girl and I was worried they would chew her up and spit her out. And myself? I was *not* going to be one of those hovering, demanding mothers, exuding a narcissistic attitude of "no one matters but *my* girl!"

The city of Toronto was—to us—big, noisy, dirty, and not what we were used to. The hotel where the pageant was held was in the city center and I felt Erin got swallowed up by the organizers and all the events leading up to the big night. There was so much going on: photos, pre-competitions, costuming, sponsored lunches. Every morning, I turned her over to the care of the chaperones and organizers and I could see her discomfort when I looked longingly back at her. She didn't feel like she belonged but she seemed determined to try her best.

Finally, the night of the pageant arrived, and I was overwhelmed with pride at how she conducted herself. She was exhausted but beautiful, determined but out of her element. And gracious above reproach.

To me, she shone like the brightest star there. She achieved a "most congenial" award, which I thought was well deserved. Despite the haughtiness of the more experienced girls, Erin held her own, was kind to everyone, and kept herself in check—even when they made snide remarks about the country-bumpkin girl.

Once we arrived back home, Erin was subdued and confessed the pageant was not what she had expected. Being raised on a farm and never exposed to that kind of life, she felt belittled and concluded that pageants might just be for the "snooty" girls. We laughed together and life wiggled back into the groove of working, schooling, friends… and then the dark secret she'd been carrying started to manifest itself into something I just could not manage or understand.

CHAPTER EIGHT: MOM AND ERIN

EGGS CAN BREAK WINDOWS, AND FRIENDSHIPS (2001)

MOM

It was just past dark, and I was walking out of my home office at the front of the house on the second floor, heading for the kitchen to start making supper. A loud bang on the glass patio door sent me scurrying and covering my head with my arms. It sounded like the sharp retort of a rifle. Another loud bang startled me but this time it was coming from the living room windows on the other side of the wall. It was followed by several other loud bangs, ending with a crash. I heard glass shattering. I ran into the living room, sure we were under attack by who-knows-what, and saw broken eggs running slowly down the panes of glass, pieces of shell sliding and sticking on the mullions in the windows. The furthermost window was broken in the center, a direct hit from a well-aimed egg and the contents were lying on the carpet amid the pieces of glass.

Both Erin and Ryan had come running from their bedrooms and I shouted at them, "Get back, there might be more!" The three of us cowered on the floor and once I figured there were no more eggs, a quiet rage took over me. I ran down the stairs, threw open the front door, and dashed into the front yard to look for the perpetrators. Of course, they were gone by then, but I heard high-pitched laughter from down the street. I chased the noise and saw three young girls, running down a side street and out of sight. I wasn't going to be able to catch them.

As I walked back to the front of the house, my rage turned to tears at the sight of my brand-new Mustang convertible, also pelted with broken eggs—yolks, whites, and shells—still dripping down the vinyl top, side, and hood of the car I had dreamed about having for decades. And worked so hard for. I looked up at the windows of the house, devastated to see the mess and the curtain blowing inwards from the broken one. Such a quiet neighborhood, great people, no crime—what in the world did I do to deserve this? No other house had been hit, so I deemed it a targeted hit.

Ryan and Erin stood in the light of the open front door and Erin was so angry, tears of rage coursing down her face as she shouted, "I know who it was, Mom!"

ERIN

I stuck my nose in where I shouldn't have, I guess. I went to school with a very mixed group of kids from all walks of life and I was in that place where teenage girls' whole purpose is to fit in and be a part of the popular crowd. And I'd made it. Even though I was uncomfortable with some of the girls' behavior, I felt like I was a part of the group and overlooked some of what I saw and heard. That particular day, the dynamics of the group were challenged and then changed forever. A boy—who admittedly was way behind in his maturity, along with the other boys—was trailing ahead of me and three of my "cool friends." We were quickly catching up to him and two of the girls began taunting him with names, putting him down for his small size and an unfortunate collection of pre-adolescent pimples covering most of his face. He looked terrified. Girls mature much more quickly than boys and the fact that he was two years younger than we were didn't help his cause. It got ugly very fast. I found myself standing between my friends and the boy, not sure what to do or how far to go without jeopardizing my place in the hierarchy.

I turned around to ask him what his name was and was immediately ashamed to see huge tears running down his cheeks, and that's when something snapped in me. I don't claim to be a martyr, but I didn't have it in me to see him so broken by these mean girls who, in retrospect,

I now recognize as being the worst type of bully. I stood my ground between the predators and their prey and told them to stop. Big mistake. One of the girls, who towered a good three inches above my height, placed her huge hands on my shoulders and shoved me backwards into the boy. He and I both toppled to the sidewalk. His backpack saved his head from smacking the concrete but he still got the wind knocked out of him from my weight coming down on top of him. I scrambled to my feet, not noticing the scrapes on my hands and tiny stones embedded in my palms from bracing against impact with the ground. The boy was loudly crying and I was overcome with rage at the injustice and unfairness of everything tumbling around me. I later recalled that I shoved my taller friend back, then spun around to face my other two friends with all kinds of cursing and yelling coming from my mouth, which was so out of character for me. I had to ask myself, *Who was that?*

I knew at that moment I was no longer a part of the popular girls' group, and it took many years for me to acknowledge that even though it came at a cost, I did what I should have.

MOM

When Erin told me the story of what happened that day, I had to assume the egg-throwers were the same girls. They were getting their revenge by punishing her and making a statement that she was no longer accepted. Her self-esteem, confidence, and need to belong were more damaged than my car and our windows and I didn't know where to turn. I finally decided to call the local police station and tell them what happened, asking what I should do because I doubted insurance would cover an egg bombardment and a single parent's budget doesn't usually include a budget for something like this.

Fortunately, it was a slow night in the middle of the week and a very helpful officer (who eventually became a very good friend to us) came over to take a report and get some photos of the damage. When we gave the names of the suspected girls to the police, it didn't take long for them to admit their culpability the police visited them the next afternoon.

The three girls and their parents met with me and Erin in a process called restorative justice, in which the families work together with the investigating police officer acting as mediator. Costs were recouped, apologies were made, hands were shaken, and we moved on. But there was no repairing the broken friendships. Eventually a level of peace was grudgingly offered at school but Erin was never allowed back in with the cool kids. I worried about her, but she seemed to be managing okay. Still, I could sense her loneliness, not knowing at the time that this had already started many years before the egg incident.

CHAPTER NINE: MOM

EARLY SIGNS (2001)

It had been a difficult year. I knew we were likely in for a rough ride as teenage girls are tortured in their own ways with raging hormones, shifting allegiances during the transition from middle to high school, and general angst at not knowing who they are. I'd been a teenage girl myself and I remember the upheavals of friends and school, but that was at a much simpler time. In 2001, the world was changing so radically and life for young people was proving to be a roller coaster of hope, despair, and everything in between.

Erin's early teen years had already been overly stimulating with the teen pageant, her societal outcasting from school friends after the egging incident, and the negative timing of my work. I had been working as a home-construction lender with a prominent bank and the pressure was on as we were in a building boom with extremely high sales targets. I was working seven days a week, and even with a home office I was on the road a lot. My two teenagers were on their own while I was away, and when I was home my phone was constantly ringing as I put out logistical and administrative fires. I was distracted, trying to be a single parent and present at the same time. I did not see my girl starting to slip. By the time I felt the distance between us growing, I felt it was time to take the first vacation I had in three years and book us a trip to Hawaii. By then Erin was almost fifteen and Ryan was seventeen, and I wondered if they would even want to hang out with their mom for a couple of weeks. But the tropical lure of Hawaii was the ticket and all three of us looked forward to the trip.

Our last vacation together had been to Disneyland in California, and we had taken in every sight we could see and every adventure we could find. The kids were only nine and eleven at the time and Erin had cried several times during that trip, claiming her legs and knees hurt. She had also broken out in watery blisters on her legs, so I took her to our family doctor when we got back home. All the tests were inconclusive. "Probably just growing pains coupled with a bad reaction to a food," said the doctor. Looking back, external symptoms can be indicative of internal pain—and hindsight is definitely 20/20.

So, I was looking forward to this Hawaiian trip for the three of us. I had been doing well with my job and making more money than I ever thought possible. We had everything we needed and more. I felt it was the best trip we'd ever been on as we soaked up the sun in Maui, snorkeled, and swam in the warm waters of Molokini. Erin and I even shared a tandem parasailing adventure. She and I were the same that way, seeking fun and adventure, and always pushing toward that element of excitement and danger. I remember looking over at her in the sailing harness and feeling a sense of overwhelming love, pride, and satisfaction that all was right with the world. But all was not right with her world. I didn't notice or perhaps out of fear I unconsciously chose to overlook why she seemed to be awfully quiet. That shadowy time from years earlier was still haunting her.

CHAPTER TEN: ERIN AND MOM

MONEY DOESN'T SOLVE EVERYTHING (2001)

ERIN

Life was getting to be too hard; I wasn't sure how much more I could take, and this went deeper than anyone knew. Sometimes I wanted to just shriek at my mom, "You are *SO* clueless!" I often questioned whether she truly didn't know what was going on around her or whether she chose to ignore the signs because she couldn't handle even one more thing that would possibly tip her over the edge. I didn't want to take responsibility for that happening.

One of my closest friends, Megan, had been diagnosed with ovarian cancer. She was sixteen! How is that even a thing? She was in treatment, and I could only rarely talk to her on the phone. Our conversations were short, and I could hear the fear in her voice. I was sickened with the thought of losing her.

I felt like the world was crashing down around me. I had lost so many people that I loved in the past few short years—grandparents, uncles, and now my beautiful friend Megan might die. It seemed like everyone was getting younger as they died, and I just couldn't cope. There'd been too much. And in the shadows over it all was my frightening childhood memory—so much hidden pain, nothing I could share. It was always eating at me. I felt brittle inside and everything seemed to hurt.

And then I met Christine. She was new to our school and gave off an air of being completely unapproachable with her crude remarks and don't-give-a-shit attitude. I kind of admired her and wished I could put up that impenetrable wall around myself. I think she saw that I was giving her something other than a disgusted look, like most of the others in high school. My look was more of curiosity, and I was still trying to be the girl who fit in, so we naturally gravitated to one another. When she invited me over to her place one Friday after school, I thought *What the hell, Mom always works late and won't even notice me gone until dinner time.* Mom always liked to know where I was, who the parents were (if I was at a friend's house), and when she could pick me up. Riding the bus was rarely allowed—freaks and creeps rode the bus, you know. She might be the busiest, most distracted mom on the planet, but she was an expert at helicoptering. That's what my brother and I always said to her. "Just because you missed your dream of being a helicopter pilot, doesn't mean you should be in a holding pattern over us all the time, Mom!" We'd all laugh but the undertone was Mom's lack of trust and strong need to control. Ryan didn't care, he was a total geek with only one good friend (equally a super geek), and he was constantly planted in front of his video games or the TV. He was about as likely as the pope would be to get into any kind of trouble.

It took only a nano-second to tell Christine that I would walk to her place after school. We kidded around and talked smack about the other teenage girls like nasty teenage girls usually do. Looking back, I realized I had been trying so hard to impress her with my coolness that I was totally out of my zone of comfort. She was thoroughly impressed that I had been a winner in a beauty pageant a couple of years earlier and I knew I was in.

When we arrived at her place, I had my first gut feeling that this was not going to go as I had imagined. Her house was well known as a place the cops ended up at often. The yard was full of junked cars, country music was blaring out of the rundown shop on the property, and Mom could have made a mortgage payment with all the empties thrown everywhere. As we climbed the steps to the house, the smell of rotting compost and old oil was enough to make me gag. How to get out of this situation? Mom would have a fit.

Christine showed me to her room, which was another example of a careless, abandoned, don't-give-a-shit lifestyle. She quickly dropped her backpack on the floor, reached under the bed and pulled out an almost-full twenty-six-ounce bottle of booze. I think it was a cheap brand of whiskey. Not that the quality of the whiskey was even on my radar, but it was the prequel to what would turn out to be a night of horror. And a sequel to my secret memory, scarred into my soul. Like I needed more scars. . . .

I had had a couple of drinks before in my early teens, unbeknownst to Helicopter Mom of course, so I didn't hesitate to take a couple of shots out of Christine's bottle. And then a couple more. And then a couple more. I didn't know how quickly my sadness/depression/anxiety or whatever it was that was darkening my days, would take a back seat to the warm, numbing, and bliss-based glow of alcohol.

We were giggling like the schoolgirls we were when the bedroom door crashed open, its handle firmly re-wedged into the hole in the wall I had noticed earlier. So that's where that hole came from! This obviously wasn't the first time the door handle had become one with the drywall. Christine's obviously drunk dad stood in the doorway, a beer in his hand and a sloppy grin on his face. One of his buddies was peering over his shoulder, an equally creepy and sloppy grin on his face.

"What's going on here, girls?" Drunk Dad slurred. I felt instantly sober. He crawled on his knees over the end of the bed, reaching for the collar on my sweatshirt. I backpedaled on the bed, trying to figure out how I was going to get around him and out the door. I knew I was in the company of a perverted molester and I turned my head to shout at Christine to help me. Dad's buddy was already making his way around the other side of the bed where she was sitting. "Come on, sweetie, you didn't say no last time, gimme just a little feel. See if you've grown anymore," he chuckled. I could see he had a dribble of chewing tobacco stuck to the side of his mouth. Christine just sat there, looking like she had no intention of stopping him.

My head was suddenly throbbing and I crossed my arms over my chest and shut my eyes. And I felt her dad's hands on me, pulling at my arms, his rank breath wafting into my face. "Don't be shy, what's your name?" he asked, his disgusting hands working their way around my waist as he tried to pull me toward him. I pushed as hard as I could and he slipped off the edge of the bed onto one knee, then fell backward onto the floor, hitting it with a solid thump. His arm reached up, hitting the upside-down laundry basket that was serving as Christine's night table and his abandoned beer flipped over onto his legs. That was my chance to run for the open door. I grabbed my backpack off the floor and bolted as fast as I could out of the house for the main road. The last thing I heard was Christine yelling, "Erin, don't you dare tell!"

God, I felt so sick. My stomach threatened to turn inside out and my vision blurred. I didn't know whether it was tears or the effects of the booze. All I could think about was getting to the payphone I knew was at the gas station on the corner.

MOM

It was seven o'clock in the evening and I was starting to pace. Where was she? Erin had been morose lately and I had chalked it up to her grief and now her worry about her friend Megan. And those damn teenage hormones. But she was always home by dark, and it was well past that by now. For the first time, I wished I had gotten her a cell phone. She'd been asking for one for months, but I didn't see it as good parenting to give your kids every new gadget that came out. She was a short bus ride home from school and anyone she usually hung out with was within walking distance of the house. Even though we lived in a safe neighborhood, I still tended to want to pick her up, especially if it was getting dark.

Something was wrong this time. She hadn't called my cell from anyone's house to let me know where she was so I could pick her up. She hadn't told Ryan where she was going and my calls to her usual haunts brought no results. I started to drive, my heart pounding, and tried not to panic. I alternated emotions—fear to anger and back again. She'd been a bit combative lately, which was against her nature, so maybe this was in retaliation to my rules?

My thoughts turned back again to Mom's intuitive warning from when Erin was three years old. "You have to keep a close eye on her. She has something extra special about her and I have a terrible feeling that someone will try to take her… someone foreign, not from here." *These thoughts aren't helping,* I said to myself as I turned down the main street leading to the school. Kids weren't allowed to hang around the school after extracurricular activities but I'd run out of options. I hadn't seen her on any of the streets around the neighborhood.

There were no lights on, no one around the school at all, and the knot in my stomach tightened. I jumped at the sound of my cell phone ringing on the seat beside me. It was Ryan. Erin had called the house and he said she was crying. She needed me to pick her up from the pay phone at the gas station that was only about a five-minute drive from where I was sitting in the school parking lot.

As I pulled up to the phone booth, I was trying to decide whether to be angry or simply relieved. I could see she wasn't hurt.

"Erin, I've been driving all over hell's half acre, trying to find you!" Okay, maybe I was going to be angry. "Are you alright?" *Shift from anger, make room for concern,* I told myself.

"I'm fine, I just want to go home," she said, her voice breaking, fresh tears running down her cheeks. I started to drive toward home, wondering whether I should continue to push or give her some time to gather herself.

Not being the most patient mother, I again asked, "Where were you, who were you with, and, most importantly, why didn't you call me? I was worried sick." Maybe guilt would make her talk. I knew that wasn't likely to work but a mother has to try.

"I made a new friend at school, and we just hung out. I lost track of time," she said.

"But where were you hanging out?" I asked.

"Just around, Mom! Drop it!" she shouted.

This was so not like my girl. "Well, you're crying, Erin," I said. "And you're not telling me a thing, so I have a right to be concerned, okay? Don't get lippy with me."

I was met with silence as we pulled into the driveway. Erin opened the car door and stepped out, slamming it in her wake. How was this my fault? I'd give her a few minutes and have a mom-daughter chat in her room once she'd calmed down. For now, I was just relieved she was home and safe. Later, we'd get to the bottom of what was happening with her.

Erin claimed she wasn't well the next day and, given the circumstances, I agreed she could stay home. I happened to be working from home that morning and thought I'd take a chance and see if she'd open up to me. I knocked gently on her bedroom door just before lunch.

"Honey, do you want to have lunch with me?" I asked. Silence. I knocked again and turned the knob, not surprised to find it locked. "Are you okay in there? I have a meeting this afternoon and I'd like to talk to you before I have to leave. Come and have some leftover pizza with me, please."

"Okay," said a small voice on the other side of the door. When Erin opened the door, I was dismayed to see how swollen her eyes were. She was wearing a huge old sweatshirt and had her arms crossed over her chest as she shuffled out of her bedroom.

As we pulled stools up to the kitchen counter, I offered a little light banter about a difficult client I was dealing with, hoping to help her relax. It had been so long since I had heard a genuine belly laugh from my little girl. I missed it.

After some gentle probing questions, Erin finally broke down and told me who her new friend was and that she had been at her house. I was horrified because as part of a small community, I knew that place. It was known for a lot of drinking, the cops were always being called, and the dad had a reputation of being a taker who never paid his bills and continually fleeced his customers. Erin would not tell me what happened in that house, only that she hated it and was scared. I told Erin that her friendship with Christine was over, and I did not want her to ever go near that house again. For once, she didn't argue with me—almost unheard of from a teenage girl when parents start issuing orders. That told me more than anything she had said.

At a loss of what to do to help her feel better, I said, "How about we take a day to go shopping and you can pick out some new clothes? And we can maybe talk about taking another vacation, perhaps Hawaii again? Or somewhere else?"

Her baby-blue eyes turned dark as she spun toward me on her stool and shouted, "God, Mom! Why do you think spending money will fix this? Money doesn't solve everything and nothing will get better! Do you get it yet? Just leave me alone!"

She slid off her stool and ran crying down the hallway into her bedroom, slamming the door, and shortly after I could hear her music playing and drowning out the sound of her sobs. I was thoroughly stunned and thought to myself that I knew absolutely nothing about raising a child. She was probably right about the money. I didn't know how to get through to her and find out the root cause of her sadness and anxiety so I had hoped to "buy some happiness." Really, I was clueless and ill-equipped to figure this out.

I couldn't help myself. Almost with no thought, I drove into Christine's drunk dad's yard on the way to my meeting. I sat there, car idling as I debated going into the shop where I could see him standing at a workbench. Should I confront him with questions? My palms were sweaty and my heart racing as I began to imagine what had happened in that house and likely had been happening for a long time. I felt a rage boiling up inside me, but I also knew I had no proof. I'd only be putting Erin and myself in a dangerous situation as his reputation was one of violence. I backed out of the driveway, wondering if I'd regret not confronting him one day. I also wondered how his girl Christine was going to be as she grew up.

Sadly, many years later we heard that a family friend had seen Christine on the downtown streets, and she was obviously in very poor health. She was begging for money—probably for drugs, based on her appearance. So much damage and so much sadness came from that house. And my little girl took some of that with her on that horrible night.

One good thing that Erin took from her experience was a profound awareness of the effects of alcohol and drug use. In those days, it seemed as if everyone in high school was smoking pot. She would come home from school and tell me how scary it was that so many people she knew were using weed as much as regular cigarettes. She decided to join the "Say No To Drugs" school group and see what she could do to spread the word.

Erin was a resilient girl and after a few weeks, I gratefully noticed she was smiling again, enjoying her committee work with the anti-drugs campaign (her artistic talent at work on posters and advertising), and we got back into our easy mother-daughter ways. I thought we'd left it all behind. But truthfully, nothing gets left behind. It just gets buried deeper. And I would remember, many years later, her enthusiastic drive to be a part of the "war on drugs."

CHAPTER ELEVEN: MOM

A FUNNY STORY: THE MUSTANG GETS IT AGAIN (2002)

My Mustang convertible was my dream car, and I had worked hard for it. It took me some time to get over the fact that three little girls had deliberately given it a new paint job with eggs, just a few short weeks after I had bought it. If you've ever been "egged," either person or property, you know it quickly dries like super sticky paint. Add in the artistic texture of eggshells caked into the hardened yolk, and you've got a major cleaning project in store. I was so terrified of scratching my Mustang that I did the cleaning myself, not letting anyone touch it, until it was spotless enough to just be a bad memory. But I was fussier with my Mustang after that incident than I had been when I first drove it off the lot.

When Erin got her learner's permit for driving, I knew I wanted her to be a good driver and that only comes with experience. But please, no practicing in my formerly defaced and precious Mustang! Being a one-car family didn't leave us much choice and my friends weren't that eager for her to gain experience behind the wheels of their vehicles—beater *or* beauty.

So, into the Mustang we went. Living near Victoria on Vancouver Island, I chose a parking lot at the beach as the place for Erin's inaugural drive. I figured with the forest on one side and the ocean on the other, what could possibly go wrong? Play chicken with a massive cedar or see if the car could float? I thought it was a better choice than taking my precious daughter and my precious car into a populated neighborhood with people, pets, other cars, houses, and various inanimate or animate objects to become potential victims of a speeding red bullet.

We pulled into the parking lot and I got out of the driver's seat, motioning to Erin to switch with me. After a quick look around to see if there was anything that could potentially pose a hazard, I carefully got into the passenger seat and gazed longingly at the floor, hoping to conjure an additional foot brake like the driver training schools have in their cars. No such luck, only Erin's suitcase-sized purse, which I hoped contained a first-aid kit. You know, just in case…

After adjusting the seat and mirrors, I gave her a run-through of all the gadgets and gauges and a *thorough* explanation of gas pedal versus brake, and which was appropriate for which situation. Not rocket science, I thought at the time.

"D for drive," I said. "Gentle on the gas, sweetie." And so we started the driving lesson. Nice and slow, her hands at two and ten o'clock as instructed. "Okay, ease off the gas and then gently press on the brake." My voice sounded amazingly calm in my head. This was going so well! Maybe Erin was a little hard on the brake, but she'd get used to the feel of it. A few runs forward, the dreaded "R" for reverse, and we ended up in the same place we started.

"I think we're good for the first time out, let's celebrate with a walk on the beach," I said. "Just pull ahead one more time, aim for the parking barriers, and you can finish practicing slowing and nudging the car up to that cement curb."

"I feel so powerful," Erin said, and I turned my head to see her face lit up with joy and confidence.

"Okay, but don't let that feeling make you reckless. Here's the barrier coming up, press on the brake," I said, as she carefully turned the wheel to bring the car into a parking spot. Was she coming in too fast or was it just my heightened sense of impending doom?

Suddenly my head was pinned back against the headrest, my feet were slammed against the floor, and all I could see was shrubbery and trees with the hood of the car at an unnaturally high angle. And the motor was revving at top speed. Why weren't we still plowing into the trees? I felt the car tilting gently up and down. It was subtle but I felt that heightened sense of doom again. It felt like we were on a teeter totter.

I pried my hand off the door handle; my other hand was planted on my chest. Was I having a heart attack? I could feel the rapid pulse of my blood circulating through my whole body, particularly in my ears. And in the calmest voice that still amazes me to this day, I turned to Erin and said, “Take your foot off the gas. Good. I’m putting the gear shift in park, okay?” My voice stayed eerily calm. “Now, open your door. Yes, good. Please get out of my car, okay?” I realized afterward that this may have sounded mean but given the circumstances, I could have said much worse.

I shut the car off and got out to examine why the car was at such an odd angle and what was causing the teeter-totter effect. I knelt to look underneath the Mustang and saw a mangled parking barrier about halfway down the chassis. The wheels were off the ground—first the front, then the back—and as I fought the urge to lose my lunch right there, the car finally settled on the front wheels. Mustangs are notably front heavy with those big motors—no junk in the trunk to provide a ballast.

I stood up and looked for Erin. She was standing about twenty feet from the car, hands over her mouth, looking as if she had just witnessed a brutal murder. Erin always had big, beautiful blue eyes but at that moment they were saucers. I’ll never be able to explain the human psyche when it comes to reactions, but I started to laugh. And I laughed until I was on my knees, tears running down my face, arms across my belly, and unable to stop.

“Mom? Are you okay? Am I in deep, deep trouble?” Erin’s voice brought me out of my hysterical state, and I looked up into her terrified face. I loved her in my deepest core at that moment. She was truly devastated (and most likely sure she had broken my brain and that was why I was laughing like a hyena).

“No, sweetie. Shit happens and nice cars get launched into bushes all the time.” And I broke into more laughter but this time she joined me, although her chuckles were a little reserved in case her mother had definitely lost her faculties this time. “I’m pretty sure you hit the gas instead of the brake and I'll probably be doing the same if I'm still allowed to drive when I'm in my eighties. It's a common mistake with new drivers as well as elderly," I said as the reality of the situation slowly returned.

"I'm going to call a tow truck," I told her. "I think this is going to be a challenge to get the car off that barrier." By this time a few beach walkers had arrived, and some men were examining underneath the car. "Your frame is probably bent," one wise guy said. "Probably a write-off." Crap. Erin was now crying and pacing as I greeted the tow truck driver. I was honest and told him what happened, and he was amused enough to swear to keep our secret that an unlicensed driver was behind the wheel. "Geez, I didn't even think of that!" I said gratefully. "Thank you so much."

After a jackhammer and a lot of freaky and scary maneuvers, my beautiful red Mustang was sitting in the middle of the parking lot. Like nothing had ever happened. The tow truck driver assured me he didn't think the frame was bent and I could drive it home. *There you go, macho man,* I thought as Mr. Your-car-is-a-write-off hopped into his pickup and took off.

"Let's go home Erin," I said as I slid gratefully into the driver's seat, adjusting it back to my height. I doubted it would ever need to be moved again as I couldn't see letting my precious daughter back behind the wheel of that car. Not in this lifetime. It was a very quiet car ride home, with the huge bill for the towing sitting on the console between us. "I'll pay the tow bill," I heard her say quietly, her tearful gaze down at her lap. "I don't think you can afford it, hon," I said. "Not with your one-shift-a-week job at the fish-and-chips shop. And I'll have to get the hood and front bumper of the car painted as it's pretty scratched. I'll see what insurance will cover."

I didn't want to make her feel worse than she already did but there were lessons to be learned. That statement she made, "I feel so powerful," probably gave her a bit too much confidence and I hoped she learned that vehicles are *more* powerful and require a driver's full attention and caution. And she was always a very careful driver from then on. Enrolling her in driving school was something I should have done in the first place. Let her launch someone else's car into the bushes! The would-haves, should-haves, and could-haves became haunted words for me later, but we continued to laugh about the Mustang incident throughout her remaining years. It's one of those rare happy memories that still makes me smile, thinking about that day of Erin's first driving lesson.

And then a family tragedy left a wound so deep in all of us, but particularly Erin, and the loss pushed her further into a shadowy place of aloneness, fear, and insecurity.

CHAPTER TWELVE: ERIN

MY COUSIN, MY IDOL, MY CHAD (2003)

When I was little, my cousin Chad was my absolute and foremost idol. He was twelve years older and like a much bigger and older brother than my own brother, who was only two years older than me. He was kind, funny, caring and he told us the best jokes! We rolled around on the front lawn at Grandma and Grandpa's place, and he'd let us think we were beating him up. He was hilarious. I don't know what it was about him, but he could instantly make anyone feel at ease and we couldn't wait to see him every chance possible. I really missed him when we moved to the west coast.

"Chad is really sick," Mom told us as we sat on stools across from each other at the kitchen counter. "He's been dealing with some liver issues, and it looks like he'll need a transplant. He was born with a defect in his liver and it's creating further problems within his body," she said with tears in her eyes.

"Is he going to die?" my brother asked.

I wanted to hit him. Of course, Chad wasn't going to die! He was my rock, my other brother, and my favorite cousin. I had just been through the fear of losing Megan to the ovarian cancer diagnosis. She was still fighting but now from so far away where she and her parents moved to be closer to an advanced treatment center. This was all too much. Surreal. There was a chance I could still lose my best friend and I had already kind of lost her to distance. The last I heard, she wasn't coming back to the island and she no longer returned my messages. I was hurting and worried, so I wasn't going to accept losing my favorite cousin Chad, too.

The highway stretched out ahead of us into the flat horizon, seemingly unmoving, shimmering on the pavement ahead of us. The radio was on, Ryan was reading, and I was thinking about a poem in my head that I wanted to get on paper. We were going home to where my mom was originally from, where I had been born as well, and to all the family. We had rented a car at the airport and wasted no time getting out of the city because we wanted to get home for my oldest cousin's wedding and then back to the city again to visit Chad in the hospital. He'd had his second transplant; the first liver had been rejected by his body. He wasn't doing well but supposedly was hanging in there with optimism. By this time in his life, he had a wife and two very small children. He was twenty-eight and had his whole life ahead of him.

Mom's cell phone rang, and she pulled over to the side of the highway, an unusual move for her as she usually ignored it when driving. I could see the worry on her face as she checked the incoming number and answered it, her voice wavering as she said "Hi, is everything okay?"

It was her oldest sister, delivering shocking news.

Nothing was ever okay again. Chad had died. There was cancer throughout his abdomen, discovered when he had his second surgery. My brother's face was pale and tears silently poured from his eyes when Mom told us the tragic news. All I remember from the rest of that long drive back to our original home was my cheek pressed against the upholstery of the back seat, my knees pulled up to my chest, arms wrapped around them as I cried loudly, feeling more like I was six than sixteen. Memories of Chad played in my mind, and I couldn't grasp the reality of him not being here anymore.

CHAD, MY IDOL by Erin Gray (With allusion to "The Misery" by Sonata Arctica)

I write the lines you want me to,
with the words I dare to use.
All the ones that you have taught me,
along the years.
You cast a perfect shadow on the paper,

yet you fade away with sunlight.
I fear the way you know me.

You steal my only hope
and make me stay awake another night.
I wish you to bear with me, stay near me.
I can't do this without you.
If you fall I'll catch you
don't be scared,
you'll be safe, this I swear.
I can do this without you
to make me strong.

Burn the paper, every lie
for them I cried.
You can't unbreak a heart
no matter how hard you've tried.
We love you so much, though it's too late to say.
I thought I had tomorrow, but tomorrow's gone away.

I ask myself so many questions, like "Did u know I cared?"
Or when you were sick in bed, why I wasn't there with you.
We miss you so much, we didn't even get to say goodbye.
I think about the past we shared, and wondered
why all the good ones are taken from the world.
I can't help but think about you, day by day.
I'll never forget you, Chad.
I didn't get to say we love you, that day just never came.
But always and forever, we'll love you just the same.

CHAPTER THIRTEEN:
MOM

THE TATTOO (2003)

Chad's death devastated all of us but especially affected Erin. To commemorate his life, some family members decided to get the same small Japanese symbol-of-life tattoo that Chad had. I never thought I'd support one of my kids getting a tattoo, but this seemed right. Erin and I booked an appointment and went for our first "inking" together. Mine went on my hip as I was still a little nervous about anyone seeing my mark and Erin decided to get hers on the back of her shoulder. It was a fun afternoon as we giggled our way through the experience, feeling like "bad asses" and healing our grief at the same time. We enjoyed that day, even though the meaning was somber. In the years to come, we both got a couple more tattoos, getting a little braver, and excitedly showing each other our new "tat." Little did I know then that the most precious tattoo on my body now would be the one I got in her memory. I look at it every day and send her my thoughts of love.

CHAPTER FOURTEEN:
ERIN AND MOM

THE SERENE YEARS (2003 TO 2008)

Some people believe that we completely physically and mentally regenerate every seven years, that we change in ways that lead us to new paths and new lives. We were given the gift of a relatively peaceful five years. But toward the end of that fifth year, I learned the hard way that those paths can lead to a fork in the road and the people we meet can push us down the wrong one.

ERIN

Grief and buried trauma have been my constant, unwanted companions but as I passed my sixteenth birthday, I began to feel like maybe I was coming out of a long, dark tunnel. Everyone thought of me as outgoing, friendly, happy, and simply energized by life. It's truly exhausting to keep up that facade. But lately I had been feeling like it wasn't such a facade anymore. It felt real, genuine, and exceptionally liberating. I had so much to be thankful for—lots of good friends, a beautiful place to live, and my high school grades weren't too awful, considering I was such a social butterfly. I'd had a couple of different boyfriends after that disaster with the first guy who broke my heart and inspired my first poem. Now I looked back on that with a different lens from a bit of growing up. But I also knew those new boyfriends were a product of my sadness and desperation as they were not nice guys. I just could not figure out why I kept attracting guys who ended up being such jerks. But I wasn't the only one struggling with relationships. Mom had a couple of "bad boyfriends" over a few years too and I can say we almost bonded over our poor ability to meet nice guys. The odd time she or

I did find someone nice who treated us with kindness and respect, we unconsciously managed to find a way to end the relationship.

Around the same time in 2003, both Mom and I decided that single life was the way to go. She worked too much to waste any more energy on creeps and weirdos and I just lost any desire to have a boyfriend. I knew it was unusual to not be pouring all my social energy into getting a boyfriend as that seemed to be the goal for the rest of the girls my age.

Then Mom and I found a common interest we could share when she made the sudden decision to let go of her career and step into something new. A hair salon of all things! This was going to be a fresh start for both of us as we were closing in on what had been a hard year. It's amazing how a change in energy can attract good things. Mom, even though she truly did not want to meet anyone, agreed to a blind date arranged by a close friend. The friend insisted it wasn't a set-up but, flying in the face of Murphy's Law, the blind date turned out to be one of those rare, nice, and decent guys who she managed not to kick to the curb. He became a wonderful husband for her and a loving, caring stepdad for me. Finally, all was going in the right direction and hope was on the horizon. Maybe it would soon be my turn to meet a great guy. But I had lots of time, and I was also looking at establishing myself in a career that I would love. The future was looking pretty exciting.

MOM

A happy time in Erin's life was when I bought a hair salon shortly after she turned sixteen years old and she became my right-hand helper. Thinking back, it seemed like a very quick and surreal decision to buy a salon, considering I wasn't even a stylist, but my friend was the shop owner and confided to me in the chair one day that she needed to sell her business. She was having serious personal problems and wanted to move back north to her family. I was feeling burnt out from my lending job and the idea of owning my own business again was so exciting that I found myself signing a sale contract within a matter of a couple of weeks.

The next two years were a whirlwind of learning how to manage a very diverse staff of long-time employees and an ever-evolving business of helping people feel beautiful. Some days I felt I was totally out of my element and losing control of a herd of feral cats, but things were going well and I expanded the business to include spa services. Even though the days were long and the shop only closed one day a week, I could go home after locking the shop door and not be bothered by anyone.

Erin was in her element. The girly-girl in her came out in full color as she learned how to book appointments, clean the shop, give an excellent shampoo and conditioner treatment, and even talk to fussy customers. She was a natural. I would laugh out loud sometimes, looking at her in perfect hair and makeup and socializing among the staff and customers with an ease that truly amazed me. The tomboy that was my little one so many years ago had been replaced by this new and polished example of brightness and beauty. A client once told me she reminded her of a butterfly floating around the shop. That conversation inspired me to jot down a few thoughts I had about butterflies, how very much Erin reminded me of a butterfly with her ethereal ways, and how much seeing a butterfly could affect the viewer.

Butterflies flutter gracefully from place to place. And when you see one, you stop. You watch, admire, and smile. You are transformed by this moment of surreal beauty and wonder.

One evening I sat down and expanded on those words, writing a piece that I intended to give to her at some point in her life. Maybe her birthday, or a time when she might need it, with the hope it would remind her of her true nature. I did not have the knack for poetry that she had and just scrambled together my thoughts and feelings into a whimsical bit of writing. I felt a bit awkward with it as the craft seemed to come so beautifully to her. I tucked it away, unaware then that some hard, dark chapters in our lives would come along with the opportunity to give it to her.

Erin's experience in the hair salon led to a burning desire for her to be a stylist too. Right after her graduation from high school, she went to hair school. I'd had the salon for more than two years by then and near the end of the third year, I was approached by an interested buyer who particularly wanted my business at that location. Even though I hadn't been thinking about selling, the offer was a good one and I felt I was ready to move onto something else. It was almost the same time as Erin graduated from hair school that I handed the salon keys over to the new owner. Erin was sad about the sale, but she quietly supported my decision to sell in an effort not to "upset the proverbial apple cart." We both felt there was a lot of opportunity for her out there as she was skilled and sociable. But I still felt guilty as she bounced around, working as a stylist at two or three different salons, even renting a space for herself at one point. It seemed like her spark had dimmed. She couldn't seem to settle.

Maybe she was more like me than I realized, needing substance in her work and unafraid to do career hops when she wasn't getting it. So, I wasn't entirely surprised when one day she announced that she was tired of the hair-care chemicals and the high maintenance of clients. Being the natural caregiver she was, she soon found herself looking at other work opportunities and ended up working for a family friend in a care home for mentally-challenged young-adult men. She excelled at the work and loved her clients, putting in extra hours and excitedly looking forward to every day. It was an outlet for her desire to take care of others and my beautiful girl was the absolute best at what she did.

Looking back, I wonder where we would be now if I had declined the offer for the salon and Erin had settled into her role as stylist there, eventually taking over the management of it. That had been my original plan for her. Instead, the last place she ended up working at, the care home, was the catalyst or the fork in the road that took her in the wrong direction. Because she cared too much.

CHAPTER FIFTEEN: MOM

THE QUIET ONE (1987 TO PRESENT)

Maybe now is a good time to introduce the quiet one. My son, Erin's brother Ryan. He is two years older, and you couldn't find two more opposite personalities. Where she was an extreme extrovert, he was an equally extreme introvert. Erin loved being around people, she could be quite loud and *never* stopped moving! Standing still was challenging for her, and she always looked for an adventure, being outdoors as much as possible, and thriving as the center of attention in a crowd.

Ryan loved books, movies, games, and generally just being engaged in sitting-down type activities. He matured slower (as it is with boys versus girls) and we used to tease him about Erin having to tie his shoes for him when they were getting ready to catch the school bus. He was one happy boy when Velcro runners came about!

When they were still little kids, Erin had loved riding our pony Dusty, but the last time I encouraged Ryan to get on her he ended up clinging to the saddle *underneath* her! And swearing he'd never ride again. Which he didn't. Erin played sports and Ryan did not, even though we registered him for boys' softball. He hated every minute of it and one day, watching him miserably trudging around the bases, I gave in and let him quit. It was time for us to acknowledge that our boy was not going to be the stereotypical kid and we just wanted him to be happy. He is very creative, kind, and thoughtful and I was, and still am, just as proud of him and his endeavors as Erin's.

Despite their obvious differences, Ryan and Erin grew up being best friends. She looked up to him and, from the time she could crawl, followed him everywhere. They made up skits together, sang the same songs, and sat with their heads pouring over the same childhood books. It was only as they grew older that she began to tease him about not being sociable. They were growing up and growing apart as siblings often do.

Ryan has been there, quietly in the background of all that was going on, through all the years, good and bad. His river runs deep and I may never fully understand what caused them to drift so far apart as adults, but he did want to be his sister's best friend again. I will never forget his words when we clung together in grief: "I thought we had more time."

CHAPTER SIXTEEN: MOM

HAPPY BIRTHDAY, ERIN (2008)

In June of 2008, I decided that Erin and I would have a true all-girls weekend to celebrate her twenty-first birthday. I booked us a room at a posh hotel on the mainland that had a casino, thinking it would be a fun treat as she was now of age to gamble a bit! This would be our "intro to being-of-age-to-gamble" weekend, a rite of passage and I was thrilled to be a part of it. Not that I wanted my daughter to become a gambler, it just seemed like an eventful milestone we could commemorate. Like when I took her to the beach to commemorate her first menstrual period, and we chanted to the rising sun and heralded her transition from girl to woman. She was horrified. My intentions were good, but the poor girl was so embarrassed. A ghastly but funny mistake on my part!

I remember being very excited to spend this weekend away with my adult daughter but before we hit the casino, we had our first treat: a couple hours in the hotel's deluxe spa. Massages and mani-pedis as we sipped on champagne and giggled like friends. Then onto the gambling floor. The casino was fun as I led her around, "showing her the ropes" (not that I had a lot of experience gambling, but I did know a blackjack table from a one-armed bandit).

What a gracious girl. On the way home after our fun weekend, joking about our huge loss of twenty dollars each, but also reveling in the pampering we had indulged in, she said to me with a cute smile on her face, "Mom, are you aware that twenty-one is not the legal age for gambling here? It's nineteen and I've already been to the casino a couple of times at home with friends. But I appreciate the sentiment!" Once again, I made a ridiculous but funny mistake. However, there were so many benefits to that oversight, and I will always treasure the memory of that weekend away with my girl.

It was the last memory we had together that was pure and fun.

PART TWO:
LIFE, UNRAVELING

CHAPTER SEVENTEEN: MOM

THE CHARISMA OF HIM. A MOTHER'S INTUITION (2009)

Life was perking along quite well as we looked forward to the coming new year of 2009. I was in a happy marriage and my adult children seemed to be doing well. Erin was working at a job she loved while renting our basement suite, surrounded by good friends and a fun social life. Ryan had moved to the mainland a couple of years before and met the love of his life. Were the struggles of our past behind us permanently? Everything we had been through seemed trivial, a means to an end, building our characters and making sure we were all on the path we were supposed to be traveling. Looking back, our lives seemed quite normal. We were far from thinking we were going to become part of a terrible movie in which bad things only happen to other people.

One of the young women that worked with Erin at the care home invited her to go see some new puppies, as she hoped to be able to buy one. Being a dog lover, and having her own beloved Harley, the German Shepherd we adopted, Erin was all in to go with her friend. I was more worried about Erin wanting to bring a puppy home than anything else, but they were apparently a rare and expensive breed from Africa, so I didn't think she would give in to temptation.

That evening, she did not rave about the puppies; she raved about the man who was raising them. I was quite amused by how enamored she seemed to be of him and thought it was harmless as she was between boyfriends and hadn't dated anyone for quite a while. The usual questions asked by parents resulted in rather vague answers, but I assumed it was because she didn't know him well enough. Which she didn't. But that all changed over the course of the next several weeks as she was home in the evenings less and less, spending more and more time with this mysterious stranger. We'll call him D.H.

Christmas was coming and we were hosting dinner that year for my husband Al's family. Everyone was able to come so I called Erin on her cell phone and asked her if she would consider bringing him, D.H., this elusive guy she was spending all her time with. I thought it might be a bit much, launching him into our loud, raucous family even before he met her parents, so I was expecting a firm "no thanks, Mom." After she discussed it with him, we were pleasantly surprised when she announced they would come for dinner. She seemed as surprised as we were, but we were happy to finally be able to meet him. I could tell she was worried about how things would go, so to soften the introduction into our typically chaotic-but-fun family gatherings, I asked them to come early so we could have a couple of getting-to-know-you hours before the rest of the dinner group arrived. I also had not seen Erin for two or three weeks by that time, so I was excited to have her home again, even if it was just for dinner and a visit.

This memory is as clear in my mind as if it had been just yesterday. I was in the kitchen and heard the front door open. "We're here!" Erin called from the entrance.

I came around the corner, drying my hands on a towel, and there he was, standing in the doorway, leaning nonchalantly against the door frame with one hand on Erin's shoulder.

Erin introduced us. "This is D.H., and this is my mom," she said quietly back to him. She was watching me anxiously as I extended my hand to shake his. I noticed he gave Erin's shoulder a tight squeeze and she winced slightly, then he reached for my hand with both of his, grasping it warmly. His eyes were directly on mine and his super-white smile took me by surprise. I'm not sure what I was expecting but I was impressed with his manners and good looks. Could I have been worried about nothing?

"And you!" I said as I turned to Erin and wrapped my arms around her. "I've missed you so much!" She was wearing a bulky sweatshirt and a pair of jeans that looked brand new but underneath the bulkiness of her top, I was shocked to feel her sharp shoulder blades below my forearms as I hugged her tightly. And she felt so much smaller—narrower through her back and shoulders. She tensed and I heard her suck in her breath. I pulled back and held her at arm's length, noticing that she had really thick makeup on and underneath I could see how tired she looked with poorly disguised, dark circles under her eyes. She was looking directly over my shoulder, where D.H. had moved farther into the room behind me. She nodded slightly and smiled. Where had my daughter's brilliant white teeth gone? I had caught a brief glimpse of grayish-white teeth, and it made no sense as she prided herself on looking after them after a couple of years in braces as a teenager. It had only been a few weeks since I'd seen her this close up and I was shocked at how she had let her appearance go. This was my girl who spent hours in front of the mirror and never left the house without perfect hair and makeup.

"Are you feeling okay?" I asked her.

"I'm fine," she replied. "I had a really bad flu for a while but I'm all better. I'm looking forward to a big turkey dinner!"

I was so naive then.

I turned around to D.H. and said, "I'm happy to finally meet you. Come into the living room and have a seat."

As they sat on the couch together, I took a seat on a chair across from them, preparing myself to hand out the mother's inquisition, when he began to speak first.

For the next half hour, he spoke eloquently about how much he admired Erin, how beautiful she was, and how he could see where she got her beauty from.

Typical, I thought to myself. Schmooze the parents and don't let me get a word in edgewise to ask questions! Al came in the front door and introductions were made again. By the time our other guests were arriving, I still hadn't managed to find out any more information about him than I had before. Which was very little.

D.H. continued to monopolize the conversation as he met the family, and it felt like the dinner table was a stage for him. But despite my concern at not being able to find out more about who he actually was, I found myself beginning to warm up to him. I could see Erin's attraction to him. He had gorgeous brown eyes, thick black hair, and his skin was a beautiful dark cream color. I remember wondering what his background was. His voice was inviting, with just a hint of an accent. He spoke to everyone at the table with a level of interest that, at first, seemed to be so nice, especially when he was zeroing in on my sister-in-law. His direct gaze just shifted slightly, from interested to leering, and I felt a chill run down my back. His behavior was too much, almost creepy, and I felt the first pang of worry.

Something was just not right with this guy. I was trying my best to be open minded but a mother's intuition is strong, and I had to figure out why I was feeling so much trepidation. What confused me most was Erin's behavior. My bubbly, talkative girl was quiet during the entire visit, and I wondered if she felt the same way with him that I did. That we couldn't get a word in with him talking non-stop! He seemed very overprotective of her as well, constantly asking her if she was good. She would nod and say, "Yes, I'm good," but I noticed her glance directly at me as she spoke.

Dinner was over and there was an abrupt change in his mood. He went from congenial to impatient, insisting he was tired and they should leave. He made a trip to the washroom, giving me a brief moment alone in the kitchen with Erin. I grabbed both her hands in mine.

"Are you really okay?" I asked her.

"For sure, Mom, do you like him?" she asked.

"Well, he is very good looking, but he never stops talking so it's hard to learn anything about him." I replied. "Is he always like this?" I expected him to come back into the kitchen any minute, so I continued to ask her questions in a hushed voice. "How old is he?" I whispered. "And I still don't know what he does for a living." I could tell he was older, but with those good looks it was difficult to put a number on him.

"For God's sake, Mom, does that matter?" she said loudly. I knew before shifting my gaze that he was standing behind me in the doorway to the kitchen. He did not look happy and jerked his head toward the front door. "Let's go, Erin," he said quietly. And they were gone.

CHAPTER EIGHTEEN: MOM

THINGS ARE GETTING WEIRD (2009)

It started with Erin not coming home on weekends. Every time she did come home, she would leave with "just a few things" as she was spending more and more time with D.H. They'd been dating for a few months by then and I was questioning my own intuition. She seemed to be quite happy, so why was I still twitchy about the relationship? We would call or text each other every couple of days and I was doing my best to set my fears aside, deciding I was still being a helicopter parent.

Or was I?

Sometimes she would show up out of the blue and seem to be in such a rush to run in, grab more of her stuff, and run out again. He would be sitting behind the wheel in his diesel truck, not even shutting it off while he waited for her. She claimed they were always in a rush to be somewhere, but I noticed she was no longer making any prolonged eye contact with me.

One day, she showed up by herself. I was just baking some bread and she said she was hungry, so I suggested she stay for lunch. She was wearing another long, bulky sweatshirt that was obviously D.H.'s and it was hot in the kitchen. "Take your sweatshirt off and stay," I said. "You look like you are truly sweating in that thing!"

As she pulled it off, I couldn't hide my shock when I saw how much weight she had lost. I knew she'd dropped pounds when she first brought D.H. to meet us at Christmas but I thought that had been because of the bout of flu she'd said she had. Now I could see her collar bones sticking out and I noticed her face seemed smaller with cheekbones more prominent than they used to be.

We sat at the counter and I asked her, "Erin, what is going on? You've lost so much weight. We rarely see you. I'm really worried." Silence. I gave her time as she was ravenously devouring a grilled-cheese sandwich, her favorite food on the planet. As a little girl, when it was snack time, she always asked for "just melted cheese on a plate please." It was a unique request but she loved it, so we indulged her. And now my little girl was a young woman, diving into the adult version of melted cheese on a plate and avoiding my probing questions.

I met silence with silence, giving her time to finish eating and think about her response. I recall holding my breath, knowing we were about to embark on a whole different conversation. She finally looked up at me and said, "Mom, he's getting a little bit weird."

"Like what? What do you mean by weird?" I asked. She didn't answer so I followed up with, "Erin, you have to get out of there. We'll take my vehicle and go pick up your things. Is Harley still at his house? We need to grab him too!" I was already looking for my wallet and keys when she stood up and said, "Oh, forget it, Mom, I'm the one being weird. He's fine, he treats me really well and I love how he looks after himself. Look at these pictures," she said as she punched her code into her cell phone.

I looked at the images and tried not to be a prude; they weren't the typical images a daughter shows her mother. He was obviously posing and I could see just his torso, naked from his jeans' very low waistband to the hollow in his throat. He had a lot of tribal-type tattoos down his arms, across his chest, and down both sides of his ribcage.

"I've never dated a guy who worked out so much," she said proudly, gazing at the photos. "He keeps himself so strong and fit. He sure does look good, doesn't he?"

I didn't know what to say. I could see why a young woman would be attracted to him with his looks and charm, but my mother's intuition was screaming at a decibel level I couldn't ignore.

"Erin, something is not right with this guy. You know it, I know it, and you have to get away from him."

"You don't get it, Mom. I'm not breaking up with him! I just can't. He's everything I want in a guy. He comes from a wealthy family, he's drop-dead gorgeous, he has a successful business. I love him," she said, her tone getting more defensive with each word spoken.

My heart dropped when she said she loved him. "Okay, well, tell me then, how old is he? What business and what wealthy family are you talking about?" I asked.

"He's fourteen years older than me, and I'm happy with that as every guy I've dated up to now has been a selfish, immature dweeb. His family has a successful business overseas and he also has a successful construction-supply business here." Erin was still speaking defensively, but I could also hear an underlying tone of pleading. She really wanted me to believe and support her.

"Then why did you say he was getting weird?" I asked, really wanting to know what she was referring to.

"Forget I said anything. I have to go," she said as she glanced at the time on her cell phone. I really did not want her to leave, but after a few more minutes of trying to convince her to let me go with her to pick up the dog and her things, she'd had enough. And out the door she went, slamming the door on her car, gravel flying as she drove down the road.

And that's when things really started to unravel.

CHAPTER NINETEEN:
ERIN

A BAD MOVIE. AND I'M THE STAR PLAYER (2009 – 2010)

Things were so good at the start. D.H. was adoringly attentive, always asking me what I wanted or needed, his hand touching my face, arm, or back with what seemed to be complete worship and caring. I was so excited to be with someone who seemed to have so much going for him. He told me he had lots of investments, his father was very well off, and my future would be one of love, security, and a lifestyle to match none of my friends. I wouldn't have to work, just help him with his business occasionally, and we would travel the world. What a dream.

My only misgiving was my failing relationship with my family. They didn't believe me or D.H., and Mom was becoming a raving lunatic with her insistence that he was bad news for me. D.H. told me they were being selfish, and I began to think he was right. Why would Mom, especially, deny me the right to be happy and married to a rich, good-looking man who wanted us to have children and travel the world? He wasn't perfect. He had a couple of weird quirks that made me question my beliefs and upbringing. He repeatedly told me that in his world, men and women shared their loved ones with others and I just couldn't get my head wrapped around that. So far, he'd respected my wishes when I said no to him inviting other men or women over for "special encounters." Mom would have had an absolute meltdown if I'd actually told her what I meant about him getting weird. But if that was his only vice, I guess I could get used to it even if I was in no way ready to try something that seemed far too foreign and kinky for my tastes! As the weeks went by, D.H. got more insistent that I give it a try but I still balked at the idea. It was starting to get uncomfortable and cause arguments between us.

I don't remember any details about that first night. D.H. had ordered take-out food and brought home a couple of bottles of wine as we were going to have a "super romantic evening." He wanted to clear the air and start fresh so we wouldn't argue anymore. I was definitely on board with that as I had been having thoughts about moving back to my suite at Mom's house. I wasn't a big drinker at the time but started to relax after my second glass of red wine. I was feeling pretty woozy but also really happy, so I don't think I knew when I went from being lightheaded to barely conscious. There were voices and I could hear Harley barking frantically as D.H. shut him in the garage. Why did he do that!? But I seemed incapable of getting up to rescue him.

Faces, voices, laughter. Lights in and out, people moving. *Why can't I talk? My tongue and lips don't want to move. But I'm still floating on a cloud of numb contentment. What is this? And then something hurts, but it rarely registers as I feel someone putting another glass of wine to my lips. I'm really thirsty. Where is Harley? And then it's all black.*

The next day I woke up with a horrible headache and my whole body hurt. When I stepped out of the shower, I could see bruises on my neck, arms, and chest and I was so sore from my groin to my ankles. *What happened last night?* I must have been so drunk but when I asked D.H. about it, he just laughed and said we "all" had a good time. I felt sick.

That was the beginning of the end. My life, as it had been, was over. As 2009 rolled into 2010, each day was a round of lies, drugs, threats, physical and mental torture, and control. I zig-zagged back and forth between just giving into the constant drugging to keep me quiet and vowing to find a way to get myself and Harley out of this situation. But D.H. seemed to know when I was plotting, as the threats would increase along with the abuse. He would taunt me by holding a knife to Harley's throat as my poor dog howled and tried to struggle out of his strong grasp. D.H. told me that if I left, he would go to my parent's house in the middle of the night and burn them in their beds. I truly believed he would go that far. Oddly, I felt that the man I had met, who swore his undying and everlasting love for me, was still in there. I had to find out what changed but when I tried talking to him, every word he hurled at me felt like the bite of a venomous snake.

SNAKE BITE by Erin Gray

Sometimes, your words
strike at me like a viper
Piercing, stinging, venom burns my heart
When from the blue
Your poison spews
Ripping me apart.
What makes a lover turn so quick?
Striking out at lightning speed.
Is there a motive hidden,
Or something lacking that you need?
Treading ever cautious
Never knowing when you'll strike
Spewing out your vile words
Like a deadly cobra bite.
You coil up in anger
Laying there in wait
For the unsuspecting movement
When your target can't escape.
Your poison fangs kept hidden
their tips so razor sharp
Injecting deadly venom
Deep inside my heart.
Leaving painful scars
That are always slow to heal
And though not always fatal
Sometimes that's how it feels.
Penetrating deep inside
Your eyes flash full of hate
When you strike me with your evil ways
the bite of a poisonous snake.

How much time had passed? I had no idea that a full nine months had passed since I last physically saw my mom and stepdad. Or since I'd talked to my own father who lived in another part of the country. No one was ever able to reach me. I lost track of the days, weeks, and even the months as I grew sicker and sicker. I couldn't stand to look in the mirror anymore as I saw my sallow complexion, dull eyes, and horrible "crack acne" creeping across my entire face. I didn't even know what drugs he was feeding me but somewhere along the way, I had begun to welcome them. When I was high was the only time I didn't feel the pain. Or the shame.

I know he took my phone and laptop away. I would hear him answer my phone and say things like, "Oh, she's fine, Mom." (Was he actually calling my mother *MOM!?*) "She's out getting groceries and forgot her phone. She's a bit of an airhead, you know."

And then the ultimate cover-up. One phone call he answered for me went like this:

"It would be great to have you guys over for a visit, *MOM*. But we are just renovating and everything is a mess. How about we come over in a couple of weeks, I'll bring my dirt bike, and we can ride it on your country road? I want to teach Erin how to ride, so it's the perfect spot. You know, *MOM*, I always give her your messages but, for some reason, she said she doesn't want to call you. I'm really sorry, I'm not sure why she doesn't want to talk to you. But I have a surprise for you. I want to tell you that I love her so much and I'm going to marry her."

He's such a liar, I thought from my drug-induced state on the bed. I rarely left the bedroom anymore except to find my way to the bathroom. I don't remember the last time I had a shower except for once when D.H. pushed me into the bathroom, telling me I was dirty, and no one would want me. Which wasn't good for his business. I kept getting flashes in my more lucid moments of a tiny butterfly under glass, wings fluttering as it kept bashing itself against its prison walls. I could even hear the soft ticks of its little body each time it tried. Was that me under the glass?

At that point, I was out of hope. All I had was my dog and the numbness that the drugs gave me. I never knew from day to day what kind of drug he was going to make me take. It seemed to depend on whether he wanted me nearly comatose, when he abused me himself, or coherent enough to say and do what he told me to do while others were abusing me. Each day I slid further and further down that slippery slope into complete dependency on the drug of the day. It's hard to explain how it felt. The first few moments were fear and resistance and then suddenly I was being wrapped in a warm blanket of comfort where the pain wasn't there and the knowledge of what was happening did not exist. I began to miss that blanket terribly when he withheld it.

"We gotta get you cleaned up, visit your stupid bitch of a mother and get her off my back." D.H. was panicked, I think he knew my mom wasn't going to stop calling and had often said she would just pop in one day. He wasn't concerned about her popping in at the house we no longer lived in, where she likely thought we still were, but he wasn't so confident that she wouldn't find us somehow. He had moved us to a cheap, no-questions-asked motel by this point as the bank had foreclosed on his house. So much for Mr. Moneybags, his rich family, and his successful business. The construction-supply business was actually a drug-supply business, which was also failing. Things were really going south for him, and I was his only source of income, so he had to keep me functioning. And keeping my family away was key to that.

I had brief times during those months when I tried hard to plot my escape, when I could be sure no one would die because of it. There were times when I felt I wanted to die, but then I'd get a little fight back in me—not for myself but my family who was under threat if I tried to get away. But I didn't know how to get myself to safety without him finding me.

One night in terrified desperation, before I was sent out to "work," I confronted D.H. and told him I was going home and would call the police and shoot him if he came near my family. The punishment that night in the hotel was brutal on the garbage-covered floor.

I REMEMBER THE GARBAGE by Erin Gray

He would run his hands through my hair only briefly,
before clasping my strands so tight and
pulling back in a velocity I could only compare
to the abrupt snap I received, getting rear-ended on the highway
at eighty kilometres per hour.
But more than that, I remember the garbage.

He would strangle me from behind with his bicep
so tight I would go deaf and blind
until I dropped like a book, pages flailing
from the top shelf.
To teach me what other men may do
given the chance.
But more than that, I remember the garbage.

He would extort me to ingest chemicals infused with fluid
just to see if it would burn.
I would collapse, searing and screaming,
fire inside me.
Leaving me coherent yet lifeless on the ground
until the next concoction was ready to snort.
But more than that, I remember the garbage.

I remember the way his body would feel
like dead weight on my back,
trying to buck him off me like a wounded foal the herd had left behind.
I ran across the wrong wolf.
His way of punishing me like a child, eating my soul like an animal.
But more than that, I remember the garbage.

He slowly turned my life against me.
A game of pretending to be me
until the last goose took flight, migrating in time.

My time had pressed pause as they flew,
my neck limp in the wolf's mouth, bones crushing,
constant pressure, slowly suffocating.
But more than that, I remember the garbage.

As the weeks went by, I no longer heard or envisioned the butterfly under glass because there was no escape from that solid, structured prison. I figured that beautiful, trapped butterfly had died, broken into a million pieces. A new sense of who I had become started to creep into my mind and I saw myself as a ragdoll. I had no substance. My body had become so thin, and my hair, nails, and skin had the appearance of someone already dead. I knew my days of being useful to him were coming to an end.

The following is from Erin's journal:

> *Tonight, I know I'm going to die. I walk fearlessly down the sidewalk toward the hotel where my captor waits, confident that I will return to him as I have become the obedient once-beautiful doll he has destroyed. But I see the look of disgust on his face, so I know, I'm going to die. Walking, stomping, catching soggy maple leaves now soaked and draped on my shoes as I march. Tiptoeing around flopping, squawking bar patrons at the bus stop, bumping my hip on a waist-height fence. The rusted metal with splashes of green where the paint hasn't worn off is only a four-inch diameter between me and a twenty-foot honor plunge to my death. Briefly, I feel it would be less torture than what's waiting for me behind the door in Room 140.*
>
> *Two a.m. Trembling, shaking, I walk slyly through the front sliding doors and casually, slowly walk toward the front desk. My shoes squeaking louder than the desk clerk Amanda could type, she looks up and I smile and turn away. She saw me. I make sure to walk in front of the cameras lining the long hallway, turning to show my face as I head toward the gates of hell. Room 140.*

As I stand paralyzed with defeat before the door, I take note of the nicks and cracks I see and admire the imperfections. I pull my hands up to my face and feel my withering, pale skin, wrinkled at twenty-two. I smell the garbage again. Death and decay, the rotting smell that leaks through the crack in the door. I compare it to the smell of my hair and confirm no difference. I remind myself of the charcoal grey coating where my gums straddle my yellow, cotton-covered teeth. I smile, remembering how I had the world four years ago and tonight I face ominous anxiety of being murdered. I stand and wonder where I'd be if I was born a redhead.

I used to be so pretty. The perfect little girl. I had long, natural blonde hair once, at the beginning of my captivity. I had a perfect body, mesmerizing icy-hot blue eyes, full lips, and those perfect teeth that my daddy had paid to straighten.

But then he took me.

Just a little while ago, I fell upon jealousy for the first time in my life when I saw a woman who society would deem unattractive, unsymmetrical, and deeply undesirable. How little she knows how I would murder to have been born another way. How jealous I was that she would never know the hurt of being taken and used, trafficked with no mercy, because I was "pretty" and "polite."

Had I known what I know now, I would've realized it was something written on my face besides eyes that match, but at twenty years old, I was naive and that's why I was tortured, molded, and made into a ragdoll.

RAGDOLL by Erin Gray

But the book could still look nice,
set on a shelf for rent,
with a sticker and a price.

It is met with craving eyes,
and minutes passed, they are content—
but the book could still look nice.

Perfume and heels will entice,
for the book itself has pages bent—
with a sticker and a price.

Its value lessens after the vice,
and back on the shelf with another's scent,
but the book could still look nice.

I began to try and record what was happening while I was fully drugged. Many times, I was sure I wasn't going to survive this torture and wanted someone, anyone, to hear what had been happening. He had given me one of his burner phones to use in case I needed to call him when he was out, but he always made sure to give me enough drugs to keep me pretty much comatose until he returned. I did notice he was no longer locking me in toward the end of our stay in his repossessed house and now he wasn't physically able to do that at the hotel. I felt maybe he was confident that he had me enough under his control that I wouldn't try to run away. But to make sure, he still forced me to consume a cocktail of uppers and downers, always timing it so I was depressed, drowsy, and weak when he had to be out.

I gradually came to be vaguely aware of those times where he needed me to "entertain" him or his customers. He would force me to take more drugs, typically GHB, commonly called the date-rape drug, which numbed my brain and slowed my body so I couldn't fight back. I practiced portraying a quicker reaction to the drug and would wait until he was out of the room, setting the hidden phone under the bed to record before I lost my ability to move. Those recordings proved to be crucial evidence in the years to come.

Leading up to the visit with my parents was so difficult. I always thought that when I was rescued or managed to escape, I would be so happy to be off all the drugs. Yes, they took me away when I was being used or beaten but I always knew, at some level, they were slowly killing me. The next two weeks were incredibly painful as he weaned me off enough drugs to make me appear to be mostly together.

But not so much so that I regained my ability to fight back. I was still highly alert to his threats and didn't doubt for a moment that he would carry through. I was in a vague state of trying to stay alive while also keeping alive my dog and my family. This would be the performance of my life as we went to visit my mom and stepdad. I hadn't seen them for almost a year. That's when I realized that I needed the drugs as badly as he needed me to perform for him during "working hours" and to keep my family off the scent of deceit. I was learning a very hard lesson that a person can't just make a choice to quit taking drugs. That's where the devil lies and the body dies.

CHAPTER TWENTY:
MOM

CUT OFF (SPRING 2011)

After a few more weeks of excuses and delays, Erin and D.H. finally arrived for a visit, trailer towed by his diesel truck and loaded with a frighteningly decrepit-looking dirt bike. My heart was pounding as I saw Erin step out of the passenger side of the truck. She did not look anything like my girl. Her hair had been dyed black and the protective gear she was wearing for her motorcycle lesson must have belonged to a child. She was so tiny and pale. I barely said hello to D.H. and brushed past him to hug Erin. She was like a statue in my arms but eventually put an arm around my waist and said "Hi, Mom." Her eyes and skin were dull, her words were slurred, and as her hand brushed hair back from her face, I saw the tremors. Both her hands were shaking so badly but when I asked her what was wrong, she simply told me she was nervous about learning how to ride a bike. Being a tomboy and risk taker was part of her DNA so I could not believe she was frightened about doing some slow trips up the road with three experienced people—me, Al, and D.H.—helping her along the way.

With the bike off the trailer and her helmet on, she went up the road at a snail's pace, D.H. guiding her as he refused to let us be a part of her learning experience. I was looking forward to them being finished so we could take them into the house for a coffee and visit. I should have known not to get my hopes up. The next time she looped back to the house, Erin dismounted, took off her helmet, and wearily crawled up into the passenger side of the truck as D.H. loaded the bike back on the trailer.

"We're going home," she said when I asked her to come in for coffee.

"But we haven't even had that visit you promised us!" I appealed to both her and D.H. Al got involved and told D.H. that we hadn't seen Erin for months and it wasn't fair to just leave.

"It didn't go as well with the bike as I thought," D.H. said bitterly. "She wouldn't listen and obviously isn't going to be good at riding, so we'll write this off. She's tired, I'm tired, we're going home. You've had your visit."

I cried silent tears as I watched them drive off down the road. I felt officially cut off from my daughter.

CHAPTER TWENTY-ONE: MOM

A PLEA FOR HELP (SUMMER 2011)

I had become a desperate stalker. It had been several weeks again since we'd seen Erin on that heartbreaking day with the dirt bike, and I kept trying her phone multiple times day and night. Eventually I got the message that the number had been disconnected. I had D.H.'s number from the times he had called to assure me that "everything was just fine" so I kept punching it in, but it mostly went to that dead-zone voice telling me the voicemail was full.

It was time to try and get some outside help. I had driven to D.H.'s house where I thought they were living, but the property was completely enclosed in construction fencing and the house was being demolished. A worker on site told me he thought the developer had bought it from the bank. And my worst fears were realized. D.H. was not the person he claimed to be, and my daughter's life was in danger. I called the local police station and spoke to an officer on duty.

"I believe my daughter is being held against her will and I need help getting her back," I said. "She began dating a guy who is not who he says he is, and now he has cut me off from any contact with her. She looks really ill, is not herself, and seems terrified."

"How long has this guy been dating your daughter?" the officer asked.

I struggled to remember the exact dates, so I told him approximately a year and a half.

"And you're just calling us now?" he replied.

"You don't understand," I said. "He is a chameleon, charming one minute, and brutal the next. He says he's good to her, but she looks like she is being horribly abused."

"Have you asked her to leave him?" His half-interested tone sounded like he was reading from a script.

"Yes, on many occasions, but now she doesn't talk to me because he won't let her." I was desperate for him to understand how serious this was.

"Are you sure she isn't just being rebellious because you don't like her boyfriend? How old is she?" He was beginning to sound annoyed with me.

"She's twenty-two and vulnerable. She's not the rebellious type, she's more like someone who would do anything to help someone else," I said, hoping he'd change his attitude.

"I'm sorry ma'am but she's an adult and if you've seen her and asked her to break up with him, there is nothing we can do. We don't get involved in family disputes unless there is a threat of violence and it sounds like she has made the choice to be with this guy, whether you approve of him or not."

My heart sank. "I don't think she *has* made that choice. I think he is forcing her to stay with him. There must be something you can do. I don't even know where they are anymore. His house has been foreclosed on and I can't get in touch with either her or him." By this time, I was sobbing into the phone, not something I would be reduced to normally, but I was terrified and desperate for help.

"I'm sorry ma'am, if she was a minor we could help but, in this case, it sounds like you and her will have to sort this out on your own." It was clear that the help I needed would not be coming, at least not from the police. I would have to keep trying on my own.

My own health was failing quickly. I'd taken a leave of absence from work to spend more time trying to find Erin and do some work on myself to help alleviate the anxiety. I was sleep-deprived and jumped at every sudden sound. And then I began to have heart troubles. I was experiencing heart palpitations to the extent they were causing me to almost lose consciousness. I was nauseous and terrified. I spent a full month getting a complete heart workup, fast tracked due to the high level of heart disease in my family on both sides.

Up until all this had begun, I had kept myself in relatively good shape but I was also entering the menopausal years and the perfect storm was building with the shifting hormones and extreme anxiety I had day and night. After all the blood tests, X-rays, ECGs, and whatever else poking and prodding was done to me, my heart was determined to be healthy and functioning and the reality kicked in that it was Erin's disappearance and not knowing whether she was dead or alive that was killing me.

I couldn't help her if I was dead, so I needed to make some changes in how I was managing my life while in this state of stress. I slowly began some stress-reducing practices with nature walks, calming music, and my already-established yoga routine, and I began learning to meditate. Meditation does not happen overnight, as I quickly learned. With a tortured mind like my own, coming into a calm and quiet place to rest my brain was, for me, like the movie *Groundhog Day*. I'd get settled, begin my breathing and relaxation, and then Erin's face would pop into my mind and I'd have to start again. I had to start over and over and over again. And then one day, I realized I had gone through the whole twenty-minute meditation, coming out at the end of it feeling just a tiny slice of hope, relief, and clarity. I could focus on a more constructive way of getting through my days and nights.

My closest friends were my rocks and my salvation through the whole process. Al did his very best to keep me level, while struggling with the anxiety and worry himself. He had been Erin's father for fifteen years and they were bonded like a dad and daughter. Ryan was angry that Erin was, as he verbalized, "putting us through this," and he distanced himself from the pain and the understanding that perhaps she did not have a choice in what was happening. But I had a strong network around me for which I will always be grateful. Because I needed to lean on them even more in the darker days to come.

CHAPTER TWENTY-TWO: MOM

GONE FOREVER (FALL 2011)

Several weeks went by with only one quick phone call from Erin, an unknown number coming upon my screen. "Mom, D.H. and I are camping at the beach," she said. "We didn't want to leave the animals at home, so I need your help as we have too many to keep with us. We have two cats and two dogs, and I think something is wrong with one of the cats. Can you come and get her?"

Camping? I stopped myself from telling her I knew they no longer lived at his former house because it had been repossessed. I knew she would hang up and my brief window of opportunity to see her would be gone.

"Erin, remember you already dropped off one cat, Mocha, several months ago. We already have two and another one will turn this house into a battleground of fur and angry felines!" I didn't want the cat, but I desperately wanted to see her. "We'll come this afternoon. Where exactly are you?" I asked. She gave me the lot number at a campground on a nearby beach.

"But Mom, we're going fishing, so I don't have time for a visit. Can you just come for the cat? And don't start asking a bunch of questions. D is grumpy today and he wants to get out in the boat, so I don't want to upset him, okay?"

I couldn't help myself. "Are you okay?" I asked her. "Your voice sounds really gruff, like you have a cold or something."

"I'm fine, it's just this medication I'm on," she replied. I wondered what kind of medication would turn what used to be a sweet girly voice into one that sounded almost manly.

I confirmed the time with her and then started doing what mothers do. Putting together a care package of baking and a couple of warm sweaters for her. The weather was quickly turning into chilly autumn, and I couldn't imagine what camping would feel like, especially that close to the water. I felt helpless and scared, not sure what seeing her this time would be like.

We pulled into the campsite and took stock of what we could see was obviously not just a camping weekend. This was a home. There were two dogs in the back of the diesel truck, Harley and another small bulldog named Reckless. Harley bounded over to my SUV and jumped up, wiggling with excitement. He was a German Shepherd cross, so he almost reached my chin on his hind legs and he was desperately trying to lick my face, covering my neck with happy dog slobber. As I rubbed his sides, I was concerned at being able to feel his ribs.

Then my concern shifted as Erin came out from the other side of D.H.'s truck. Even though she was wearing a thick fleece, I could see she had lost even more weight. Her eyes had dark circles and her dyed black hair was so lank, thin, and dirty looking. This was not my girl who cared so much about her appearance.

"Hi, D.H. is in the tent and he's sick so please keep your voice down." Her voice was even deeper than it had sounded on the phone, her words were clearly scripted, and I could hear the stress and fear in them. I set the box of baking and clothes on the tailgate of his truck.

"This is just a few treats for you and a couple of warm sweaters. But this isn't right, Erin. It's freezing to be camping. Are you homeless now?" I asked.

The tent flap opened, and D.H. crawled out, hauled himself up to standing and shouted at me. "Who do you think you are? We aren't homeless, we are enjoying the last few days of summer camping. You think I can't take care of your daughter—that totally pisses me off!! You don't care about her. You never have and I am here to protect her and give her everything she needs. You should leave now."

His sudden tirade shocked both Al and I but it was Erin's reaction that got my blood boiling. As soon as he began shouting, she shrunk as if avoiding the words like blows to her body.

Al, being the calm diplomat, tried to reason with D.H. and bring the conversation back to civility. My hands were shaking, the dogs were both barking, and I was glad the rest of the campsite was empty. "Erin, do you want to come home with us?" I asked, hoping my eyes would show how desperate I was to get her out of that situation.

"No, I'm fine. I told you D.H. wasn't feeling well and you were rude, asking if we are homeless. That's ridiculous, I just wanted you to take the cat and not make such a big deal out of everything."

Not once did she make eye contact with me when stating this. My stomach dropped as I could clearly see what a hold he had on her and my hopeful thoughts of a rescue dissipated.

"Okay, where is the cat?" I asked, trying to defuse the situation. Erin led us to the back seat of the dual cab truck and pulled a cage out with a thin, sickly looking gray tabby looking at us in fear. I was dismayed to see another cage in the truck with a larger cat who fortunately looked in much better condition. Erin explained that one was D.H.'s cat and they were keeping him.

"She doesn't have a name, we rescued her, but she has some kind of weird skin condition. We don't want her to infect the other animals." This time, she looked at me with pleading eyes.

"She'll infect our cats too, Erin, if it's contagious. Why don't you just take her to the vet?" I already knew the answer to that one, as obviously they had no money. But I wanted to hear what D.H. would say.

"We have plans after camping, and we don't have the time to be taking her to the vet or looking after her so why can't you just do your daughter this one little favor? Is it such a big deal?" His voice had calmed but he was staring at me like he hated me. Which I'm sure he did. I was the biggest threat he had to losing control over Erin.

"I'll look after her," I said as I put the cage in the back seat of our vehicle. I was hoping Erin would follow me so I could quietly whisper a few words to her, encourage her to jump in with us, and get out of that terrible situation. She was standing halfway between our vehicle and their tent where D.H. was standing. She looked at us, looked at him, and then he put his hand on Harley's collar and pulled him close to his legs, all the while staring at her, the threat clearly in the air between them. She walked back to the tent, D.H., and her beloved dog.

"Thanks, Mom. Let me know what the vet says, and I promise I'll pay you back for whatever costs there are. And thanks for the goodies."

I could barely hear her as she tucked her chin down into her fleece. Her eyes were downcast, and I was sure she was hiding tears. My own eyes were filling up with tears and I wondered for the hundredth time if I was reading more into this than there actually was. I was questioning my own gut again. But I was also at a loss of what to do.

I walked back over to her and wrapped my arms as tightly around her as I could. "You can always come home," I whispered. I felt her nod her head into my shoulder.

"We have to get the boat into the water, it's getting late," D.H. said. She quickly pulled away from my embrace and I slowly walked back to our vehicle, Al taking my hand and saying "She'll be okay," as I got into the passenger seat.

I hoped he was right but another piece of my heart broke as we backed out of the campsite. I didn't know where they would go from the campsite, where they would end up living. How would I ever find her if he kept all communication cut off?

And then the day came when I no longer had hope that she would show up, bags in hand, asking if she could come home. It was a Saturday, and I was working in the flower garden in the front yard. I heard a diesel coming down our small, rural road and looked up to see D.H.'s truck pulling up to the front of the house, a long hauling trailer hitched to the bumper. Erin climbed out of the passenger seat, and he drove away. In that brief moment, my heart soared. *He's brought her back and he's leaving. She's staying!*

"Is he gone? You're home to stay?" I asked excitedly.

"No, I'm not home to stay. He's just turning the truck around at the end of the road. Mom, we're moving to Prince George to stay with someone in D.H.'s family who lives there. And we won't be coming back. There's nothing left for us here and he has a business to run, moving parts to oil rigs up north. We can do that from Prince George easier than from here."

Her words were flat. Rehearsed. Not for a minute did I believe D.H. was running a legitimate business. By this time, even though we tried to understand and accept that she wanted to be with him, I never came to terms with it. It rang false in so many ways; it was an act on her part, and she was inextricably trapped. I was sure he was involved with criminal activities and had no ability to lead an honest life.

D.H. had pulled the truck up again to the front yard. He stepped out, barely looked at me, and asked Erin where it was.

"What are you looking for?" I asked.

"Erin's furniture, we're taking it with us to PG," he responded. There was a couch and chair in our basement that we had given to her brand-new when she first moved into our suite.

"You can't take that," I cried. "That's for her first house, a gift from us!"

"Well then, it's hers, isn't it? And we are moving into a house. Tell her, Erin."

"Mom, we don't have a couch and chair, so I want to take it there. And all my boxes are stored downstairs too." she said, her eyes not focusing, looking somewhere over my shoulder rather than at me.

Now I was angry. Furious that they were leaving, taking the few things that still tied her to our house, declaring they would not be back. My feelings about her going were being disregarded and the finality of it filled me with fear that I may never see her again. At least with her still here in the city, I had some semblance of hope that she would find her way back home. Now a twelve-hour drive away, she'd be completely isolated from her family and remaining friends. She used to be surrounded by many friends but over the past several months her absence in their lives and D.H.'s continual erosion of those relationships had left only one or two still willing to be a part of her life. And now those would be over as well.

My anger welled up again. "Go ahead, take your furniture and the rest of your stuff. You know where it is." I fumed and paced as they were loading up the couch, chair, and half a dozen boxes of precious memorabilia including photographs piled on top without even a protective tarp. It was like Erin's life, her future, and my memories were haphazardly being tossed up and away. Maybe forever.

My anger then turned to desperation. “Please Erin, this is not a good idea. I have a feeling things will go very badly, and I’ll be too far away to help you.” I had my hands on her upper arms, pleading with her, tears streaming down my face by this time. She looked so detached, so cold, so devoid of hope. I dropped my hands, and she turned around to get into the truck.

As I stood in the middle of the road, watching the truck and trailer drive away, my cries became guttural, and I clenched my fists into my stomach. My last vision was D.H. looking at me through his side mirror and grinning like a Cheshire cat. He had won.

CHAPTER TWENTY-THREE: ERIN

NO HELP (FALL 2011)

I will never get the sight of mom out of my tortured mind, as she stood crying on the road while we drove away and out of her life. I was numb on the cocktail of downers that D.H. had given me, but I wasn't so far down that I couldn't see her pain. But I couldn't feel my own pain and that was alright with me. It was a long drive ahead of us and I was so tired.

Within the first two weeks of our arrival in Prince George, the glimmer of hope I'd had that things might get better was dashed by the treatment I received from his family. It was a house filled with violence, yelling, drugs, and filth. I looked at my nice new couch and chair in the almost empty living room and watched it deteriorate with spills, cigarette burns, and worse. Everything that I had brought with me was thrown in with the communal kitchen things and my boxes of pictures, memorabilia, journals, and poetry were tossed haphazardly down in a damp basement. I wasn't allowed to go through them as I was told it would only remind me of what a terrible family I had, who didn't care about me and had abandoned me when I needed them.

Every week was the same. I'd get woken up by D.H. and told to get my ass outside and help load up the truck as we were taking another shipment of parts up north to the oil rigs. It didn't take long to figure out the "parts" were drugs and his business was dealing to the oil-rig workers. Once all the deliveries were done, we'd start the long drive back to Prince George and the fighting family members, filth, and verbal abuse. They called me every name possible, including D.H.'s "whore."

Prior to moving to PG, I was subjected to drugging, sex trafficking, forced into exotic dancing, and held hostage with the constant threats of harm to me, the dogs, and my family. At some point those threats became secondary to my need for access to the drugs he supplied. In PG, the threats continued but at least the sex trafficking stopped, although now I had become a partner in drug trafficking. The drugging did not stop but was doled out only enough to keep me compliant and in a weakened state. The combination of drugs and the lack of healthy food was quickly breaking down my body—and my mind was along for that terrible ride. The verbal and physical abuse doubled once D.H.'s brother decided I was his property too. I guess that's what I had become, and I could no longer deny that they owned me and my soul.

And then one day everything changed. I don't know what triggered it except it might have been a bad drug deal as D.H. and his brother got into a huge fight about all the money being "gone."

We took the bare necessities in a few bags, loaded up his truck, and started the long drive back to the island. I was going home.

D.H. was in the worst frame of mind I had ever seen him in. He checked us into a run-down motel that had long-term rentals and we moved into a one-room space with our now *three* dogs, one cat, and a few clothes in a bag. He continually freaked out about where to get money and blamed me for everything. And it was going to be my responsibility to get back the money he had lost.

"You stupid cow, you have to work to make up for this." He was shouting at me and I looked longingly at the tin with a line of cocaine on it, inviting me to escape from his hateful words and the gut-twisting feeling of combined helplessness and hopelessness. He saw me looking at it and said, "I can't afford to let you have that. You have to earn it." He began to withhold all drugs and for the first time, I experienced what full detox felt like.

I was begging him. "Please, I'm in so much pain. I should go to the hospital."

"Suck it up, Princess," he smirked. "You are in this because of your stupidity. I put out an ad and you'll start earning money tonight. Then you can have all you want."

That was the first time he had pimped me out without the reality-numbing mask of anything. No cocaine, no crack, no GHB, no stolen prescription sedatives… nothing. It was horrific. I was so weak. I couldn't walk or even move. I tried to make my mind go to other places, but the physical pain kept dragging me back to the present. It was a long, tortuous night of the door opening, another strange man hurting me, the dogs whining in the bathroom, and then D.H. waving money in my face in the morning. And my reward? A couple of hits to soothe my aching body and help me to forget the nightmare. I was covered in bruises and vomiting from still detoxing. I welcomed the comforting blanket as the hit warmed me and took me to a quiet, still place of no pain and no fear.

And so, it carried on, until he managed to get himself back into the drug-dealing market. By this time, I had lost most of my looks through the brutality, lack of food, and drugs. D.H. began to berate me as becoming "unmarketable," so he increased the dose of steroids he had already been giving me, stating this would help me muscle up faster and get rid of the skinniness. My voice had already been altered by the steroids and taking the extra-high doses was further robbing me of what little health I had left. I had lost any ability to even think about escape and spent most of my days lying either on the bed with my dog or lying on the bathroom floor, praying for death. He watched me constantly, suspecting I was having suicidal thoughts. Days rolled into nights and then weeks and I lived in a state of stupor, all thoughts of ever again living a happy healthy life gone. I would die here, and he'd toss me in the ocean one dark night, moving onto his next victim.

It was the thought of this next victim that lit a small spark of defiance within me. I had come to know the buyers and sellers of the drugs he was trafficking but one day a new guy showed up. I was usually made to wait in the bathroom while they did their "business," but on the day I first saw him, he and D.H. were in the parking lot talking. I was never allowed to stand in the window, but something made me open the curtain part way and as I looked right at this guy, Harley jumped up beside me, putting his paws on the sill. I glanced down at my beautiful German Shepherd and noticed how terribly thin he was. Then I turned my head and looked at myself in the mirror on the dresser and saw how terribly thin I was too. It was at that moment that I knew I needed to risk it all and try to get away.

D.H.'s back was to the window and I looked long and hard at this new man's face, trying to get his attention and convey a silent message of "help me" to him. I was desperate and taking a chance he was a decent person. He glanced over D.H.'s shoulder, held my gaze for a brief moment, and as D.H. started to turn, he put a hand on his shoulder to get his attention long enough for me to quickly close the curtain. Did he sense I was begging for help? Or was I imagining things? And then I heard him get in his car, the door closed, and he backed away from the building, taking any hope of rescue I had with him.

CHAPTER TWENTY-FOUR: MOM

LOSING MY MIND (FALL 2011)

Because my thoughts were so fantastical—something out of dark, terror-filled movies—I found a few family members and even friends suggesting that maybe I was imagining scenarios that didn't exist. It was obvious to them that after all this time, Erin had made a choice and I just didn't like that choice.

But a mother's intuition about her children is rarely wrong. I've always had an active imagination as a writer of short stories and humorous articles meant to engage and entertain. But now I felt I was writing a horror story. I was starting to have doubts about my acuity and even starting to believe that my daughter and I were estranged forever. I needed help from an outside source to provide some perspective. I needed someone impartial to please tell me I wasn't losing my grip on reality!

I sought counseling, hoping someone unattached to my story could help me. On the fourth session out of the six that we had planned, I decided my first counselor wasn't getting me anywhere. She was jokey, constantly trying to make me laugh, and I just couldn't get my head around how the circumstance of my missing daughter—probably being held against her will and forced to ingest and traffic drugs—could possibly be alleviated by having a good chuckle.

And, at that time, during my first counseling session, I had absolutely no clue that she actually was being sex trafficked. My thoughts hadn't gone that far, so if I had known that was happening it would have broken my brain forever. So no, dear counselor with the jokey sense of humor, sometimes laughter being the best medicine is just a load of crap.

My second counselor was through a government-assisted service that alleviated costs because I was running out of money since I was no longer able to manage a full-time job. Therapy is expensive. That second counselor lasted one session after she spent the entire hour looking at the clock and taking phone calls while I cried out my anxiety to a distracted and robotic sub-human. As I left her office, refusing to book another appointment with the busy receptionist, I was determined to figure this out myself. Where had my intuition gone? Where was the little voice that steered my insides? Why and when had I begun to question my gut feelings? It was time to go back to searching for answers within.

In the weeks following Erin's departure for Prince George, I paced, monitored social media (complete silence on any of her accounts), dialed and re-dialed every number I had for her or for D.H., and jumped for my cell phone every time I heard a ping. My anxiety was doing its own dialing, farther and farther up the scale where sleep only came when my mind and body reached a point of exhaustion. Even those brief exhaustion-induced coma-states were interrupted by every little sound I heard in the night.

What I didn't know as the days melted into nights was that Erin was no longer in Prince George. She was back in the city. Living a life of absolute terror, brutality, and sickness.

CHAPTER TWENTY-FIVE: ERIN

EVERYTHING BURNS (EARLY WINTER 2012)

All desire to be or do anything was gone. As I laid on the floor with Harley, once again crying into his fur, I began to pray. I'd felt months ago that God had abandoned me, and I carried the burden of believing I didn't deserve His love and guidance because I had allowed myself to be in this prison of drugs, abuse, and criminality. I was using drugs, selling drugs, putting up with being sold to other men, and even sometimes helping D.H. plan how to scam people.

How had things reached this point? It's all a blur and with the constant ingestion of so many different types of illegal and prescription drugs, I wondered how my heart was still beating and how I could still take a breath. Without the drugs, though, I'm sure I would have died a brutal death by now. Either from D.H.'s and other men's beatings or maybe by my own hand. But if I died, what would happen to Harley and the other dog, whom we had named Rufus? The third dog had already been taken away by animal control after biting other hotel guests. That poor dog had never had any hope other than being violent. I had grown to love Rufus as well as Harley and wanted to protect them both because we were all terrified victims together. I was sure D.H. would just kill them if I wasn't around as a buffer. I was trapped.

I wonder what Mom is thinking now? I mused. Did she really give a shit about me? I'd lied so much about what was going on and then he'd cut me off completely from my family and my friends, so I was sure they thought I was a total selfish bitch. She might be mad at me but why wasn't she working harder to find me? *She probably thinks I'm still in*

PG so imagine her surprise if I manage to just show up on the front step of their house one day! But … what if I didn't get there and warn her about D.H.'s promise to burn it down if I left him? She'd want to go to the police and then they'd find out my part in all the drug dealing and, oh my God, the shame of what has been done to me. It was all too much. So much time had gone by, and I was getting deeper and deeper into this pit that was surely hell.

My hands were shaking and I was sweating. The craving is indescribable. It's a hunger that reaches its greedy fingers down deep into your brain and your soul. It is pain, it is desire, it is unrelenting. I needed a fix to help me get through the disappointment of missing my chance to get the attention of the guy outside—and to numb me for what would likely be another night of abuse.

The hotel room door opened and D.H. walked in, shouting into his cell phone. "What the hell happened, you idiot! Where's all our stuff? Did you get anything out of the house?" He was beside himself with anger and obviously frantic with worry. He listened to the other voice for another minute or two and then said, "Just get yourselves the hell out of there, call me later once you find a place to go."

"Please D.H., I need something. I'm hurting." I was begging and he wasn't listening. I was more concerned with how I was feeling at the moment than with what I assumed was likely a drug deal gone south.

"Who was that on the phone? What happened?" I asked, still hoping he'd look at me and be able to tell how much I was suffering.

"Shit, shit, shit!!! The goddamn house burned down in PG. My brother is taking off; he doesn't know what happened, but it's all gone. Everything burned. Including all your crap in the basement and the furniture. We definitely have absolutely nothing now." He picked up a plate from the table and threw it across the room, pieces shattering against the door.

"Pack up your shit, Erin, we gotta get outta here. But I need to do my run tonight and get some cash. And I don't need to remind you, do I? You try to sneak out of here, I'll find you and end you along with your stupid dog and your asshole family. Got that?" He was spitting as he shouted at me, raising his hand to make sure I did get it. Harley barked and stood in front of me, sensing danger. For once, he wasn't locked in the bathroom while D.H. took his anger out on me. D.H. dropped his hand and went over to the hotel safe in the wall, opening it and taking out a package that was either money or drugs. It was routine. Same time, same night of the week, and same package from the safe. I knew I'd be alone for a couple of hours and felt relief, but I also knew I'd be in severe withdrawal by the time he came back. He left without looking at me, as I pulled my knees up to my chest and hugged myself tight to try calm the tremors. I called both dogs over to where I was curled up on the floor and they settled, one on either side of me. My whole body hurt, and I wondered where we would end up by this time the next night.

I must have fallen asleep and thought I could hear a soft knocking in my crazy dreams. Harley whined beside me and Rufus gave a short bark. They got hit if they uttered a sound when D.H. was around, so I figured he was still out. The knock came again. Too soft to be D.H. if he had lost his key. I crawled on all fours to the door.

"Who is it?" I whispered as loudly as I dared.

"It's Bruce. From last night. Out in the parking lot. I know D.H. isn't here but he could come back any time. Are you okay? Can you open the door?"

"Bruce? I don't know any Bruce. You have to leave before D.H. comes back." Was this the new guy I had been trying to send a signal to?

"I think you might be in trouble." he said quietly through the door. "I can help but you gotta come out right now!"

I should have been more scared. But something told me my chance had come. I grabbed my purse, opened the door, and pushed the dogs ahead of me.

"No, no dogs. You have to leave them. He needs to think you've just gone out for a walk or something. If we take the dogs, he'll be on our trail too fast." He was pushing the dogs back in through the door as they whined and barked to be let free too.

"I can't leave them, he'll kill them!" I shouted.

"No, he won't. They are his ticket because he knows you'll come back for them. Come on! He might come back any time!" He was starting to panic but I was thinking, this guy is huge, he could take D.H. in a heartbeat. Then I remembered the package from the safe. Maybe it was a gun. I knew D.H. carried a knife and I had never seen a gun but that meant nothing. D.H. was a master of deceit.

I was still standing in the doorway, one foot toward freedom but sick to leave the dogs. If I left now, I could wait until D.H. went out again, maybe tomorrow or the next day, and come get them. I felt sure D.H. wouldn't leave the city to go wherever he had been planning on taking us—not without me, his meal ticket. I was sure he would be out looking for me and if I left, I had to make sure to call Mom and let her know she needed to call the police for protection.

Now that I had someone on my side, I felt a glimmer of hope that maybe this was going to work! My body was still wracked with pain and I was shaking uncontrollably from withdrawal, but my thoughts had become crystal clear with the anticipation of escape. I wrapped my arms around both dogs and said "I'll be back in a day or two at the most and get you out of here. I'm so sorry, I'm so sorry," I cried as I pushed them back into the room. I stumbled into the corridor and immediately fell to my knees. My stomach cramped sharply, my head was pounding, and I was shaking so hard, I couldn't even push myself back up. I had been too long without food or drugs.

I felt Bruce pick me up as if I weighed nothing and then I felt the cool air on my face as he hurried us out the back exit. He settled me into the passenger seat of his car and asked me, "Are you high right now?"

"No, but I need something. Have you got anything? Can we come back tomorrow for the dogs? Where are you taking me? I need to phone my mom right now. He's going to kill my whole family in a fire!" I could hear myself rattling off questions, panicking, and going into full detox mode.

"No, I don't do that shit. You're going to have to muscle through this. Erin, right? You look really rough. What has that fucker done to you? Never mind, you can tell me later. I'm taking you to my house." He put the car in gear, and I could feel the tires spin on the pavement as we left the hotel parking lot.

"Don't freak out," he said. "I'm not going to hurt you. But first, you need to eat something, so we're going to a drive-thru. You're gonna eat and then you're gonna sleep, and we'll figure out things in the morning. He ain't going to go after your family tonight, he'll be too busy driving around trying to find you walking the streets."

Bruce, I thought. *Did he say that was his name?* I didn't think I'd be able to eat but the sleep sounded good. I could call Mom tomorrow and start figuring out what to do next. Was it finally over? My head rolled back against the seat and just as I started to close my eyes, I asked Bruce a question I had been wondering for weeks.

"What month is this?" I asked.

Bruce turned his head to look at me, disbelief written on his face. "It's February. February 12th, 2012. You honestly don't know that?" he asked.

"I missed Christmas again," I mumbled as my eyes closed and darkness washed over me. I had been held hostage by a monster for almost two years.

PART THREE: A LONG ROAD TO RECOVERY

CHAPTER TWENTY-SIX:
MOM

HOPE IN THE NEW YEAR (2012)

Christmas had come and gone and the empty chair at the table sat foremost in my mind. I tried my best to celebrate with the family but the knot of anxiety at the base of my stomach and the ever-increasing headaches from worry were taking their toll. It had been almost two years since my daughter slipped out of our lives and I still felt alone in my belief that she was gone against her will. If I was honest with myself, there were times that my fear, anxiety, and worry escalated to anger. If she was truly being held against her will, why didn't she find a way to reach out to me?

I had spent hours studying cases of women who developed Stockholm Syndrome, when the victim begins to identify with her captor and support his initiatives. I learned it was rare for victims to develop this condition and I had a hard time accepting that my strong-willed, resourceful girl could be a case. Something else was keeping her away from us because I was so sure she wouldn't support and encourage what I believed to be his criminal activities in drug running. If I'd only known then that the drug business was only a small component of his evil lifestyle.

The days went by with my body and mind functioning at a bare-minimum level. Each morning started the same way. I went through the motion of someone opening their door to pick up the daily newspaper, but I held my breath as I checked the front step. Not for the paper, but for my daughter's body… hopefully quietly sleeping, waiting for me to wake up and come to the door so she could come in and return home. The sight of the empty front step defeated my hope every damn day.

I wrote a card to Erin on Valentine's Day. It simply said, "I miss you sweetheart. Wherever you are, I love you, I miss you, please come home." And I tucked it away in a dresser drawer with the one I had written to her in 2011, the same words, the same agony of loss.

It was Monday, February 20th, 2012. When an unknown number came up on my phone, I deliberated not answering, thinking it was yet another sales or scam call. But then I answered just before it quit ringing.

"Hello?" I answered.

"Is this Wanda?" A strange man's voice was at the other end and as I moved the phone away from my ear to press "end," he said, "Are you Erin's mom?"

A hushed silence fell as the world began to waver in front of me. Everything came down to this exact moment. "Yes, who is this?" I asked.

"I'm calling to let you know that Erin is here with me, safe. She's not with D.H. anymore, I got her out of there. She's not feeling good, but she wanted me to call to let you know."

"Where are you?" I shouted into the phone. "If she's really with you, please let me talk to her!"

I could hear his muffled voice talking to someone. He must have had his hand over his phone or pressed up against him. "Just say 'hi' to her cause I think she thinks I'm lying."

It was a female voice I heard answer him, but it sounded much more gruff, deeper than Erin's voice. I shouted again into the phone, "Who is this! Please. This is cruel if it's a joke."

I heard a muffled groan followed by a sigh and a shuffling noise, followed by the sound of breathing in the phone.

"Hi Mom, it's me."

"Oh God, Erin? Is that really you? What's happened to your voice?" I knew it was her, but the tone and depth were so different. "Where are you? What's happened? I'm coming to get you." Everything was coming out of me in one sentence, my breath leaving my body with the words.

"I'm not ready to come home yet, Mom. I'm pretty messed up and need some time to sort out what's happened."

"Erin, it's been two years with almost no communication! Do you have any idea what we've been going through?" My frustration and anger was starting to surface and I struggled to get it under control.

"You have no idea what I've been going through either, Mom. I said that I need time to rest and figure out what I'm going to do. I can't do that with you. You're way too out of control."

Her words hit me hard. But how could I help her if she wouldn't let me come and get her? All kinds of visions were flashing through my mind. Was she beat up, bruised, physically altered in some way? And what the hell had happened to her voice? It was so raspy and so deep, much deeper than the last time I had physically talked to her.

"Do you need to go to the hospital, Erin? I can take you now." I was so desperate to see her for myself and know firsthand why she didn't want me to see her.

"*No!!*" she shouted in that deep, almost unrecognizable voice. "No hospital, I told you, I just need time. I'll come home when I'm ready. I don't want to be sorry I had Bruce call you, Mom. Please just back off until I call and tell you that I'm coming home."

Bruce? I wondered. I'd never heard that name. I doubted she would give me his last name, but I'd try. "What is Bruce's last name? How do I know he's not hurting you?" I asked.

"He's not hurting me, Mom. He rescued me. He's keeping me safe. I'm back in the city and no one knows where I am. I need to keep it that way while I think things through. It's not safe for me to be at your house."

"Why not? Is D.H. looking for you?" I asked.

"He probably is, so you have to be really careful, Mom. Keep the doors locked and watch for his truck. He's probably watching your house to see if I show up there, but I doubt he'll come to the door. He knows he's busted, so he'll be keeping a low profile."

I couldn't believe what I was hearing. What kind of nightmare movie were we unwillingly characters in now? My intense relief at knowing she was safe felt like a breath of fresh air and I didn't feel worried or fearful at any possible confrontation with D.H. Was I actually having thoughts that my little handgun I used for target practice at the firing range might come in handy on the home front? I shook that thought off and tried once more to convince Erin to come home—to no avail. She was determined to stay put until she was ready. She promised she'd call me in a few days, and I had no choice but to accept that. I was feeling an extreme rush of gratitude and optimism only slightly overshadowed by my worry over her health and the sound of her changed voice. When she hung up, I quickly moved to call my husband Al and give him the good news. *Erin is alive, she's in the city and she'll be home soon!*

CHAPTER TWENTY-SEVEN: ERIN

WHAT HAPPENS NOW? (EARLY WINTER 2012)

When I ended the phone call with Mom, my thoughts were so scattered. I did feel safe with Bruce, whom I had started to look at like he was my guardian angel. My hero. My rescuer. He was older than me and I had no fear of him. It didn't feel safe going home because D.H. might see me there and carry out his threats of burning my parent's house in the night—this time with me in it too. I was his main source of income with the sex trafficking and the forced drug dealing but it was his psychotic need for control that had me more concerned. He was not going to let me go without some kind of payback. That was the way it worked in his world. I would need to be punished for leaving. And what about the dogs? Was he feeding them? Taking care of them? I preferred to think so, but I also needed to make sure. I was so stressed. I didn't know what to do. Should I go to the cops? Tell them everything? But what if they looked at me like an accomplice? I could go to jail!

And then another horrible thought came into my head. With me gone, the first thing D.H. would have to do is "recruit" another victim to take my place. My stomach turned at the thought. He would need to be stopped. Was I willing to sacrifice the dogs' lives and risk going to jail if I went to the police?

I couldn't seem to control my thoughts. And then there was the other thing I was trying to hide from everyone. I had been a week without drugs and it had been brutally painful. Bruce did his best to keep me from harming myself, but I was so sick. In those last few months with D.H. I had been taking so many steroids that it had changed my voice and ruined my skin and hair. I knew I looked like hell—another reason I didn't want Mom to see me yet. She'd freak out and rush me to the nearest hospital and it wouldn't take them long to figure out I was drug dependent. I didn't want her to know that. I would tell her that quitting was really easy once it wasn't being forced into me. She knew nothing about drugs and would probably believe me if I told her I was just experiencing symptoms of trauma from the hostage taking.

Even Bruce thought I was going to be able to stay clean after this week of detoxing at his house. I had found some pretty strong painkillers in the medicine cabinet in the bathroom next to the room he had put me in "to get healthy again." If I was careful, they might be enough to get me through the next few days, as I claimed I was just so tired and worn out that I couldn't function. The thought of deceiving him and Mom made me sick, but I knew I could let go of the cravings once I had time to figure out what my next steps would be. I fully believed I would get through all of this, D.H. would be dealt with, and I would lead a long, healthy life. Maybe get married and have kids.

But first, I needed to write everything down about what had happened to me over the last couple of years. It would be brutal, yet probably cathartic. I could use it as my statement should I decide to go to the police. I prepared myself for reliving the nightmare, pen in hand (Bruce had no computer, weird). I just needed to make one phone call first—once I ran it past Bruce. I'd need him to get me a burner phone so the call that the number came from wouldn't show up on the other end.

"Hi, it's Erin," I said quietly into the phone.

"You treacherous bitch! Where the hell are you? You owe me money and you stole drugs and all my money too, you thieving cow." I had done none of that, but he was convinced I was a snitch and a thief. D.H. was shouting into the phone and I could picture him spitting as he yelled, hair standing on end, and probably kicking things around the room. His temper would have had plenty of time to build in this past week or so and I worried about the dogs.

"I didn't steal any money, you know that. And how would I have stolen drugs from you? Everything was in the safe," I said, hoping he'd realize what he was saying was impossible. "I'm really sorry but I was feeling so sick and so tired, I just needed a few days of rest to get better. I need a break from the work you keep bringing in."

My heart was pounding, and I felt sick to my stomach with the effort to stay calm and placate him. "I promise I'll come back as soon as I feel better," I said into the phone. And the next words would be the most practiced lie I could manage. "I really miss you. I'm no good without you but I have a lot of bruises, and my energy is just gone. I was working too much and not sleeping. I'll be that much better, and we can make more money to make up for what I'm missing now. Please understand."

I didn't think I could keep up this facade much longer and I could see Bruce sitting on the couch across the living room, fists clenched and face purple with suppressed emotion as I spoke to D.H. He didn't agree with my methods but understood the need to try placating D.H. so he didn't think that I'd just left him high and dry. I didn't think it would be totally unbelievable to my captor that I might go back, considering what a narcissistic control freak he was. He honestly didn't think I could survive without him and for too long I had believed the same. His luring methods, followed by the gradual mind and body control, were honed from plenty of practice with his previous girls.

"How are Harley and Rufus?" I asked.

"What did you think I would do with them?" he sputtered into the phone. "You just left Harley, and I shouldn't have to look after *your* dog! They're a pain in the ass so you better get your ass back here right away and look after them. They are your job, not mine."

My heart dropped. He probably wasn't feeding them properly or letting them out. And then they'd get a beating for making a mess inside. I absolutely *had* to get them back. Harley was mine and Rufus was his, but they were both bonded with me because I protected them. And now I had left them. I was consumed by guilt and worry.

"Give me a couple of days and then I'll come back. I promise. And please, please, please feed the dogs and I'll make it up to you as soon as I'm back. Okay? Please. I love you." Those last three words felt like shards of glass passing through my throat—they were so painful, so hard, and so wrong. But this had to work.

"Where are you?" he demanded into the phone.

I'd already worked out a response for that question I knew would be coming. He might not just back off and give me a few days, he might hunt me down and drag me back by my hair.

"I'm not at Mom's, I didn't want to go there. I have a place to stay where it's quiet and I can just sleep. No one is here." My lie hung in the air between us, and I held my breath, waiting to see if he'd pursue it further.

"You're so stupid, Erin. You don't know when you've got it good. But because I love you too, I'll give you a couple of days. Then you better get your ass back here and make it up to me." His idea of love made me want to vomit. But I breathed out, thanking him and ended the call quickly before he could go off on another rant.

I needed to work fast. How was I going to put everything together and hopefully convince the police to arrest him within a few days? My statement was almost ready and in my desperation to rescue the dogs, this meant that I would have to ask for help. But not from Bruce this time—I didn't want to get him involved. I would need to call Mom. I could not do this on my own.

CHAPTER TWENTY-EIGHT: MOM

A BRAVE GIRL (EARLY SPRING 2012)

Every fiber of my being was in a state of shock and disbelief. This had to be the plot of a terrifying and violent horror movie with my daughter playing the part of the victim. I was being pulled along on a wave of surreal events that just don't happen to ordinary people like us. The reality of what Erin had been going through the past months did not register with me. I think that if I had allowed her story to penetrate the protective wall of shock that surrounded me, I would have simply died from the pain.

But here we were. Waiting together in an interrogation room at the police station, our fingers intertwined and terrified of what would happen next. I had a silly thought as I looked through the glass walls that surrounded this room. On TV, the rooms are always four walls with a one-way mirror where the investigators and other police could watch the suspect being questioned. Why would there be so much glass? Here, I could see across a wide hallway into another identical, cubicle-like, glass-walled room where a young officer was reading what we knew to be Erin's statement. We had been told to wait while they had a chance to go over what she had written. It was several pages long and she had refused to let me read it. She told me I would never sleep again if I did. I would hear that once more a few months later, this time from the Crown prosecutor, and I would understand the reasoning behind it. But for now, I had heard the story of her horrific life from my daughter, and I thought those words couldn't be any more painful or shocking.

"You're a very brave girl, sweetheart," I said as I put my hands on either side of her face, wiping tears away with my thumbs.

"I'm so scared, Mom. No one knows what he's capable of."

Her fear was palpable, and she seemed to be falling apart again. My thoughts were jumping all over the place. Oh, God, how did we get here? And why is it taking so long?

As we waited, I thought back to the day before when Erin had called me. She was coming home and needed to tell me something. I was scared and excited at the same time. The last time I had seen her was when she was going to Prince George; she had been so thin, her hair brittle, and her skin so pale. And I was furious at this man who claimed to care so much about her but didn't give her the time to look after herself. She had been so beautiful with her big blue eyes, blonde hair, and healthy and fit body but after all those months with him, she was barely recognizable. She couldn't possibly be in worse condition now, could she?

I had paced, anxiously looking out the window and waiting for a car to pull up. She said her ride "buddy" would not be coming in and I was to wait inside until she came to the door. When I saw a car pull up to the front fence, I couldn't wait. I opened the door, forcing myself not to rush to the car, and went down the steps as slowly as I could. I saw her get out of the passenger side, turn to say something to the driver, then she closed the car door and turned to face me. I only briefly saw a hat pulled low over a man's face, but I did get the impression of someone quite large. My full attention turned to Erin.

Her hair was still black but looked freshly washed and she had a bit of color in her cheeks. Her eyes were huge, filled with both trepidation and tears as she paused at the top of the sidewalk and looked at me. Such intense love filled my heart as I ran toward her. I had almost given up hope, thinking she didn't want to be a part of the family anymore. And then I lost more hope when I began to believe she wasn't with D.H. willingly.

I felt her emaciated body within my hug and held her tightly, never wanting to let go again. She wiggled out of the hug and said we needed to go inside to talk. The exact conversation eluded me now as I sat beside her in the interrogation room. It was as if I had been in a tunnel, not walking, yet the end of the tunnel kept getting farther and farther away from me. My ears burned. My breath was caught in my ever-tightening chest. I truly thought I was having a heart attack. She cried and let out her story in a voice I barely recognized, it was so deep and broken up with her tears and gasps for breath. All I could register were horrible words like hostage, beaten, raped, sold for sex, drugged, tortured. *No, no, no.* I remembered shaking my head and repeating *no* as if that would have stopped what I was hearing.

As she sunk deeper into the chair and cried uncontrollably, I knew I needed to get myself together and give her my strength, rather than sit there denying everything she was telling me. I took her hands in mine and said, "We have to go to the police."

She reached into her purse and took out a thick wad of papers, holding them tightly in her hands and said, "This is my statement. I want to go to the police, but we have to go right away. He'll kill the dogs if I don't go back, and I have to do this, so he doesn't take another girl."

That surreal feeling settled over me again. Was this really happening? I had just begun to feel the relief of her being home, trying to digest what she'd been going through for the last two years when, suddenly, we were heading to the police station. She was exhausted and I had wanted her to wait until morning so she could be somewhat rested before facing the daunting task of spending what was sure to be many hours being questioned. She had been insistent on leaving right then but I was really concerned about her mental health and demeanor. Her hands had been shaking uncontrollably and she was slurring her words. Her face was swollen from crying and I had begun to absorb her sense of panic.

"I just need to go to the bathroom, and then can we leave?" she said.

"Sure, I'll call Al and tell him you're home and where we are going. He'll want to know what's happening. What can I tell him?" I asked her.

"Please don't tell him some of the worst details I told you. He'll want to go with us, and I know for sure he will lose it. I can't handle trying to keep him from yelling at the police to do something. I'm not even sure I'm not going to be arrested, Mom," she wailed with a fresh set of tears.

"Okay," I said resignedly. "Let's just go then. It's getting late, you're exhausted, and I want to make sure you get something decent to eat and a good sleep tonight. I can't imagine you've had a decent sleep in such a long time!"

I just wanted to get this over with as much as she did. I had begun to process what she had told me, and my horror was slowly being overtaken by a growing anger and need for justice. Erin would need a long time to heal and the sooner we handed this over to the police, the sooner she could begin the long, painful road to recovery from the brutality she had experienced.

I thought back to how Erin had seemed so much better when she came out of the bathroom. She no longer shook as she reached for her purse and the statement, and I hadn't questioned her resolute calm that seemed to be in such contrast with the way she had been just ten minutes earlier. I had been so anxious to get in the car and take this nightmare to the police station where I believed we could just leave it and get on with our lives. I was so naive.

CHAPTER TWENTY-NINE: MOM

VICTIM STATEMENT (EARLY SPRING 2012)

As a police officer came into the room where we were waiting, I brought my thoughts back from remembering the day before.

He slowly sat down across from us. "We have an officer going over your statement, Erin. I'll need more information to get your file started. Can you please give me the accused's full name, address, and date of birth as well as some of the approximate dates of the crimes you are wishing to press charges for?" His voice was soft, and I breathed an internal sigh of relief. I had been worried she would be either disregarded or treated like an accomplice. I glanced over at the other room, hoping the other officer was nearly finished—it seemed to be taking him so long!

I could see the officer who was reading the statement staring into space in front of him, the top of Erin's statement showing just above the window I was looking through. I was surprised to see his hand that held the papers was shaking. He was hunched over the table, and now his shoulders were also shaking. What was happening?

The officer in the room with us glanced where my gaze was fixed and excused himself, getting up quickly and going over to the other room. He beckoned to his colleague and they both walked down the hall out of sight. My anxiety level was climbing rapidly.

After a few very long moments, the first officer came back to where we were waiting.

"Erin, we've had a chance to review your statement, and we want to express how much concern we have with what we've read. This has been beyond horrific for you, and we would like to give Victim Services a call to enlist their help. I'll finish taking the rest of the information we need and then we'll get you some help. You are very brave in coming forward with this and I want to reassure you that we will be putting all our efforts into apprehending D.H."

He turned to look at me and said, "Wanda, your daughter is going to need a lot of help. Thank you for bringing her to us, but this is just the beginning. I want you to know these investigations are thorough but not quick. I'm so sorry you are all going through this."

His voice faltered and I took a deep breath as I could hear Erin's sobs intensifying. "How do I keep her safe? Keep all of us safe?" I asked. My own voice was starting to break as I struggled to stay collected.

"If you have any contact from him, call us immediately. Call 911 and give them the file number. We will be assigning a watch to be put on him and detectives who will be doing the investigation will be in touch with you tomorrow. Or maybe even later tonight. We understand the urgency of this and will be doing our best to move as quickly as possible."

"Can we go home now?" I asked. I was feeling a bit of relief, knowing D.H. would be under surveillance.

"Absolutely, get some rest if you can," he said sympathetically as he led us back to the main entrance of the police station. "The detectives will be in touch with you tomorrow. I'd like to strongly encourage Erin to see a doctor as soon as possible to make sure she is healing and will be healthy enough to face what will be coming up."

I hadn't even thought of that. Of course, I'd take her to our family doctor as soon as I could get an appointment for her. She was shockingly underweight and there could be any number of underlying issues resulting from her treatment while in captivity.

Erin was very quiet on the ride home. There comes a time in trauma where nothing else can be taken in. It is all overwhelming and the raw emotions have been laid bare so even talking brings more hurt. I was lost in my own thoughts of what was yet to come as we parked in the driveway and walked slowly into the house.

Little did we know then that things were going to get much harder and that there was still more pain and trauma to come. It was the beginning of an eight-year journey into light and then into the deepest dark.

CHAPTER THIRTY: ERIN

ANOTHER SECRET (EARLY SPRING 2012)

Mom was hovering. Constantly. Sometimes I soaked it up but as the days went by, I began to resent it. She was handling most of the phone calls from Victim Services and the two detectives assigned to my case, and for that I was grateful. But I really needed time to myself to sort out my thoughts. And I had to face the truth, deal with how to manage what I now knew to be my dependency on drugs. I thought once I got out of D.H.'s clutches, it would be so nice to not be drugged and my need to be medicated would go away because I wasn't being abused anymore.

It ate at my conscience as I found ways to score hits, sneaking out by borrowing Mom's car and telling her I needed a few things from the store. As the days went by, our fear of D.H. showing up began to wane because of the constant reassurances from the detectives that he was being monitored as they built a case against him. Mom relaxed her vigilance over me slightly, but it was getting very difficult to keep my secret hidden.

"I'm having fugue states from the trauma, Mom." I would tell her. And that my frequent episodes of vagueness, slurring, and dissociation were all "normal" behaviors for someone with PTSD. We had been going to family counseling and I had my own therapy sessions with trauma counselors. My diagnosis was complex post-traumatic stress disorder (PTSD) and that came as no surprise. My night terrors were constant and I woke up several times, only able to sleep in short bursts. I heard noises, voices, and movement around the house at night. Mom would get up and find me huddling in the armchair, shaking, crying, swearing people were outside. I honestly don't know how she survived it as she was sleeping less than I was! I had the benefit of my hidden stash of drugs to take away my anxiety and let me sleep. She had refused sleeping pills from the doctor to be alert and hear if I needed her in the middle of the night when things were extra rough for me.

On top of the nightmares and hiding my secret, my anxiety over the dogs was overwhelming. While the case was being built against him and charges were being prepared to have him arrested, I had been advised by the police to keep D.H. calm by telling him I was sick but that I would be coming back to him as soon as I was better. He was, by then, holding both dogs hostage to ensure that would happen. Any effort by me or anyone else to get them would incite him to possibly harming the dogs. In his sick mind, if he had them he had that hold over me. This ate at my soul every day, not knowing what kind of condition they were in or if they were still alive. I worried about Harley especially and this increased my already over-stimulated anxiety level. And, in turn, that increased my need to quiet that anxiety.

Illicit and anxiety prescription drugs are a mystery to most people. No child ever announces that they would like to be addicted to drugs when they grow up. I had been the queen of placing stigma on people who used drugs. I was even the president of the "Just Say No" committee in high school. In the 1990s, Nancy Reagan's tagline was on everyone's lips. If only it were that easy. *Just say no.* I wasn't allowed to say *no* during that time when I was a child, and I wasn't allowed to ever say *no* to D.H. For most people, the pain in their lives takes that ability away. By the time I was trying to survive what had happened to me, "Just Say No" was in the history books and it was becoming known that addiction is a disease.

I didn't think Mom would understand or know how to cope with the fact that her little girl could no longer function without the crutch of drug use. I had sworn to her that I had easily kicked the business of drugs when I was free from D.H. and that I no longer had any desire for any kind of upper or downer. I kept insisting that my symptoms were all related to my diagnosis. My shame at lying and using became a part of me over which I had no control.

CPTSD has a myriad of effects on the people who suffer from it and results in a wide variety of behaviors, all based on the severity of the trauma and the individual trying to live with its debilitating aftermath. I had many severe effects from the trauma I'd experienced, and I clung to the belief I would get better at coping with my pain in time. I just needed to get through these next few months and then I'd quit using. Addiction was, in my mind, the only way I could cope with the trauma and pain, because all the counseling I was taking didn't seem to be helping. The craving controlled me, and I was becoming a master at covering up my dependency.

It was such a hard conflict for me because I had always been very open and truthful as a child and as a young adult. Even though I kept a horrible childhood secret from everyone and believed I would take that secret to the grave with me, I had previously always lived a life of truth. This shame and secrecy were slowly killing me, but how could I possibly tell my family?

Mom started to suspect I was lying to her, and even though she was trying to give me some space, the suspicion was making her hypervigilant about my every move. And then I came up with an idea after my last meeting with the detectives. I had been asked to transcribe all the recordings from the time I had been trafficked and try to remember dates, times, places, and names of others involved during my hostage life. All this evidence was being used to lay charges against him and build a strong case of sexual offenses, hostage taking, animal abuse, and drug dealing. It was a huge undertaking and, according to the police, they needed to make sure they had everything possible nailed down to ensure a successful arrest and prosecution. In the last few months of being D.H.'s hostage, I had been secretly audio recording him and his episodes of abuse, hiding a phone under the bed, and this was an integral part of the evidence for the arrest and for court.

No one will ever understand the toll this was taking on me. It was like living each and every nightmare over and over again. But it had to be done. I had to help any way I could so he would not walk free. Trying to do this while staying with Mom and Al was really hard. With every recording I transcribed, I had to live through the terror and pain over again. My drug use increased. I devised a plan where I would go to my friend Chris's place every day and hunker down to go over the recordings. It was quiet, no one was around, and I could also hide the fact that I was regularly using cocaine to stay on top of the work I was doing.

Mom met Chris once and instantly decided she didn't trust him. I couldn't realistically tell her anything about him, but her instincts were keen and she had every reason to feel that way. Yes, he was generous in letting me use his place to work on my case but he was also my regular supplier of cocaine or whatever drugs I needed to either stay awake or wind down.

I had found an old car to buy, with help from Mom, as D.H. had forced me to turn over every penny I had ever saved within months of taking control of my life. My intention was to stay long enough at Chris's, after working on the recordings, to sober up and drive home. But every day got harder. I started to not go home at the end of the day and Mom was frantic. I was drowning under her calls and texts and eventually I shut my phone off. I felt I was successfully keeping my addiction hidden while at the same time helping the detectives build their case against D.H. His arrest would be any day, and he would be convicted. And then I would quit using drugs, live a sober life, and work through my trauma. It was a good plan.

I was as naive as my mother.

CHAPTER THIRTY-ONE: MOM

OVERDOSE (APRIL 2013)

It was hard to believe that more than a year had gone by since Erin came back to us. The events of these past twelve plus months were all welded together with anxiety, fear, confusion, anger, and frustration at the amount of time it was taking to make an arrest. I could not come to terms with the fact that our lives were on hold and D.H.'s existence was still controlling our daily lives.

Erin was struggling with the side effects of trauma and all the anxiety medication she had been prescribed. We had been going to family counseling and she had regular sessions with her own counselor, but we didn't seem to be making any progress. I resisted the notion that she could be using any kind of street drug as she had so many pill bottles of anti-anxiety medication—why would she need anything else? But her regular disappearances, her continuing weight loss, and her abruptness with me were escalating. Things were quickly spiraling out of control.

It was April 13th. Erin had had a particularly rough morning. All her evidence had been turned into the police and she was feeling the anxiety around the pending arrest. Against my advice, she had a different male friend, James, pick her up to take her out for the day to "take her mind off things." I didn't like this guy either, just like I didn't like Chris, the friend whose place she had been using to work through her case evidence. My worry, hypervigilance, and fear were taking a toll on me. I no longer trusted anyone, and I spent most of my time worried that my own mental health was on a rapid decline. Soon I'd be no use to anyone. But that didn't stop the loud braying of my intuition about James, the friend who had just led Erin to the passenger seat of his car in front of our house.

As I watched her drive away with him, I did a quick inventory of my own life. I was hardly functioning at work. My friends had quit trying to hold me up and a wedge of silence had fallen between me and my husband. All I could do every minute of every day was try prop up Erin while still letting her live her life. She was in her twenties, not a child anymore, but I couldn't seem to release my overbearing scrutiny or my thoughts that something even more terrible would happen if I didn't constantly monitor her and keep her safe.

I had been pacing and calling Erin's phone to no avail. I tried the breathing techniques I'd learned from my counselor, which had been marginally working for me to calm my worried mind and give my adrenal system a rest. It was getting late, we'd had dinner without Erin, and the TV was droning in the background as I took another loop around the house, looking for distraction.

The front door opened and Erin came in saying how sorry she was to be late. And that she was hungry. The level of slurring in her voice and her unsteady stance told me things had just taken a turn for the worse.

"What happened to you?" I asked her. "You're barely understandable!"

"I took an extra Ativan, Mom. Don't freak out."

If I didn't know my daughter and sadly hadn't been getting used to her ever-increasing episodes of rambling and slurring, I wouldn't have been able to decipher what she was saying.

Why would she do that? I wondered as I steered her toward the kitchen, propping her up on a stool against the counter while I put the kettle on. I also wondered how a cup of hot tea would cure anything. I was at a loss. When lost, I made food, boiled water for tea, and tried not to show my own level of anxiety. It wasn't helping the situation.

"Let's go out on the deck. I made you a sandwich and a tea and I think you need the fresh air," I said as I helped Erin into a patio chair. She was honestly so uncoordinated and, as I watched, she lifted the sandwich to her mouth but could barely steer it so she could take a bite. Her head rolled back and when she brought it upright, her eyes were closed. I was feeling sick, watching her try to feed herself, eyes closed, and head lolling as if her neck had become rubber.

"I think the best thing for you right now, Erin, is bed." I could think of nothing other than to get her in bed to sleep off that extra Ativan… if it was just one that she took. She must have really been at the end of her rope to take more than what was prescribed. The pills usually made her calmer, more collected, and able to sleep, but this was beyond that.

I tucked her into bed like she was four years old again, pulling the comforter up to her chin. She was fully clothed but seemed cold. I shut the ceiling light off, leaving a softer table lamp on, and noted again what a disaster her bedroom was. Maybe tomorrow I'd help her clean up a bit. I left the door cracked, glanced at the clock on my way to the kitchen, and saw it was almost eight o'clock at night. It felt like a hundred o'clock in my head and I told Al I was also going to bed. Maybe reading for a while would take my mind off things. I planned to check on her hourly, knowing my own sleep was going to be pretty messed up that night. I couldn't wait for morning when I could ask her to tell me exactly what happened that day for her to end up like this.

I knew I had been fast asleep when I heard an insistent voice. "Wake up!" It was so familiar. I couldn't quite grasp whose voice it was. As I struggled out of a deep sleep, I wondered if it was part of a dream. "Wake Up! Wake Up!"

I shot up in bed. "Mom?" I asked. It sounded like my mother's voice but was now more like a soft echo, fading away into the night air. Al was in bed next to me and his soft snores told me he was sleeping deeply. Exhaustion had overtaken both of us, even though I had been sure I would not sleep that night.

I slipped quietly out of bed and down the hall to look in on Erin. The soft glow from the night table lamp gently lit up her face. She looked like she was resting peacefully but she was so quiet, I could hardly hear her breath. I watched for the rise and fall of the comforter across her chest and saw no movement. There was no breath.

I recall a sense of drawing back into myself and then rushing forward. I grabbed her shoulders with both hands and gently shook her, just in case I was mistaken, but I didn't want to panic her. Nothing. I shook harder. I shouted her name. I lifted her eyelids. She stared blankly back at me. She was an ashen color except for a blue tinge around her mouth.

I heard myself scream. "Al! I can't wake Erin up!" I heard him get out of bed, run down the hallway, and into her bedroom.

"What's wrong with her?" he asked. He was groggy and not comprehending what he was seeing. And I was struggling to come to terms with what was my daughter's apparently lifeless body beneath my hands.

A strange sense of calm came over me as I told him to get the phone and call 911. As he made the call and we waited to be connected, I felt a shudder from Erin's body. She took one breath. And then stopped. When we had an emergency dispatcher on the line, I was shouting as Al held the phone towards me.

"My daughter isn't breathing. She just took one breath and then stopped again. I think she may have taken too many of her anxiety pills. She has CPTSD and lots of prescriptions." In my head, my voice sounded calm but my heart was pounding out of my chest.

"Okay," the dispatcher said. "What is your name and her name? And how old is she?"

I rattled off our names and her age as I continued to try and wake her up. *Why is it getting so cold in this room right now? Why do I feel like I'm sliding backward through a long tunnel?* All these strange sensations were moving through me, and I wondered if I was going to pass out. I struggled to not give in to the panic. I needed to stay on top of this or I would lose her.

"How often is she taking a breath?" the dispatcher asked.

Al and I listened together. There was about one breath every eight to ten seconds.

"You have to help her breathe," he said quickly. "Do you know CPR?"

"Yes," I replied. I had just taken a refresher course a few months ago. I was shaking so badly as I started to position her body to begin.

The dispatcher's calm voice spoke again. "Okay, I'm with you, Wanda. I'll talk you through this and we'll get Erin breathing again together. The ambulance is on the way."

As I worked through compressions and then gave her a breath, I was vaguely aware of the sweet taste of peppermint. The remains of the tea I had given her a few short hours ago.

I had no idea what time it was as I fell into the rhythm of chest compressions and breaths. I wondered if Al was waiting for the ambulance outside as I could no longer sense him in the doorway behind us. I briefly turned my head to see if he was there and was enveloped in a wall of cold air. The door was closed and a loud hum filled my ears. What was happening?

I turned back to Erin and gave her another breath. That's when I felt a strong pull on my right shoulder, like someone was trying to yank me away from her. There was no one there. I sensed a darkness closing over us and I cried out loud, "*No!*" Again, I felt the pressure on my shoulder and pulled it away quickly. There was something in that room with us, something dark and evil. It wanted her life and soul, and I was in the way. I heard myself chanting "No, no, no, " over and over again.

The bedroom door suddenly opened and a small, red-haired female police officer stood in the doorway, one hand on the frame and one on her gun. The invisible hand and the cold immediately disappeared.

"Oh God, she's doing CPR!" she shouted. Then she turned and ran back down the hallway toward the front entrance. A bang and commotion followed, then two EMTs and a stretcher showed up in the hall.

"I've got her," one of them said to me. "We've got to get her on the floor, you can stop now."

"No, she's dying. She was dead but I think I got her to breathe again. We can't stop." Now I was crying and begging, babbling. He gently lifted my daughter's thin body off the bed and placed her on the floor where they started compressions again and one of the EMTs gave her an injection. Later I would learn it was naloxone , the life-saving drug given to people in an overdose situation. Then she was on the stretcher and heading out the front door.

As I followed them out, the EMT said, "You can ride in the front of the ambulance, Mom. We'll be leaving shortly. We're just getting her settled." I turned back, saw Al standing in front of her bedroom door and asked him to call Ryan. They would have to meet us at the hospital.

"What the hell are they doing?" he said, looking into Erin's bedroom. As I rushed to see what he meant, I was horrified to see the police turning her room upside down, looking under the bed, in the closet, tossing everything around.

"We have to make sure there aren't any weapons or illegal drugs," the police officer with the red hair was explaining as she searched the night table drawers.

"I can't believe this, I can't deal with it," I said to Al as I ran back to the front of the house to get in the ambulance. "Find out what's happening. I'll call you from the hospital."

I only vaguely recall the ride to the hospital. We stopped once to bring another EMT on board. I know they lost Erin again at least once on that ride and I felt hope slipping away with the miles on the way to Emergency. And I thought with horror about that cold, evil encounter with whatever malevolent spirit was in the room with us. Had it won? Was it going to get her soul? My daughter believed in God and was innocent. Maybe (I hoped) I had imagined it all.

CHAPTER THIRTY-TWO: MOM

THE DAYS FOLLOWING (APRIL 2013)

I was kneeling on a cold floor in the visitor's washroom outside of the Emergency Department at the hospital, my hands bracing the floor as I vomited into the toilet. Would it ever end? My head was pounding, and every heartbeat felt like a giant slam against my breastbone. I had been left waiting and told I couldn't go with her into the emergency room.

I was alone at the moment. Al wasn't there yet with Ryan. They had to wait for the police to be done with whatever they were doing in the house. I had called Erin's dad in Regina, terrifying him, unable to give him any more information other than she had apparently overdosed. He needed time to catch a flight and was likely already on his way. We were all coming together over the worst possible circumstances with an unknown outcome. I couldn't get my head wrapped around the fact that my daughter might not be able to be saved or, if she was, would be horribly damaged by lack of oxygen for too long.

Eventually I was able to stand up from the floor, grip the edge of the sink, and look into the mirror. "I'd sell my soul to save her life," I said to my reflection. My eyes spoke volumes of regret and hope at the same time. My words to the devil hung like thick strings on the surface of the mirror, slowly running down but leaving the remnants of my damnation as testimony to my desperation. My insanity was teetering on the brink as I could see the same demon from Erin's bedroom behind me. He laughed, greedily ate my insecurities with joy, and followed his meal with a long cold drink of my fear. And then he turned and walked away.

The mirror was empty except for my face, which I no longer recognized. I loved too much, and this was my punishment.

Did this vision really happen? Did I imagine it? Feeling like I had briefly lost consciousness, I washed my face and hands and went back into the waiting room. Faces around looked at me with curiosity. There I was. In pajamas with a ghostly white face, raw with tears, and wondering if my next breath would be my last one. At that moment, if I lost her I did not believe I would survive the tragedy.

Finally, a nurse came out to get me. Al and Ryan arrived at almost the exact same time, and we all followed her into the ICU. The sight of my daughter's small body on life support is something that will haunt me to the end of time. She had no color in her face, the lower half of which was covered by the intubating apparatus, and there was no movement. *This must be what death really looks like*, I thought to myself. I heard a low moan start deep down within me and I reached for the end of the bed, gripping it tightly as I felt my knees begin to buckle. The nurse made a movement toward me and I shook my head at her.

"I'm not going to pass out. Please tell us what is happening." My voice sounded like someone else's, calm and collected, while on the outside I was shattering like glass.

"The doctor will be in shortly to let you know everything we know at this point." She sounded as calm as my voice did but when I looked into her eyes, I saw she was a mother too. There is a knowledge between women when one is suffering and the other lives the pain alongside her. She took another look at the monitors surrounding Erin's bed and quietly left the room.

Time stood still. The three of us never spoke. The beeping of the monitors spoke, letting us know there was a heartbeat and each breath mechanically entered and left her lungs. My own breath became so shallow, I felt the room begin to swim around me again. I made a vow with myself that if the monitors stopped beeping and the artificial breathing stopped, I too, would stop breathing. My heart would stop beating and I'd leave with her as there was no living here without her. A daughter needs her mother. How could I possibly let her spirit simply float away all by herself? Hadn't she been abandoned enough in her lifetime? I wouldn't abandon her at her time of death too.

Ryan's voice broke the silence. "Dad is on his way. He caught the earliest flight he could. We'll go get him from the airport this afternoon."

I nodded, thinking that he might not get here in time. Why did two provinces away suddenly feel like the other side of the world? He deserved to see his daughter still alive, even if that state was being kept artificially with machines. I wondered how awful his trip would be, leaving Regina and then sitting in Calgary, waiting for his connecting flight to Victoria while every precious moment counted. I also wondered whether we'd be standing together as they disconnected the life-supporting equipment from our daughter's body, her brain shut down forever.

I shook off my dark thoughts and said *No!* to God and to that dark presence I'd felt in her bedroom as I was giving her CPR. *No one is taking her. Not yet. She has a life to live, and I WILL NOT allow her to be taken before her time.* I felt my breath come back into my body full force and I stood tall, reaching for Al and Ryan's hands, gripping them tightly.

"She is coming back from this," I announced.

Two men came into the room. One in doctor's scrubs, the other in a suit and holding a file folder.

The doctor cleared his throat. "I was the attending physician in the ER when your daughter was brought in. She is suffering from a very serious overdose, and we found a significant quantity of methadone in her blood work. Methadone is typically used in treating heroin addicts. Is your daughter using heroin?"

"No," I replied. "She was the victim of a violent, prolonged crime and is on several anti-anxiety medications due to her CPTSD. That must be what she took too much of?"

"We could see the other medications, but the amount of methadone in her system is alarming. Unless she was using heroin, methadone would be a very dangerous substance for her to take as her body is not used to it. Could she have been given it from someone who is a recovering heroin addict? They are quite often prescribed methadone as part of their recovery."

My mind went back to the "friend," James, who had picked her up that day. Or was that the day before? I was getting confused about the timing of events. I couldn't even remember what day it might be or even what time it was. I glanced out the window and saw it was daylight, the sun in the east, so it must be mid-morning. What had happened to the night?

"She had a guy pick her up yesterday, I think. I didn't want her to go with him. He seemed really twitchy, but she assured me he was just a friend, trying to help keep her occupied. She's going through hell again right now, getting ready for court as the police will be arresting her hostage taker soon."

"Well, wherever she got the methadone, it was a dangerous quantity for her," said the doctor as he looked at each of us with sympathy. *She isn't just another addict overdosing in the emergency ward. She's a real person who has suffered a horrible tragedy.* All these thoughts were racing through my head as I imagined what he was thinking. Or maybe he wasn't thinking that. I just needed him to understand! She was a special case, and she would not have taken methadone on her own.

"I'll be honest," he continued. "We don't know yet how much damage has been done to her brain or her internal organs. The methadone worked to slow and then shut down the part of her brain that tells the body to breathe. I understand you discovered her only taking occasional breaths and then none and that's when you began CPR. We will count on those measures keeping enough oxygen flowing to her brain to mitigate any extensive damage. But we won't know until we try removing the breathing tube and see if she can take a breath on her own. We'll try that in the next couple of days once she is stable and only when we think she might be ready. But please know that if we remove the tube and she can breathe on her own, it may take a while to see if she has full function of her brain and her body."

"You mean she might be brain damaged or paralyzed?" Just uttering those words made me feel like I might be inviting them into our lives, but I needed to know.

"We really don't know what the outcome will be until we can take her off the machines that are sustaining her right now. Let's wait and see. I'll keep you informed as we move along."

He gestured to the man in the suit that had come in with him. "The doctor here will speak with you about next steps and I'll be back in a little while to check on her. Let the staff know if you need anything."

"You are Erin's mother, correct?" the suit-man asked. "I'm Dr. Morgan and a clinical psychologist. I assist in these types of circumstances to help you understand the process and where we can go from here. Why don't we step into the family room at the end of the hall, and we can talk about things."

"I'm not leaving this room," I said. "We can talk here."

"Alright," he said. "Let me ask you some questions. Was your daughter ever diagnosed with ADHD—attention-deficit/hyperactivity disorder as a child?"

I stared blankly at him. "No, why would you think that?"

"Quite often, drug users and addicts have a history of family trauma or ADHD. If she was diagnosed earlier on, we can then recommend an appropriate treatment going forward. It helps to know a little bit of her history." He stood poised with pen in hand, ready to write down whatever I told him in his little folder.

I'm not sure why I was so offended by this man, but I felt my defenses rising. Was he actually blaming her family or her upbringing for her condition now?

"Like I told the doctor, she has been the victim of a horrific crime that went on for a long time. She was lured and held by a sex trafficker who drugged her, beat her, raped her, and sold her. *That's* why she is on so many prescription drugs. She can't sleep, she's anxious, she's been hurt in ways that no one should ever have to even read about, never mind live!" My voice was breaking, tears were coming fast and furious. I was angry, insulted, and disgusted by this stranger's analysis of my daughter, when he knew absolutely nothing about us.

"I understand," he said in his practiced soothing way. "We can talk more when we know what Erin's prognosis will be. But in the meantime, we can talk about choices of what to do if or when she recovers and is able to function on her own. Assuming she has her full faculties—and we all hope she does—we can't just allow her to go back into her life without the proper support in place."

Now he was making sense, I thought. I was so desperate for help, and I couldn't let myself think of anything but a positive outcome when she was weaned off the life-support equipment. I hadn't even thought ahead to that moment but now that I had, how could I just bring her home and presume everything would go back to normal? Not that anything had been normal for such a long time, but this was out of my area of capabilities.

"I'm sorry," I said to Dr. Morgan. "I'm just so terrified and I don't know what to do. But I don't think this is a byproduct of her upbringing. She grew up on a farm and was well loved by her whole family. Her dad and I had an amicable divorce, and she was loved and supported by both of us throughout. Not every kid coming from a divorced family ends up here, so I think we need to look at what has been done to her over the last couple of years and treat that part of it. We are trying; she has counselors and a supportive family doctor, but this is a lot of trauma to deal with."

"This has been a terrible thing for Erin, you, and your family to deal with," he acknowledged. "There is a real chance this experience may have affected her in ways that no one has seen or recognized yet, so it helps to have some options moving forward."

"What options?" I asked.

"There are two," he answered. "One would be to get her into a good drug rehabilitation center and, if she refuses, the only other option would be to admit her to the psychiatric hospital."

My gaze moved back to the back where Erin was lying on the bed, unmoving. Choices. What choice did she have that had resulted in her being on life support, our lives crumbling around us like walls in an earthquake? I was still trying to wrap my head around being told she had overdosed on an illegal drug, not the prescription drugs she was taking. Had she willingly taken methadone and, if so, why? Or maybe she had been unknowingly drugged, just like before with D.H. when he took her on a "date" and slipped GHB, the date rape drug into her wine?

Dr. Morgan's quiet voice brought me back to the present. "Let's wait to see what happens when the doctors say it's time to remove the breathing tube. Then we can see if she is able to communicate and talk about the options. I'll leave you now but please have the nurses contact me if you have any questions. I'll come back once they advise me that she is awake."

I felt a pounding at the back of my eyes as my headache returned with a vengeance. Stress and exhaustion permeated my body; when was the last time I'd had a drink of water or something to eat? A couple of hours went by. Ryan had left to pick his dad up at the airport and the nursing staff came in to run some tests on Erin. It was the first time I'd left her room but I needed some fresh air, so Al and I stepped outside into the parking lot, where I looked up at the blue sky and prayed harder than I ever had in my life.

Just as we were about to go back into the hospital, I saw Ryan and Ken, Erin's dad, walking toward us between the cars. As they drew nearer, I saw the raw pain on Ken's face and we clung to each other in a fierce hug, pouring all our fear and sorrow into that hug as we cried over what was happening with our little girl. Then we went back up to Erin's room in the ICU and positioned ourselves around her bed. Life? The prospect of a very hard road ahead. Death? The end of everything for her. And for me. Now we wait.

CHAPTER THIRTY-THREE: ERIN

AWAKE (APRIL 14, 2013)

I was having the best sleep I'd had in such a long time. Years maybe. There were no dreams, just endless quiet and a darkness that superseded everything that had been haunting my conscience. Gradually, I felt, rather than heard, quiet movements around me. *Oh no, please, I don't want to wake up yet!* A vision floated in front of me. I was wearing my little pink pajamas I had as a kid—they were my favorite. So warm and cozy. But I wasn't in bed. I was floating! Way up in the corner of the bedroom. Not the bedroom I grew up in, but the room where I was staying at Mom and Al's house. I looked down and saw Mom leaning over the bed. When she stood up, I saw myself lying on the bed. But I was no longer a little girl in pink pajamas. The "me" on the bed had dark hair and was older than the little girl in pink pajamas, floating up in the corner.

What was Mom doing? Her upper body was randomly moving up and down over me and now I could see that she was doing compressions on my chest and then sometimes giving me mouth-to-mouth breathing. So weird. Was it a bad dream? And why was it so cold all of a sudden? I turned my head farther to the left, sensing a presence and a movement on the wall behind Mom's back. The wall was the original stucco of an older house. I could see a pulsing in the material, like a breath moving in and out. The wall was breathing. As the stucco stretched, a face-like protrusion began to appear, pushing out of the wall, mouth outstretched in an O shape. I heard Mom scream as she reached her left hand over to her right shoulder, as if she was trying to push something away. "*No*!" she cried loudly, resuming compressions on me, stopping to give me a breath. Over and over. Between breaths, she was muttering, "You aren't having her! Oh God, please help me!"

From where I was floating up in the corner of the bedroom, I could only calmly observe and didn't understand what was happening. The pulsating in the wall receded but the image of the frightening face that had emerged from it was imprinted in my mind. And would come out again later.

There was a commotion in the hallway, and I no longer saw myself up in the corner of the room. I was back in that dark, peaceful place, but it was no longer silent. I could hear voices murmuring, beeping sounds, and someone softly crying. Was this still a dream?

And then I felt a terrible pain in my chest and throat, my body lifting slightly up with the force of whatever was pulling me upward. And then it let go so my body drifted back down into what I sensed was a bed. *Oh, that's better. That really hurt!*

"Erin? Erin?" I could hear someone calling my name, tapping on my wrist. Where was I going? A bright light was warming my eyelids, and I wondered if I was supposed to open my eyes. Or would it be blinding? Should I keep them closed and follow that light as it moved back and forth and then away, leading me somewhere?

A sense of peace and knowing settled over me and all I had been, was now, or would be, seemed sharp with clarity and direction. I opened my eyes. I was in a bed and standing at the foot of it was Mom, her hands clasped at her chest. She looked completely devastated … a ruined ghost of the woman I knew as my mother. But I knew what I had to tell her. It just came out. "Mom, God has a plan for me."

CHAPTER THIRTY-FOUR: MOM

HOPE IN OUR HEARTS (APRIL 2013)

The next forty-eight hours following Erin's return to the waking world were a time of alternating joy, fear, and indecision. Joy because she was alive. Fear because we had learned a lot over the last few hours about drug use, overdoses, and the repercussions that can come with a total shutdown of the body and mind—even for a few short minutes. Fortunately, so far, there were no signs of brain damage. We were filled with gratitude. It was nothing short of a miracle. And finally, indecision because we still didn't know what the best course of treatment was going to be for Erin. It was a hard conversation.

"Erin, we've been advised that there are two choices about where to go from here," we told her. "You've been given another chance at life but there is no going back to how you were living before. You've told us what happened with the methadone, and we truly believe that you never want to be in that situation again but we have to make sure. There has to be some sort of system in place that will keep you safe and it sounds like there are only two avenues."

I looked at Ken, then Al, then Ryan, and finally to Dr. Morgan, the psychologist who would be administering the necessary paperwork when the decision was made. We were all on the same page and needed to be presenting a united front, but I already knew Erin wouldn't like either of the options.

"First option, the best one in our opinion, is to be admitted to a drug rehabilitation program up island. There is a family connection on your dad's wife's side that can facilitate an immediate intake. This is a wonderful opportunity as the wait times are a month and we don't have a month to keep you safe. This can't happen again. You almost didn't come out of your coma. I can't tell you how that would have impacted your dad and me." It crossed my mind briefly that I was bargaining and manipulating. I was desperate for her to take this option.

I took a deep breath and said, "The other option is to be admitted to the psychiatric hospital here in the city. You'll be a patient there for a long time, I know you need psychiatric help for the trauma, but I'm not sure how you'll be treated for the addiction."

"Mom," she spoke so quietly that I had to lean closer. "God has spoken to me and showed me what I need to do. I can't do any of it if I'm locked up in a loony bin. I'm not crazy. I just took a drug that my friend insisted would help me calm down, get a good sleep, and be able to finish my police report work. I'm *not* an addict!"

"Then you'll agree to going to rehab?" I asked. Hope filled my heart.

"No, I don't want to go there either. You're sending me to rehab? Where's Amy Winehouse when I need her! No, no, no!" she laughed.

"This isn't funny, Erin." I shot back at her. "It's only thirty days, the drug treatment center has got a great track record, and it's where you'll get the help you need for your anxiety and insomnia, get off the drugs, and get strong again." I knew it could very well be longer, hoping that she would be there for as long as needed. I just needed to convince her to say yes.

"You're an adult and we can't force you to go into drug rehabilitation but given the trauma you've been through and the inability to cope, you *can* be forced to go to the psychiatric hospital, and we don't have any say over that. You are a danger to yourself."

My voice was breaking and my entire body was shaking as I uttered those harsh words to her. Blue eyes looked back at me with such hurt.

"Going to rehab is a lot of money, Mom," she said. "You guys can't afford that. I certainly can't."

"Never mind that now," I assured her. "We'll figure it out, they have a payment plan, and we also have CVAP, the Crime Victim Assistance Program. They've been covering some of your prescription expenses and I can see if they have a plan for programs like rehabilitation." Hope was building again. I had forgotten about that resource and I crossed my fingers. *Please,* I thought to myself. None of us could afford a reputable treatment center, which ranged in excess of $10,000 per month!

Erin was silent. Looking down at her hands in her lap, she seemed like a small child being punished for something she didn't do or something she didn't know was wrong. My heart went out to her.

Bless Ken, who put it bluntly: "It's either a drug treatment center or the psych unit at the hospital. What's it going to be, Erin?"

"Okay, I'll go to rehab. But I won't need to stay the whole time. I don't need hard drugs. I'll prove that to you." She was being stubborn and in denial, but I didn't care about any of that. I was so grateful.

The next few hours were a whirlwind of paperwork and phone calls and, in the end, we decided we would all go in the same car to take Erin to what I was beginning to see as the answer to all our problems. I envisioned a future of picking her up again after her treatment program was finished, our funny, healthy, and beautiful daughter back to her old self. Ready to take on the world. She wasn't the only one in denial.

Our short trip up island to the treatment center is one we will never forget, as our funny girl was at her best. It was a rocky start as we got ready to leave the hospital and she began to insist that she "needed something" to calm her nerves because she was desperately scared.

"They can't just take me off all my prescription drugs too!" she shouted. She had just been informed that she needed to arrive as sober as possible at the treatment center. She would be going through a detoxification process once there, so the less to inhibit that the better. She dug in her heels and got so agitated that the doctor finally agreed to prescribe a very light dose of Ativan for her. Something I learned along this treacherous journey of recovery was that seasoned drug users won't respond to low dosage medication because their bodies become conditioned to high doses of both prescription and street drugs. However, just the knowledge that she would be given "something" seemed to tame the dragon and she left the hospital in good spirits. I breathed a sigh of relief. In about one hour, we'd be with professionals who would know what to do next.

I don't even know how this happened, but we now reflect back on it when seeking happy memories. Erin was so jovial all the way out of the city, cracking jokes, and making fun of everything and everybody she could. Not in a mean way but in a loving, compassionate way. It's hard to describe. As it turned out, we had almost no gas in the car. We had also realized that we hadn't eaten in a very long time. With my renewed optimism and faith in this rehab path, I was suddenly ravenous. Had it been two days since I'd had anything other than cups of tea, coffee, and a few crackers? My belly was certainly telling me it was a long time. Erin was also ravenous, only having had intravenous fluids and then a bit of soup and Jello.

"A big, fat juicy burger, large fries, and a Coke. *And* a large coffee, three creams, three sugars," she crowed from the back seat when I suggested we stop at the drive-thru after we gassed up the car. I laughed with sheer joy at the sound of her delight.

As the car was being filled, Erin stepped out and engaged everyone at the gas station in a comedy routine. She joked with people, told them how good looking they were, and she danced with joy. I knew she wasn't high on drugs—at that time, she was truly high on life because she had cheated death with a narrow margin. Every person who was refueling their vehicle that day smiled at her antics. I could not only see but feel the love she was sharing.

Suddenly, she said, "It's getting busy at the drive-thru! I'm starving, I can't wait."

"Erin, we're almost done, we have to get in line." I was still laughing but hoping she'd get back in the car.

Nope. She strode with confidence over to the fast-food restaurant but she didn't go inside. She took her place behind a car that was idling at the ordering window, then looked over at us and waved, shouting "Come on! Hurry up! I'm holding us a spot."

"Oh, good lord," I groaned. A pickup truck pulled up behind her, the driver looking baffled as she wiggled her fingers at him. She looked so happy, he had no choice but to shrug and put his hands up in the air, smiling at her with patience.

"I'm sorry," I said to him as I ran over, wiggling between his front bumper and Erin. I placed my hands on her shoulders and guided her over to the side, waving him to move forward.

"Well, now he thinks I'm crazy and I'm just hungry!" she laughed. I couldn't help myself. I hugged her so hard. Right there in the drive-thru.

"Okay, here's the car, jump back in and we'll get you fed, you hungry beast," I laughed. I'm glad the fast-food restaurant *was* fast food that day! We all laughed as she gobbled her food, still cracking jokes and making up stories about the people she saw at the gas station and in the drive-thru line at the restaurant. She was definitely on a roll.

Within ten minutes of finishing her meal, she was fast asleep, her head resting on her dad's shoulder. And we arrived just on time at the treatment center, hope in our hearts, and dreams of having our loving, funny girl back. In my mind, I was thinking that she would finally be safe, I could let go of my maniacal vigilance for the next several weeks and just sleep. Deep, dreamless, healing sleep.

CHAPTER THIRTY-FIVE:
MOM

THE ARREST (LATE SPRING 2013)

Erin's intake at the treatment center was seamless and I counted on some time to ground myself over the following weeks while she was in expert hands. A week later my phone rang, and I saw the name of the lead detective in her case on the screen. The evidence had all been gathered, charges were filed, and the case was solid. They were going in to make the arrest. D.H. was finally going to be taken into custody. I almost dropped to my knees and thanked God right then and there that Erin was in treatment. The timing couldn't have been better as she would not have been able to cope with the flurry of activity that would be happening.

After weeks of gathering evidence in a complex and multiple-charges pending case, the arrest was finally going to be happening that afternoon. We had been advised in advance that we could not discuss the circumstances around what had happened to Erin so as not to jeopardize the case. It had been difficult only being able to confide in Victim Services counselors and other mental health professionals, so I was nervously looking forward to this being over with. But I also knew that the court proceedings would likely be long and tortuous.

My thoughts went to the dogs. "Where is he? Does he still have the dogs?" I asked the detective.

"Yes," she replied. "Our surveillance team knows where he is living but we have not had a report of seeing any dogs with him. Regardless, in this situation where we suspect there might be pets or other animals involved during an arrest, we arrange for an animal control officer to attend with us. There are a lot of people involved with the arrest, given his record of violence and the nature of the charges." Her voice was calm yet laced with tension and excitement. "I have to go but we will call you from the arrest site once he's in custody and I'll let you know if we find the dogs." She hung up quickly before I could ask any more questions.

My heart was pounding, my stomach was rolling, and I could feel the anxiety building. Once D.H. saw the police arrive, the entire story Erin had been telling him, about needing time to get well and that she'd be back to him and the dogs soon, would be exposed as a cover up. In a matter of hours, he would know it was her who had gone to the police with her story. My first call was to the treatment center to let them know what was happening. She could be told it was happening, but she would need extra help and vigilance as this would surely ignite an emotional overload for her. I was also worried about her safety; criminals like D.H. have people in their wretched lives who have no qualms about delivering punishment on their behalf. Erin had taught me the meaning of the expression "snitches get stitches" and I had no doubt D.H. would exact his revenge if given the chance.

Not for the first time, I wondered if I was caught in some kind of horrible movie where bad things happen to good people. I hoped for the end of the show or that I'd wake up from this nightmare. I called Al at work and told him what was happening, and he said he would head for home. But it could be a very long time before they actually had D.H. in custody so there was nothing he could do to help. In retrospect, I think I wanted to be alone for that call when it happened. And I dreaded what had happened to the dogs. I took deep breaths, willing myself to stay calm, and waited for the phone to ring as I paced and watched the clock.

Later that afternoon, my phone rang, and I saw the detective's name come up again. I hesitated. Heart pounding, I answered the call. "Please tell me you've got him," I pleaded into the phone.

"Yes, we have him." she answered. "He gave us only a bit of trouble as he was taken completely by surprise." I could hear the relief in her voice. Months of investigation had led to this point for her and the others involved in the case.

A buzzing was going on in my ears as I tried to comprehend what this would now mean. Could we relax? How long until court? Were we safe? All these thoughts were darting around in my head when I realized she was still talking.

"The animal control officer has taken possession of two dogs. A part German shepherd and a bulldog-cross of some sort. I didn't get a good look at them as we were busy with D.H. but she has advised us to ask you to meet her so she can transfer ownership over to you."

"They're alive?!" I shouted. "Oh my God, I'm so relieved. Erin will be ecstatic. Where exactly do I go to meet her?"

The detective went on to explain where I'd be meeting the officer. She asked me to hurry as the dogs were already in the van. It was a half-hour drive from home to the park where I was to meet her and I was already running out to my truck, grabbing my keys and wallet and slamming the door behind me as I ended the call. On the drive to the park, I had time to slow my breathing and my heartbeat as I considered the implications of today's arrest. My hands shook on the steering wheel and tears flowed down my cheeks. Finally, justice was being served and the monster who had hurt my little girl was behind bars. I didn't know at that moment, but I would learn in a few days that she had not been his first victim. There were at least three other young women somewhere out there who had escaped and could finally break their silence, having been held by threats of physical violence and even death if they spoke out about what he had done to them. The depravity, the horror, and the fallout from his treatment of women was about to be revealed.

CHAPTER THIRTY-SIX: MOM

THE ANIMAL HOSPITAL (LATE SPRING 2013)

I spotted the animal control van sitting in the middle of the parking lot and pulled up alongside. I was so excited to see Harley, Erin's soulmate with four paws. Even though I'd never met the other dog, Rufus, I was feeling a sense of joy and relief that he had also been rescued.

A woman in a municipal uniform stepped out of the van and walked toward me as I climbed out of my vehicle. She put up a hand and asked, "You are here to pick up the dogs the police took from the residence of the accused?"

"Yes. Harley, the German shepherd belongs to my daughter. And there is another dog? Named Rufus? I can take them both," I said to her.

"When was the last time you saw Harley?" she asked.

"It's been around two years. Why?" I asked. I was getting a sinking feeling in my gut.

"They are in very rough shape." she replied. "These are two very neglected animals, and I just wanted to prepare you before opening the door."

As she slid the side panel open on the van, I saw Harley first. He lifted his head and looked at me, a slow dawn of recognition coming into his eyes. And he was trying to wag his tail although he didn't have the strength to stand. The little bulldog was lying on his side, not even lifting his head up.

"Oh my God," I cried, covering my mouth with my hand. I choked as tears began and I turned to the officer. "What happened to them? Do you know?"

"I don't know what their life has been like, but I can tell you that the residence was in a deplorable state. There was no sign of dog food anywhere and only an empty, very dirty water dish in a small room at the back where the police found them. They are both very weak. They should be seen by a vet right away. Can you do that?" she asked me.

"Yes, of course." I replied. "The emergency animal hospital isn't very far from here. I'll take them right away."

"Given their condition, with your permission," she said, "I feel I should take them there and you can follow me where I can sign them over to you and get them in right away to be examined. I will also call the detective I was working with at the scene and ask them to call the hospital to be ready for you so there is no waiting. I don't think the little one has much life left in him."

Sick to my stomach, I got back in my vehicle and followed the van as it pulled out of the parking lot. I knew she was making some calls to hasten their admission to the hospital. I prayed we weren't too late.

Both dogs had to be carried into the examination room. The animal control officer put her hand on my shoulder and said quietly, "I hope they nail his ass to the wall and he doesn't see daylight for an eternity."

I couldn't have agreed more.

I've had pets and livestock all of my life and I've never seen a vet cry. That day was the first time. She was an experienced vet and had seen some terrible things, but knowing the story behind why Harley and Rufus were there seemed to heighten her sense of compassion. Both dogs had matted coats and were staring at a jar of treats up on the counter, shaking with hunger, weakness, and fright at this new set of circumstances.

"May I?" I asked the vet, pointing to the jar.

"Of course, it won't hurt anything now," she said. "Give them a few."

Rufus struggled up onto his front legs, anticipating my outreached hand while Harley hung back just a little, waiting for his friend to get the first treat. What kind of hell had these two once-beautiful dogs been living? I could see they had become very attached, likely looking out for one another.

As I continued to give them small bites, the vet gave me her report. "I don't see any signs of physical trauma, no open wounds or abrasions.

But every rib is sticking out and they are both severely dehydrated. Harley seems to be in slightly better condition, but he is bigger and is also a tougher breed. Rufus has multiple issues. His eyelashes have curled back into the eyes and he is almost blind. All of his teeth are rotted and his mouth is so severely infected, I suspect he's been like this for some time. I've never seen a bulldog so emaciated. I'm sorry but with his accelerated decline, he has lost the use of his back legs and is showing signs of internal organ failure. We won't be able to save him."

Her words were delivered with sorrow and quiet tears slipped from her eyes. I felt myself sinking to the floor as I tried to grasp an understanding of this horrible outcome. *Why did it take so long to arrest D.H.? And why didn't we do more to try and rescue them and take care of them ourselves?* I would ask myself those questions over and over again in the coming days, weeks, months, and even years.

"What about Harley?" I asked. "My daughter is in a treatment program. She doesn't know yet that they've been rescued, and I need to give her good news. Harley is her best friend, and I know he protected her as much as he could."

"Harley needs plenty of rehabilitative food and lots of time to heal. I'll give him fluids now and he'll have to come back for more once a week until he's fully recovered. I detected an irregular heartbeat, but it may be due to his condition and the trauma of his life plus everything that's happened today. I'll keep monitoring that with his return visits here." And then she added, "We'll need to talk about letting Rufus go as he is truly suffering."

I nodded slowly. Even though I had no knowledge of or attachment to Rufus, I felt in my core how damaged he was. Erin would be devastated. I hoped in my heart that the news of Harley's successful rescue would counterbalance that. Harley would stay with us until she was well and able to look after him again herself.

I recall signing a form and asking if we could stay while Rufus was being taken out of his pain. Harley, by then, had moved over to my side and was resting his head on my knee where I was seated on the floor in front of Rufus and the vet. I petted Rufus over and over and told him how sorry I was that we were too late. I watched as he slowly closed his eyes. A silence settled in the room and I cried quietly. Suddenly Harley raised his head, stood, and moved closer to Rufus, placing his nose gently on the dying pup's side. He stayed quietly like that for a moment, and I could tell he was saying goodbye to his friend. Then he slowly moved back over to me, sank completely onto the floor, looked at me and then at the treat jar sitting on the floor beside my other leg. I smiled as I handed him another one and he took it gently in his mouth. His delicacy and manners were astonishing, given his starvation. And I knew he would be okay. But would I? Would Erin? Would any of us? The battle, a new one, was just about to begin.

CHAPTER THIRTY-SEVEN: ERIN

BECOMING CLEAR (LATE APRIL 2013)

It was late April of 2013 and the last couple of years were dark memories in darker shadows. Now I felt like I was on a high, but I knew it was artificial as one Ativan wouldn't do this for me. My thoughts were pretty clear, and it had been a long time since I'd felt I wasn't blanketed head to foot in a thick cloud of confusion, fear, shame, and anxiety. The drugs I had been using took all those emotions and instead wrapped me in a different kind of blanket—one of warmth, comfort, and peace. But it had almost killed me, and I was celebrating a victory—I had survived an overdose.

It actually felt good to not be hiding my secret anymore. My family now knew I had been using more than just my prescription drugs to cope and there was a sweet sense of relief, but also a deep feeling of remorse. And the ever-present shame. Why didn't I just say I didn't need the methadone when James said it would help me relax? I figured because he was in recovery, he was a safe person to be with. If he was okay to be using methadone, what harm could it do to me? Apparently, a lot. It could most likely have irreversible consequences for someone not accustomed to it. I was so grateful and felt I had learned a lot already. I was looking forward to all the options that treatment would bring. It would give me a new life and I would walk out of here clean as a whistle, sober, and ready to take on the world.

And court. As soon as D.H. was finally arrested, and the trial was ready to begin, I would be there to testify. I would be clear. I would help put him away for what I hoped would be many, many years.

The first two weeks in treatment are a blur to me. Those first seven days were the worst. I was in the detox area of the center and the whole time was full of pain: crying, pleading, not sleeping, and feeling like thousands of ants were crawling all over my skin, biting me. There was also an indescribable hunger of a different kind.

Then one day, I woke up feeling better. And then the next a bit better again, until just over a week had passed and I was able to join the rest of the patients for meals, group therapy, individual counseling, and to listen to speakers. I still had my moments of returning to that heightened sense of hypervigilance and feeling like I couldn't get through it without drugs. The staff were so supportive and my fellow "inmates," as we laughingly referred to ourselves, were always there by my side. There was no judgment, only love and support, and it had been a long time since I felt like someone was there to hold me up when I was about to fall.

Two weeks after my time spent in detox, I was really starting to feel like my old self. And I found I was taking on a different role as a support person when one of my new friends started to slip. I had always been a caregiver (which is likely what put me in my predator's sights). But now it felt so good, and natural, to be there for someone who needed me. I was much wiser, I thought. I would never find myself in that vulnerable position again. I could fight back with my newfound sense of self-worth. That's not to say I didn't still need to lean back on the treatment center staff or my friends at times but, for the most part, I was doing really well.

The next Sunday that rolled around was a visiting day for family members. Mom held both my hands and told me the news. The time had come. D.H. had been arrested and was awaiting trial. My heart soared.

"It will all be over soon," she said.

"Did you get Harley and Rufus?" I asked. They were first and foremost on my mind. I was sure he would have looked after them because I had been misleading him purposely, telling him I would go back to him as soon as I was well. I always pleaded with him in those rare moments of contact to please look after them and he always assured me they were in good health and that he was feeding and walking them. I remembered the conflict I felt. I was putting together all my witness evidence against him, deliberately lying to him and hoping beyond hope that he would, for once, be true to his word. I had to remind myself that he was either a psychopath or a sociopath, and which one would be determined by his psychiatric evaluation at court time.

Mom's eyes filled with tears as she took my hands in hers. "We have Harley and he's doing well," she said. "He has some heart issues though and I've been told by your counselor that I need to be honest and upfront with you. We've taken him back to the vet once already since we got him, to have fluid removed from his chest. He is thirteen years old Erin, and he wasn't in very good condition when we got him. But he's happy now, relaxed, enjoying good meals, and I've been given permission to bring him with us next Sunday so you can see him."

My own eyes filled with tears of happiness and gratitude. I couldn't wait to bury my face in his beautiful fur.

"What about Rufus?" I asked. "He would have no place to go, did you bring him home with Harley too?"

Mom tightened her grip on my hands and pulled me into her for a hug. "I'm so sorry sweetie, he didn't make it. He was very sick."

I pushed her away. "What?" I cried. "What was wrong with him?"

As she explained what kind of condition the dogs were in, both starving and dehydrated with matted fur and lying in their own filth, my heart froze over.

"Why didn't I just go back to him?" I cried. My own tears were choking me. "I at least would have looked after them! I shouldn't have trusted him. I shouldn't have listened to the police. Or to *you*! You could have got them too." In my own muddled thoughts, I knew I was placing blame where it didn't belong, but I was so filled with anger. And so much grief at Rufus's loss. As happy as I was that Harley was okay, I knew how much of a victim Rufus had been.

"Do you know what D.H. did to Rufus?" I asked Mom.

"No, I don't honey," she replied. "What did he do?"

Visions of the abuse on that poor little dog rose up in my mind. I was forced to watch, sometimes with my wrists tied together so I couldn't hit D.H. or pull him off the little guy. I couldn't tell this kind of thing to Mom. She'd snap. I sometimes think of her as being so naive, so unworldly, and I couldn't believe how jaded I was by what I'd seen, heard, and was done to me.

"I can't say," I told her. "It'll come out in court, though, because it's in the evidence. He recorded everything and if they've arrested him and gone through his computer and phone, they'll know. I just can't say it out loud," I repeated.

"Okay," she said, hugging me tighter. "Hang on to the thought of seeing Harley next week. Your counselor has told me you are doing really well but please focus on yourself. You've been putting a lot of your energy into trying to help your friends here, but you can't be strong for them if you aren't strong for yourself. And you aren't there yet."

I heard her words, but all my thoughts were on the polar emotions of joy that Harley was okay and that I'd be seeing him, and the deep sadness I felt for the loss of Rufus and how victimized he had been as well. I wasn't the only one hurt in that hostage room.

CHAPTER THIRTY-EIGHT: MOM

A PLACE IN THE FOREST (MAY 2013)

I was invited to take part in a family program at the treatment center where Erin was undergoing her own transformation. This was likely the first time since the day she'd initially disappeared that the focus was shifting onto my own recovery. I already understood through the bit of counseling I had undergone that I was a full-blown codependent. Codependency is a form of addiction. The definition from the Oxford English Dictionary online: "codependency, n. Excessive emotional or psychological reliance on another person (typically a partner or close relative), esp. one with an illness or addiction… " That was me to a T. My days and nights had become a hundred percent focused first on finding Erin and bringing her home, and second on hovering, monitoring, controlling, obsessing… trying to keep her alive. Every moment of my time had been spent trying to fix, manage, and control Erin's life. And all my codependent behaviors had almost failed when she overdosed on my watch. It was killing me. I obviously needed help in how to manage my own life and now let Erin's caregivers do what I had thought was my job. They were far more qualified than I ever could be.

The next six days at the treatment center were the most healing and nurturing time I could possibly have imagined. We were deep in the forest and my daily walks among the trees helped to reinforce what I was learning in the numerous sessions I was a part of every day. It was my favorite place to be and as all the heavy responsibility on me lifted, I was beginning to come back into my own head, take full breaths, pause things, and feel a deep sense of peace and healing come into my soul.

There were other parents in my group along with siblings, grandparents, and even close friends of loved ones who were undergoing their own rehabilitation—just down the road and through the same trees in which I had been absorbing so much healing.

In one of our healing treatment workshops, we were assigned the task of writing a poem based around a metaphor for a tree—fitting, considering where we were for that week. Poetry is not my forte—Erin had that talent—but once I sat down and really thought about it, it was clear to me that "my" tree had to be one of releasing the shackles and moving into a place of hope.

THE TREE by Wanda Gray

I am in pain.
I once was alive and growing.
But I was shackled, stunted, held hostage.
Never to sway in the wind again.

Once I thought I was free.
But my captor came again and renewed my shackles.
I can see the colors; I can breathe the air.
But I cannot move or grow.
Shadows fall around me and the sun and the moon change places.
One day, one night, one year, one decade, one century.

But now, deep beneath my feet,
The ground is warm, and the earth is fertile.
I feel a movement, a twitch, a flutter.

I can begin again, the story of my life.
There is growth, however small.
It is not insignificant.
Now I am not in pain.

During that week, we had one session with Erin's counselor, where both she and I could talk about how to move forward, guided by a professional in the room to keep us on track. I had been so excited for that session to come as I hadn't physically seen Erin for two weeks. Not since I had given her the news of D.H.'s arrest and the outcome with the dogs. She had been getting extra support with her counselor to help digest all the additional mental anguish that had come with that news. I had understood she was handling it well, despite the guilt and heartbreak she was experiencing.

I could hardly believe my eyes when I walked into the room. There she was: glowing, radiant, my little girl with the rosy cheeks and happy smile as she chatted to her counselor. When she turned to me, the smile faded. A look of worry and fear took over. Did I have that same look of worry and fear on my face too? Why did it feel like we were strangers?

The next few minutes helped us both to relax and we began to chat about her recovery work and mine as well, as I was just completing the family program. And then the conversation took a turn that stunned me to my core. Through tears and a lot of silent moments while she gathered herself, Erin told me her secret—what she had been hiding so deep inside of herself for the past two decades. She told me part of it, leaving out some of the details and older history, but it was enough to shatter my glossy memories of what I thought was her happy, carefree childhood. It explained so much about her need to seek approval, her poor choice in boyfriends throughout her teen years, and her predilection to fall into a predator's trap. These were all the earmarks of someone living with deep trauma and shame. I thought my heart couldn't break any more but along with the shattering of my memories, my heart felt like a brittle stone in my chest, ready to also shatter with the shock… and the regret that she had been carrying this all by herself for so many years.

After this one-on-one counseling session, I was glad to have a couple more days to spend with my therapy group. I needed the extra support now that I knew what Erin had experienced as a child. I would need time to think about my past, what I had thought it had been, and what had been stirring under the surface when it came to the mental health and safety of my daughter. I still had a lot to learn and even more to put into practice. This was just scraping the surface of my own trauma, and it would be years—likely forever—that I would need to keep up the good work I had been learning to do. My deep maternal love for Erin had been flawless, but I was too close and quite likely caused more harm than good during those critical times when she was wavering in her addiction.

Despite the shocking revelation, leaving the family week in the forest had restored my energy and my optimism, giving me what I needed to deal with this new element of devastation. I also had a good set of tools to use in the days when Erin would be back home after her treatment had ended. We had so much to look forward to. And so much to try to forget.*

* *Author's note: For the purpose of this story, let it be known there were other innocents involved in Erin's secret. I have chosen to keep this part forever under lock and key to protect those whose lives were also likely put on a different and very difficult path. I still have no idea how far back the abuse started but I do know that it was too late to pursue anyone involved by the time Erin revealed what had happened to her in childhood. Erin would be learning how to live with the trauma and I would be learning how to live with the knowledge of what happened, at least in part, while moving past it.*

CHAPTER THIRTY-NINE:
MOM

HARLEY IS GONE (SUMMER 2013)

Shortly after I got back home from my week in the family program at the treatment center, Harley took a turn for the worse. We had been taking him to the vet every five or six days to have fluid drawn from around his heart and he had been managing, but I could now clearly see how depleted he was when I got home. He was failing. The vet assured us he wasn't in pain, but his weak heart was rapidly declining and it was an effort for him to walk. But his tail still wagged, thumping against the floor when he saw me come into the house. I knew we were prolonging his demise, but it had been important for Erin to wrap her arms around him one more time, which she got to do during our last family visit before my week in the program. Ten days after that last hug she had with him, Al and I were taking him for his final visit to the vet. We were assured there was no hope of Harley healing even if we brought him in daily for fluid removal.

"His heart is so broken," I said to Al. Harley was lying on the floor in a room with us at the vet clinic. The staff had left us to say our goodbyes in private. My tears were flowing freely as I wove my fingers through the sweet dog's fur.

"I'm so sorry, buddy," I cried into his neck. The vet came back in, syringe ready and profound sadness on his face. Harley lifted his head, looked directly at me, then slowly lowered it down again and surrendered to the drug that would end his suffering. He was gone.

"I don't know how I'm going to tell Erin," I said to Al as we slowly walked away from the clinic. "How much grief can she handle? I'll have to call Janine, her counselor, to see if we should keep this from her until she gets home."

Our conversation resulted in a special, mid-week trip back to treatment to tell Erin about Harley. Janine was right in that it was better to break the news to her while she was under twenty-four-hour care. Erin listened carefully as I described how Harley's heart had been failing and that we had done all we could but, in the end, his quality of life was deteriorating rapidly.

Erin's grief was palpable but she understood, growing up with animals on the farm and having a generous heart for all living things. We cried in each other's arms until there was nothing left. I watched her walk slowly back to her room in the little house on the hill and I understood how Harley's heart had broken. Mine was in so much pain and sorrow for my little girl. How much did she have to lose? And would she survive this latest blow?

CHAPTER FORTY: MOM

MORE HELP IS NEEDED (LATE SPRING 2013)

It had been five weeks since Erin's overdose at home. She had been fully engaged with her recovery work at the treatment center and I knew it was getting close to when she would be discharged and come home. But I had my concerns.

Even with the devastating news of the loss of both dogs, plus her worry over the upcoming trial for D.H, Erin had been doing exceptionally well. She was praised by her counselors as more than willing and able to do the work, and she had rapidly become a go-to friend for other patients at the center. This was encouraged but also monitored with a close eye to see if she would become withdrawn from her own recovery, shifting her focus to someone else. Avoidance. If she could immerse herself in the problems of others, she had no time to see her own path of healing and travel it fully.

I knew that was a painful path to revisit her childhood trauma, her time spent as a horrifically abused hostage, and her powerful addiction to prescription and street drugs. But by not focusing on her own recovery and spending precious time holding space for others to lean on her, perhaps she was undermining herself and opening the door to adverse consequences. I didn't think she was ready to try living outside of full-time recovery care and neither did her lead counselor, Janine.

Private treatment centers were well equipped with experienced and qualified staff but came at a heavy cost. Government-funded facilities were few and far between and we had no hope of finding one anywhere nearby.

"Erin isn't ready to integrate back into an outpatient life yet," Janine said. "We are recommending that she move into another treatment center as soon as possible after she is discharged from here."

I sat in silence, staring at her kind and worried face. I had come to a meeting to discuss options but had already done a lot of research on where she could possibly go at this stage. Staying where she was now could not be forever, based on the treatment program limits and our financial resources. It dawned on me that hundreds of people "not ready to integrate back into their lives yet, whether on their own or as outpatients" did not have families and nowhere to go either. A perfect recipe for a quick relapse.

"On the list you had given me, I found one that seemed to have as much focus on trauma treatment as addiction," I replied. "But it's all the way back east, in Ontario. That's a long way from home!"

"That's not necessarily a bad thing because Erin would have to focus solely on her recovery there. I know you've been regularly visiting on Sundays here, but it might do her some good to know she has to do this on her own." Janine's words hurt but held some truth.

"Besides," she continued, "it's partially covered funding and there is also a service where patients leaving the province for treatment elsewhere in the country can get some of their flight costs covered. That would cover both you and her flying there."

That lifted my spirits a bit. Our finances had been a mess since Erin first went missing. I had left a highly demanding but well-paying career for something part time that allowed me to focus on what had been happening, and now our savings had dwindled to nothing with the cost of private rehabilitation. But getting Erin well again was the unequivocal goal and more sacrifices would need to be made. We would do the trip, but she would need to come home for a couple of weeks first until a bed was available in the treatment center. I was terrified.

CHAPTER FORTY-ONE: ERIN

I'M SO SCARED (JUNE 2013)

I was home again in Mom and Al's house and as I walked into the spare bedroom that had become mine, I was surprised to see how neat and clean it was. There was even a little vase of flowers on the bedside table. I felt Mom's arms snake around me from behind as I stood in the doorway. Her cheek pressed into the side of my head, and I cried as she spoke. I could feel the depth of her love for me.

"Welcome home, sweetheart." she whispered in my ear. "We cleaned up your room and I had to throw out a lot of stuff, making sure there was nothing that could harm you in here. You're safe. You're home. It's time to keep working on getting well."

My thoughts went to all my hiding places. Where I kept my stash of cocaine paraphernalia. And to the horrendous pile of trash that I remembered had accumulated under my bed. I felt so much shame that she had to find all that—and then deal with it. Lurking just below that shame, I felt a sense of betrayal too. That was all my stuff she threw out and even though outwardly I knew it was the right thing to do, I also felt she had no right.

I gave my head a shake. I was thinking clearly for the first time in months, and this was a fresh start, even though I knew it would only be a couple of weeks before we would be leaving for the next treatment center. During these two weeks, I would be the model child. Devoted to my daily reading, working on my twelve steps, and keeping my nose clean. Literally.

I told Mom I needed a nap, and she left me in peace with the promise that she wouldn't be far away if I needed anything. I went over all that had happened over the past several weeks.

I almost died of an overdose of methadone. I was diagnosed with ADHD and a severe addiction to my medication and illegal drugs. I was admitted to an intense drug rehabilitation treatment and that came with not just responsibility and a chance at life but also gave me the tools I thought I needed to beat this demon off my back.

But I was scared. So much else was going on. Mom now knew at least a part of what had happened to me as a child, and I could still see the bleak sadness in her eyes. There was no going back from that revelation. I almost wished there was. I still wavered back and forth between regretting telling her and hating her for not knowing or seeing what had been happening when I was little. But she only knew part of it.

I brought my thoughts back to the here and now. D.H. was arrested and I knew court would be coming up soon. He had fourteen counts against him, ranging from sexual assault and forcible confinement to bestiality. It all came rushing back and I tucked my knees into my belly, curling into a tight fetal position, my hand over my mouth to cover my sobs. Poor Rufus, dead now and abused horrifically by a psychopath. And I had been there. Helpless, yet not helpless, in my mind. And my beautiful dog Harley was gone too—dead of a broken heart. And I believed that his broken heart came from abandonment. First by whoever owned him before I adopted him, and then again when I left him with that monster. Did he watch for me every day? How could he possibly know that I didn't want to leave him but had to in order to keep D.H. on a tether while his arrest was being organized? I was overcome by deep guilt and then a sick fear. Fear because I sensed the gnawing of hunger in my soul. It was all crashing down on me and around me. That need to withdraw and dull the pain of those memories. My nerves felt like they were on the outside of my skin and my breath was coming in ragged gasps.

Stop. Push it down. You know how to get through this. Breathe, count. Meditate, don't medicate. Mom thought I was fully recovered from my substance use and I had too when I left treatment this time. The next program I would be in was to reinforce the work I'd already done and focus more on treating the trauma. So why did coming home feel so good yet so unstable and frightening? That hungry ghost I learned about while reading Dr. Gabor Mate's book *In The Realm Of The Hungry Ghosts* was lingering in my peripheral vision, reaching its dry, clawing tentacles into my mind and telling me it needed to eat. How would I last two weeks?

CHAPTER FORTY-TWO: MOM

LOSING CONTROL (SUMMER 2013)

Those two weeks at home with Erin while we waited for our flight to the next treatment center, just outside of Toronto, were filled with worry, frustration, anger, and fear. Looking back, I know now that she felt the same but amplified. She was withdrawn and accusatory. Blaming me for not knowing what was happening to her when she was a child—how could I possibly have not known? Was I that blind? I guess I was and that is a burden I will carry with me forever.

Children are so vulnerable… and so secretive when manipulated, controlled, and afraid. I was the one person she could have come to but her shame and the fear mongering she received from her abuser was overwhelming. No, I didn't know. Should I have? Probably. I was living on the periphery of all that was happening, preoccupied with work, business, school and meeting schedules, extracurricular activities, and all the other things that went along with parenting small children and trying to make a living.

But to hear my adult daughter accuse me of ignoring her abuse was a punch to the gut. She always seemed to be her cheerful self, entertaining and loving to us and all her "critters" on the farm. We hugged every day, read books at bedtime, and I truly believed we were living a normal life together.

Predators are experts at distancing their targeted victims from the ones that love them. And I knew she still had not told me the whole story. I only knew that the origin of the trauma was deeply rooted in her childhood and likely set her up as a beacon for the luring antics of an accomplished abuser, sex trafficker, and one who I would eventually be labeling a murderer.

I was losing control of the situation. Erin was finding ways to leave the house at all hours of the day and night, telling us she was meeting with one of her recovery friends. I was so hopeful that she was staying sober that I chose to believe her—on the outside. But inside, my soul was deteriorating with an inner knowledge that I wish I'd had when she was still my little girl.

She would come home well past midnight, and I would be waiting for her. "Where were you?" I would demand.

"Out for coffee with _______," she would say. It was a different name every time. "I'm twenty-six years old, Mom, you can't put a curfew on me!"

"Actually, yes I can, Erin," I would tell her. "You aren't well, I feel like you are lying to me about where you are going and who you're with." I walked closer to her and looked into her eyes.

"Are you high right now?" I asked. I felt my stomach starting to pull up into my chest. Everything was compressing around me as I could see her pupils were the size of dinner plates.

"No, I'm not!" she shouted. She stumbled as she turned to head into her bedroom. I reached out and grabbed her arm.

"We only have a couple more days to go, Erin. Please stay home, hang in there. I won't leave you alone." I was pleading with her, and I knew I was also manipulating her as much as she was doing the same to me. But I would do what I needed to try and keep her safe. She might not be so lucky with another overdose.

"I'm going to bed," she announced, weaving down the hall into her bedroom. She paused with her hand on the door frame, her back still to me. "He's out there, Mom. He's going to find me when he gets out of prison, and he'll kill all of us." Then she went through the doorway, closing it quietly, and leaving me standing and gaping at the closed door. I hadn't thought about D.H. as I was so preoccupied with keeping her safe until we boarded that plane. I didn't realize she was still so filled with fear. And hate. For what he had done to her and even more for what he had done to her beloved pets. She didn't have any forgiveness in her soul for herself and that broke my heart.

The day arrived when we were to leave for treatment center number two in Ontario. I knocked on her bedroom door and told her it was time to get up. There was no response. I opened the door slowly so as not to startle her—she was like a jumpy wild animal. My heart sank when I saw her bed was empty. It hadn't been slept in so she must have quietly sneaked out after we had gone to bed, when she was sure we were asleep. I started calling her cell phone. No answer. I was panicking. Al jumped in his truck to see if he could find her, a fruitless search as we had no idea where she might be. The hours ticked by, and we only had a couple of hours to get to the airport. We were going to miss our flight and what I thought might be our last chance at saving our daughter.

Pacing. Calling. Clock-watching. My hopes were dying by the minute when I heard a car door outside and she was at the door, fumbling with her keys even though the house wasn't locked. I whipped the door open and knew right away that she was in very poor shape.

"Oh my God, Erin, where have you been?" She just stared blankly at me. I took her by the shoulders and shook her. "We have to leave now for the airport, are you going to be able to handle this?" I asked.

She mumbled something unintelligible. She had told me earlier that she was already packed so I steered her toward the bedroom. She fell onto the bed, her back leaning against the headboard. Her head lolled to the side and her eyes closed.

"Erin!" I shouted. "Wake up! We need to get going!" I looked around for her suitcase and saw it lying on the floor under the window, completely empty. She hadn't packed. I began throwing things into it, all the while continuing to shout at her. I was losing it.

"What is wrong with you, Erin? Did you use something last night?" I was shaking, shouting, completely losing control.

"You don't get it, Mom. I'm in a fugue state. That's what my counselor told me would be happening. I'm not high, I'm not using." She was speaking quietly and slurring so badly, I had to lean in close to hear her.

What was a fugue state? This was the first time I'd heard the term. In my desperation (and, let's face it, denial), I grabbed onto that explanation and went with it. My daughter was stronger than that. I didn't believe she could still be using drugs after everything she'd been through. No way. There had to be another explanation for her behavior and a fugue state seemed likely, given the terrible trauma she had experienced. But I had no time to ask more questions or research the meaning. My mission was to get her to the airport, get through security, and get her into her seat for the four-and-a-half-hour flight.

We made it to the airport with minutes to spare, even with Erin insisting she had to go to the bathroom before we went through security. As I waited outside of the public washroom in the terminal, I closed my eyes, calmed my breathing, and counted slowly. I was close to having a panic attack, but it would all be under control soon.

As we boarded the flight, Erin stumbled again and I held her upright, steering her down the aisle to the very back of the plane. I had deliberately reserved those seats, close to the bathrooms and away from other passengers in case she had an episode of claustrophobia, fright, or whatever else. I was prepared for anything at this point.

Miraculously she slept the entire four and a half hours. She twitched in her sleep, occasionally moaned, repeatedly saying, "No, please don't." I couldn't imagine what she was dreaming but the abject fear in her voice was heartbreaking. I had watched her sleep many times over the past few months but this time I was much closer to her physical body. I could feel her frightful tremors as the dreams took her back to captivity and torture.

I heard myself explaining to the concerned flight attendant that she had CPTSD and fugue states (still didn't know what the hell that was and the attendant didn't question, thank God.). And then we were landing at Toronto Pearson Airport. Only two more hours to go once we rented a car and made our way to what I hoped would be the final destination of Erin's additional trauma treatment before she moved on to live a healthy, happy life. Drugs would no longer be a part of our lives.

CHAPTER FORTY-THREE: ERIN

NOT A GOOD PLACE (SUMMER 2013)

The room was nice. My roommate seemed nice. And Mom seemed eternally hopeful. I had successfully made the trip, although the flight and the thought of being so far away from home terrified me. That's the only reason I used "just a little" the night before and again in the washroom at the airport, I reasoned with myself. I was not well yet and, deep down, I wasn't sure I had the strength to put the work into another treatment center. But my goal was to be off all drugs—prescription and otherwise—to be able to testify at the trial with a clear mind and not miss a thing that would help put D.H. away for a very long time. I blamed him for my anxiety and my addiction, for the abuse, the torture, the sad neglect of my now dead dog. Sometimes the hatred and the anger felt almost as bad as the fear. Would I ever feel peaceful? Happy? Hopeful?

As I unpacked my suitcase for the stay in this new treatment center that was supposed to help me with the trauma as well as the addiction, I reflected on how I had ended up in this place in my life. Mom had tearfully left, grasping me in a desperate and enormous hug while extracting promises that I would put my all into the program. She even gave me something she had written for me, framed, and decorated with little butterflies. It was called "Erin Is a Butterfly." I cried in her arms with love and gratitude and wondered at her undying hope for me. And there was the shame again. And the guilt. It felt like shame, guilt, abuse, and neglect had been the stones that paved the path to this moment in time. From my childhood trauma to my chaotic teen years and then the nightmare movie of being held hostage by an abusive, unrelenting sex and drug trafficker, it all seemed so tragic and sad. Like it was someone else's life. I felt sorry for that girl. That girl in the mirror who couldn't forgive herself for falling into so many traps and staying so silent. I would give this the best try I could and prove not only to myself, but to my family too, that I was still this fun loving, resilient and caring young woman who was my true nature. Not this quivering, emaciated and beaten creature that I believed everyone saw me as. I would fly as free as a butterfly again. This was my promise.

ERIN IS A BUTTERFLY by Wanda Gray

Erin is a butterfly. When she lands, people flock to her… to gaze and admire and try to entice her to light on their finger. She is weightless yet heavy with spirit, ever-changing colors in the sunlight and inspiring happiness and awe with every flutter of her gossamer wings.

She is fragile in appearance yet indomitable in spirit and strength. She was born to this world as a human but given gifts from God as He has a greater plan for her. She will endure great hardships so that she might learn compassion and understanding and go on to help those who need her strength.

Erin rescues the helpless—from injured gophers to homeless dogs to broken people. In the process, she can be hurt as well but she rises from the rubble and fights back as she knows the plan that God has for her, is waiting.

The time is right for the butterfly to break free of the cocoon again where it has been dark and suffocating… out into the sunlight with wings spread and love enough to share with the world. With many years left on this Mother Earth, Erin the butterfly has so much to give and so much time in which to give it. Today she is healing and learning to flex her wings again—sometimes it hurts so bad, she wants to withdraw them tight into her body, but with each flutter the pain lessens, and she begins to feel the energy again moving through her.

She is courageous, beautiful, strong, loving… soon to take wing again. Erin is a butterfly.

The first week went great. I met lots of amazing people, especially one of the other patients who became a wonderful friend. He and I had a lot in common and we spent hours just talking about our lives and our dreams for a better future. I felt he could quite likely become a big part of that future I craved. I also had a lot in common with my roommate Cassie and we spent hours drinking tea in our room and talking about our histories.

But I didn't like the direction of the actual program in the center. It seemed all about group therapy and I craved the one-on-ones I had with Janine, my old counselor at the center back home. And that wasn't the only thing I was craving. I found the hunger still lurked barely below the surface and I longed to numb the pain that was coming up again as I talked about my experiences with the group. No one judged me. We'd all had a very difficult road that had brought us here. But I could not seem to shake that need for insulation—a cozy blanket of warmth and comfort that could make me stop thinking about all the horrible things that had happened to me. I fought it. I used all the tools. And I cried a lot from the emotional and even sometimes the physical pain of continual withdrawal.

We were allowed authorized outings from this treatment center as we were told we would be treated like responsible adults. Mom, Al, Dad, and the whole family were horrified. I was thrilled. Finally, I could experience some freedom without the deluge of questions and what we called "helicoptering." That constant drone of mainly my mom hovering above and around me. She was seriously codependent, and I felt she needed as much help as I did. Even though I knew she was doing it out of love and fear, it felt more like anxiety and lack of control. It was nice to know that Cassie and I could go out on a "pass" and check out local stores, hang out in the park, and just be free for a few hours.

And then Cassie called an old boyfriend. I guess she missed him, but I also knew from our talks that he was into drugs and would be a dangerous person for her (and me) to be around. With a lot of pleading from Cassie, I went with her to meet him at a coffee shop on one of our outings and my old life poured back in. He encouraged us to just have something "small" so we could have more fun. Harmless really. No one would know and we'd be normal by the time we got back for check-in at the center. I don't even know what happened. I gave in to the pressure, Cassie was all over it, and even though I knew it would undo all the good I had done, I lacked the strength to decline and head back to the center on my own. I was so mad at myself for my weakness. I wanted to protect Cassie, as there would be questions if I showed up without her, and, like most substance users, I found a way to blame others. It was my responsibility to stay away from people who could influence me with offers of drugs—my comfy blanket—alcohol, and so much pressure. Somehow, we ended up at a tattoo shop, arrived back at the center completely obliterated, hours past our curfew, and calls were made to our respective homes. We were being asked to leave treatment. I had failed.

CHAPTER FORTY-FOUR: MOM

ON HER OWN (SUMMER TO EARLY FALL 2013)

At the end of June in 2013, in time to bring her home for her twenty-sixth birthday, I found myself taking another flight back to Ontario to pick up my daughter. This new treatment center did not work. Erin had called me after I talked to the staff there and I got a completely different story. They said she was acting out, not adhering to the rules, using drugs, and she would be discharged immediately. Erin said they weren't helping her with trauma, the group therapy was not what she needed, they were giving her far too much freedom (I agreed with that), and that her roommate got her into trouble. I felt like I was talking to a fourteen-year-old, not a young woman in her twenties. I was devastated, at a loss for what steps to take next, and thrown right back into the chaos of living with a loved one I couldn't help.

Within a few days of being back home, we established a routine for Erin that was mirrored on the after-care program when leaving a drug rehabilitation center. There would be group therapy, individual counseling, regular doctor visits, and constant check-ins with her sponsor and with her family. All of her healthy "clean" friends had abandoned her. Her new community was people like her, struggling to get well and stay well. They were a great group of friends, but it only took one to relapse and it seemed like the rest would fall like dominoes, as if they were connected by an invisible thread.

"I know what my problem is, Mom," she said to me one day. "It's who I hang out with. I can't seem to find friends who aren't using or selling or both. No one decent wants to hang out with someone like me, with a history like mine."

I felt so bad for her. She wasn't wrong because of the stigma that goes with drugs. So many people didn't care about what she had gone through, what a struggle the disease was, or why she couldn't "just quit." It's lack of education, ignorance, whatever you want to call it, and it infuriated me. This is a main reason why communities of substance users develop so strongly as they are shunned by society in general.

The "drift" happened very quickly. Within a week of getting home from Ontario, Erin decided she needed to be out on her own. She had become uncomfortable at our house, citing her past and her need to develop her independence again. Honestly, looking back, I think I felt a sense of relief, mixed with a deep worry that she wouldn't survive on her own. She found a job at a car dealership and we helped her settle into an apartment of her own. She did well to start and then she got a roommate because she found it hard to pay the rent.

The bright spot of those tortuous few months of Erin being on her own was the arrival of her adopted dog Ziggy. He was a tiny bundle of Pomeranian love and devoted to her, giving her a new lease on life. My hopes lifted again as she put in a dedicated effort to stay clean to protect Ziggy. He went everywhere with her and gave her the purpose of caring for another creature. She was finding her way back to being Erin again, rescuing various abandoned or abused pets and finding new homes for them. We became the new caregivers for two cats she rescued from a known drug house—two white longhairs that we were still loving and caring for at the time of writing this story.

Erin was also seeking out healthier relationships, purposely avoiding the crowd she knew was trouble for her. Counseling was going well, and she had moved by herself into a cute little house with a backyard for Ziggy. She was looking after her new little place with pride and the world looked brighter for all of us. But life is like a roller coaster and the dips are even deeper for someone fighting an addiction. It was only a matter of time and circumstance before Erin's ride would leave the rails.

Over the next several tortuous months, life became like *Groundhog Day*. It became a pattern of moving from place to place and an ever-changing assortment of roommates and friends who were living lives that also kept Erin in a place of sickness. We would help her move, get settled, worry ourselves sick, and then do it all over again when she was evicted or changed jobs. We even went through one terrorizing stint of having her admitted to the local hospital detox center when she overdosed again in her own home and a friend took her to emergency. We didn't know about it until the hospital called us, as I was her emergency contact number. I couldn't believe we had almost lost her again. She spent ten days in detox and came out of there with a new, hopeful outlook and determination once again to stay clean and sober. She was not healthy and needed to gain some weight, eat properly, and get into a normal sleep pattern.

Erin was thrilled to have her little dog Ziggy waiting with me when she was discharged. He had spent the time she was in detox with us, worming his way further into our hearts even while he felt her absence and wandered to the doors and windows, always looking for her. Erin spent the car ride back to her place hugging him and telling him how sorry she was that she had relapsed. To her credit, even during those times when she was using drugs again, she never once forgot about Ziggy, always making sure he was safe, fed, and loved. He was the one constant who I believe kept her alive during that time.

Once again, following the ten days in detox, we started the work that she (and I) needed to do to increase the odds of a successful recovery. We both went into an intensive round of counseling where we tried to work together to address all that had been going on and still was. We both needed so much help.

I was diagnosed with PTSD, mainly thought to be from shock on the night of her overdose at home, when I lost her heartbeat until the paramedics arrived. The ongoing prolonged exposure to the continuous worry and tension exacerbated my symptoms. I didn't know what was happening to me inside until I started having debilitating heart palpitations, landing in the Emergency Department when my erratic heartbeat increased and became constant.

I was told I was experiencing PVC—post-ventricular contractions. With the significant amount of heart disease in my family it was cause for concern, but I fortunately passed all the heart-function tests. The only other explanation for what was happening was an affected heart rhythm from the persistent extreme stress I had been under. No wonder—we had been living in trauma, fear, chaos, and anxiety for more than three years by this time. It was time for me to focus on dealing with the accumulated stress, otherwise I wouldn't be around to finally see the light at the end of the tunnel: the trial and Erin's hard journey back into health and recovery. A comprehensive and holistic healing plan for stress reduction was put in place and worked relatively well for both me and Erin, with a few bumps along the way, but at least we were heading in the right direction.

We had been waiting several months by this time for the trial to begin and, finally, we were told the dates had been set. It would begin in January, right after the new year of 2014 arrived. I hoped that the energy of a new year and the promise of spring would mean a new start. We fully believed that the trial would be done and over with very quickly. And then we could *all* recover.

CHAPTER FORTY-FIVE:
ERIN

WHAT ARE YOU AFRAID OF? (LATE FALL 2013)

The detectives on the case against D.H. called me one day and said the words I had been alternately dreading and looking forward to. The court date was set, scheduled to begin in a few weeks, in January, as we had been previously told. I would need to refresh everything, reading through my witness statements and preparing myself for questioning at the trial. I would need to visit the Crown counsel office several times and work with them to ensure a successful outcome. Other witnesses were lined up and the date was looming.

One night I woke up in a sweat. I dreamed that the judge had said it was all a joke and D.H. was a free man. In the dream, D.H. looked at me in the witness box and smiled with that devil face—the one that said "I own you. And you will pay for this." My heart was pounding, I couldn't shake the fear that ate into me, the dream felt so real. *I can't do this,* I thought to myself. *I don't have it in me. I'm too broken. I'm worthless.* Everyone will hear about how I did things for him that good girls don't do. I wished I was ugly sometimes. Men don't take ugly women. I was lucky to be considered pretty, but I no longer felt pretty. Now I'm ugly, inside and out. I was just that ragdoll on the shelf, to be looked at, admired, used, and put back. No one will believe my testimony anyway.

It was an especially hard relapse. I'd hit rock bottom before, but I knew this was the worst. My lucid moments were becoming fewer and farther between. Only Ziggy, my precious little dog that I now called my support animal, kept me from making sure I took more than my body could handle at one time. I needed to stay alive for him.

After I'd ignored Mom's calls for two weeks, she took the bull by the horns and showed up at my door. I tried to pretend I wasn't home, but Ziggy kept barking and she kept knocking. The look on her face when I finally opened the door immediately put me on the defensive. I knew I had lost a lot of weight and I couldn't remember the last time I showered.

"Why have you been avoiding me?" she asked. "Court starts next week, and I got a call from the lawyer's office that they haven't been able to get a hold of you. What's going on?"

"I'm not testifying. It won't do any good," I answered slowly. I could hear the slur in my own voice. I was barely able to keep my eyes open.

Mom looked at me with shock. "You've worked way too hard to get to this point. You can't just say you aren't going to testify," she said, tears filling her eyes.

As we stood silently on my front porch, I just wished she'd go away.

"Are you using illegal drugs again? Or taking way too many prescription drugs again?" she asked.

I didn't reply.

"Do you have any idea of how terrified I am right now?" Her voice was filled with pain, and I almost let go of any sense of caring. It was so much easier to be angry with her so I could deny the way I was living.

I managed to look her straight in the eye as I leaned against the doorway, holding Ziggy tightly in my arms. "What are you so afraid of Mom?" I asked.

She stared blankly at me for a moment and then said quietly, "I'm afraid that you'll die Erin, and then everything will mean nothing."

CHAPTER FORTY-SIX: MOM

ONE LAST TRY (EARLY WINTER 2014)

Erin wasn't in any kind of condition to be present in court. She was in no condition to even be on her own anymore and I was at my wit's end. She was doing everything right—going to counseling regularly, checking in with her sponsor, practicing her twelve steps she'd learned the first time she went for treatment... what else could we possibly do? I knew she had been trying but was slipping quickly, the impending court date putting her right back in the nightmare. She was in so much traumatic fear and pain that she just couldn't seem to stay clean and sober.

I would swing like a pendulum back and forth between feeling such a deep sadness and fear for her and then filled with anger and frustration each time she relapsed. I had come to learn a lot through this process and understood that a person has to really hit rock bottom before they'll reach out for help. But she had hit rock bottom at least three times now and we were still mired in this quicksand of inescapable chaos and uncertainty. Somehow, between myself and Erin's counselor, we managed to make sure she showed up for court for the days she needed to be there. She was never in great shape, but she was trying, and we were holding her up.

CHAPTER FORTY-SEVEN: ERIN

FACING HIM (EARLY WINTER 2014)

As we walked into the courthouse downtown, I felt comforted by the presence of my trauma and addictions counselor, Janine, from the treatment center. Many counselors in her field come from their own history of physical and emotional abuse and that experience leads them to careers in helping others navigate back to themselves. They are uniquely able to closely identify with their patients, providing a level of understanding and help that someone who has not experienced such trauma may not be able to. Also included in my family of court supporters on that first day, was my wonderful counselor Kate from the Victoria Women's Sexual Assault Centre. She had been my constant from the day I went to the police with my story and was referred to Victim Services. Kate worked with victims of sexual assault, and she had a calm yet determined demeanour.

And then there was Mom. She held my hand tightly that day, almost like she thought I'd fly away if she let go. I still struggled with our relationship and what I felt it had become because of my determination to keep her from the truth of my addiction. Her amplified codependency smothered me and escalated my anxiety and had driven a hard wedge between us. Things felt so awkward, even while I knew in my heart that she loved me to the depths of her soul. We had a lot of work to do to get back to a healthy mother-daughter relationship but on that day in the courtroom, I was so grateful she was by my side.

While trying to remain calm on the outside, inside I was a shattered mess. I had doubled down on my anxiety meds with the hope it would take some of the edge off but I craved the energy and happy oblivion I felt from my white comforter, cocaine. I was quickly going through my prescription drugs. My doctor wouldn't prescribe any more, and I was terrified of living in my own head without something to dull the pain and nightmares. With my medical file flagged, I wouldn't be able to ask any other doctors for prescriptions and the drug stores would see I was limited on what I could have. I felt trapped. It crossed my mind that I could probably go to another province but that seemed like a very scary step—I couldn't really consider leaving until the trial was finished. I filed the other-province idea away for a later date. I needed to focus and keep my shit together for court.

When he first entered the courtroom, flanked by two burly sheriffs, I felt myself spinning back through time, my heart fluttering like a frightened bird. He looked straight down at the floor, and I felt Mom's fingers tighten where they were still intertwined through mine. She was shaking as badly as I was, but I knew hers came from suppressed anger while mine came from fear. Or maybe it was hatred? I'd hang onto that emotion, feeling myself sit up straight, vowing that if he looked up and saw me, he would see a survivor. Not the beaten ragdoll he saw in the hotel room that last day when I was rescued. I focused on using hate to trump the fear that was threatening to crush me again.

All the opening statements were given, and the charges were read. It was mind-boggling how many there were. Fourteen counts of which most were assault in varying degrees. And I was the victim of all fourteen—I felt like I was in a terrible movie. Was any of this even real? Voices droned on and on in the background as I was taken back to those days of being held hostage. Some of this stuff Mom didn't even know about, and I heard her sharp intake of breath when some of the charges were read. I remembered the main piece of evidence was a video D.H. had taken when he beat and raped me while I was completely drugged. It was brutal, bloody, and horrifying. I recalled that my Crown counsel prosecution lawyer told Mom not to view it as she would never sleep again. I strongly reiterated that to Mom, praying that she would never accidentally come across it as I had all the footage stored on my laptop with the other audio and video evidence.

I had hoped it would all be over in one day because this was an evidence-heavy case where there was no doubt as to what the accused had done.

We weren't going to be that lucky. Everything took so much longer than expected. I would have to come back in a few days to give my own testimony. And I spent those few days in a drugged sleep, hoping it would all be over and I could get on with my life. A clean, sober life. I truly believed that if court was done and D.H. was in jail for many years, then life would miraculously become wonderful again and I would find it easy to quit drugs, meet someone who loved me despite what had happened to me, have children, and lead a fulfilling, happy life.

Back in court again, I was slurring my words. I could hear it in my own ears, the sound of an unfamiliar voice under water. The defense was hammering me with the same questions over and over as if no one could understand or hear me. I took a deep breath and looked up, facing *him*. D.H. The monster who stole my life and hurt so many other women. He smiled at me, but I could read it in his eyes—he would find a way to kill me for this. I stuttered, crying, and tried to finish answering the question. Reality flowed in and out, the courtroom a shimmering mirage in front of my tear-filled eyes. I caught sight of Mom, leaning forward on her seat, hands gripping the back of the bench in front of her. She looked panicked. I was screwing it up and I just could not do this anymore. The prosecution asked for a recess and once D.H. was safely out of the courtroom, I was ushered out into the hallway, Mom holding one elbow and my counselor Janine on the other. I sat down on a chair in the hall, and I heard Janine ask, "What is happening for you right now? What are you thinking?"

"I want to go home. I can't do this. I feel like I'm dying," I cried.

"Maybe we could find somewhere quiet and do a little meditation," Mom said.

"Really?!" I shouted. "That's stupid. I don't need to meditate. I need to *medicate*!"

Mom's head snapped back like I had slapped her. Her and her stupid yoga and meditation, like it was the answer to everything. My world was closing in on me, I couldn't breathe and my heart was thumping like it was on the outside of my body. And she wanted to hold hands and meditate. Maybe we should sing "Kumbaya, My Lord" around a campfire too! She had no idea what was happening inside me and angry feelings of resentment overtook my common sense. She was only trying to help but in that moment of complete breakdown, I just wanted her to go away.

Janine and Kate—always centered, calm, and professional—took control, helping me re-center and calm down. I would have to come back another day and finish my testimony. Having a meltdown in the corridor for all to see wasn't going to help my credibility as a witness, especially if the judge or defense happened to see me like that.

That night I dreamed he was standing in front of me—his face a blur. Was it D.H.? Or was it the person who'd hurt me when I was little? I had such vague memories of that but the trauma of being in court and my over-prescribed drugs dumbing me down had dropped me into an unrestful sleep with terrifying and Technicolor dreams.

It was D.H. And he was leering at me, inches from my face, his breath foul as he breathed out his promise to me. "I'm going to kill you for this and I'm going to kill your family. They don't deserve to have you anyway."

I woke up screaming and Ziggy whined, tucking close into my side. I hugged him tight and cried. There would be no more sleep for me tonight.

CHAPTER FORTY-EIGHT: MOM

THE VERDICT (EARLY WINTER THROUGH LATE FALL 2014)

At the next court appearance, D.H. took his turn in the witness stand. We watched and listened, dumbfounded at the testimony he was giving. We were left feeling like all the stuffing had been knocked out of us. Who would believe his lies? A recess was called, and we shuffled out into the now-familiar hallway adjoining the courtroom. I dropped into a chair while Erin cried and talked to her counselors at the other end of the hall, the Crown prosecutor also consoling her. I could hear her telling Erin to disregard all of D.H.'s lies as the evidence was the truth.

I thought about what I had just seen and heard. It felt like we had been waiting so long for that moment to witness him finally confronting his evil actions. It was surreal for me. His words were mostly lies and at one point, he had turned his head and looked right at me. Smiling, as if I was a welcome friend in this court where his testimony was a smorgasbord of lies and deceit. I remembered when he first came into our lives and a cold hand clenched my heart and my thoughts went wild.

First, he stole my confidence in trusting my own intuition. Mothers know—like my inner soul knew when I met him in 2010—when something evil lurks at the outer edges, waiting to pounce. A powerful bond is formed in blood, especially with our children. D.H. was like a dark tendril of sickness, weaving his way through the fabric of my cloak of safety for my child. He was a maze of lies with roads leading to nowhere, forcing me to turn back and look for the good. I never did find the good in the monster that stole my little girl.

As I sat outside of the courtroom, knowing he was just on the other side of the wall, I folded my arms across my belly, my emotions running amok with fear and anger. I heard myself softly moaning as I rocked gently on the bench. Inside the courtroom, I imagined his lies and deceit were still hanging in the air like a thick cloud of poisonous fog. On the witness stand, Erin had tried to answer the last few questions and had held herself together in a grown-woman's shell but inside she was a lost, frightened girl-child wondering why the bright sunshine that used to be in life was now so dim. The trust, hope, and anticipation of a beautiful future had been stolen, along with her innocence, soul, and mind. I knew she felt broken, a butterfly with torn wings, and my inner core screamed for her rescue as she didn't believe she would ever be anything but broken.

I mourned the loss of time and innocence yet held hope for a positive future. His conviction would pave the way for her life to re-emerge from such a dark place. I truly believed that she'd regain that bright sunshine, glorious hope, and a resurrected soul. A strong, determined, and healed butterfly would flutter bravely back into the world, into Erin's new purpose of helping change lives. What also gave me peace in the hallway outside of the courtroom was knowing that no matter the outcome, there were many types of justice and his true evil couldn't continue to exist in this world. No more young women's lives would be destroyed.

Back in the courtroom, what we thought would be a cut-and-dried end to the trial, over in a few days, was not to be. The accused, D.H., repeatedly claimed illness and court had to be delayed. Then his lawyer quit, citing "ethical reasons." It was clear that even the most hardened defense lawyers had their limits when dealing with a client who continually claimed what he did to those girls was acceptable. It took time to find another defense lawyer for him and here we were—Erin, the other girls, families, friends, and the prosecution—held hostage together by the whims of a psychopath.

Erin was staying with us again during the trial, which had become a process of stop and start. The months were going by at a slow, agonizing pace and I helplessly watched Erin decline. She randomly came and went, a lost and frightened young woman, constantly worried about the outcome and worried about our safety. I had no idea how to help. I found myself constantly asking her where she was, what she was doing. I was in panic mode again, asking horrible questions and accusing her. "Are you high? What did you take? You're slurring! You have to get yourself together so you can see this through!"

Questions, accusations, and demands. That's all I seemed to be capable of and years later I would learn how very damaging that was. With all the shoulda, woulda, couldas that haunt my days, my interrogations are one of my deepest regrets. The pummeling of those questions and accusations. My fear of losing her and lack of being able to control the situation dictated my words and actions. But I didn't know any better at that time; I was still new to witnessing the destruction of a child I loved with all my heart and soul. It was like watching a car accident happening in slow motion, knowing the end result could mean losing her. I was in full codependent mode and couldn't find any other way to manage, given the holding pattern we were in, waiting for the trial to finally be over.

I wished I knew how to change my language back then. Instead of letting the fear write the dialogue, the better script was with compassion, love, and understanding. I should have simply asked her: "What can I do to help you right now, Erin?" Those ten, little, supportive, helping words may have led to a different outcome. I'll never know. But it's a lesson that I learned the hard way and my hope is to pass that bit of wisdom on to someone else struggling in the same or similar situation.

Finally, the judge had had enough of all the multiple delay requests from the defense. The game-playing by the accused was brought to an end, and the trial moved forward. The remaining witnesses gave their statements, and the defense and prosecution teams delivered their summations. On the day of the verdict and sentencing, a weirdly mixed aura of anticipation and exhaustion hung over the courtroom. The victims had been re-traumatized over and over. Erin, especially, was barely functioning in those last couple of days. No one would be able to pick up the pieces until this was over. And, finally, it was.

I was sitting beside Erin in what had become "our place" on the bench in the courtroom, holding her hand and holding my breath. We had no idea what to expect other than that we had been told D.H. and his counsel had agreed to plead guilty to five of the fourteen charges. In exchange, the prosecution dropped the other nine to bring the trial to an end and avoid further traumatizing the victims. In our minds, the re-traumatizing had already been done, but we also needed it to be over. It was a dilemma in our minds. We felt all fourteen of the charges should have held but this could have meant months and months of more trial time. We had to be satisfied with his guilty plea to five of the most horrific assaults.

The judge seemed to speak forever, and I struggled to grasp what he was saying. The multiple charges, guilty verdicts, and subsequent jail time began to sound like a life sentence. When we heard "sixteen years," I was elated and gripped Erin's hand tightly with both of mine, hearing her cry of relief. Tears were running down both of our faces and when I glanced at Kate, seated next to Erin, she held up one hand as if to say, "just wait." I heard words like "time already served" and "reduced by," and I began to wonder where this would end up.

By the time the judge finished speaking, we understood that he would go to jail, not for the full sixteen years but long enough for us to feel some justice was being served. It was helpful to hear that there would be significant and strict parole conditions when the time came. We all knew parole would not be granted easily or early because, even though he had pleaded guilty, he still had not admitted responsibility or expressed remorse. The earmarks of a psychopath. He would also be a registered sex offender, which gave us some hope he would never repeat his crimes. It wasn't the twenty-five years we had hoped for but it was long enough that we could see a fresh, clean slate ahead of us where Erin would be free to rebuild herself and her life. I took the first full breath in months. Then I turned to Erin, wrapped my arms around her and said, "You did it my girl, you are so brave."

CHAPTER FORTY-NINE: ERIN

A NEW START, A NEW IDENTITY (2014 – 2016)

While the trial had still been lagging on, I had begun to completely lose touch with myself. Each day was a trial itself for me. Just to get out of bed was a huge undertaking and I saw no reason, nor had any motivation, to get up and start living. I felt like I was damaged goods on display now that the whole courtroom (and the whole world, in my eyes) had heard the horrid details during the proceedings. Even though there was a publication ban on the trial to protect my identity as well as the other girls, there were law students, the defense, the prosecution, and my support group in the courtroom. I felt exposed, exploited, violated, and tortured by the memories and the defense's constant diminishment of my treatment at the hands of D.H.

My only hope had been that all of the charges would stick and he would go to jail for a long, long time. Where he couldn't reach me. I still worried about his siblings who seemed to be supporting him. One of them had made an appearance as a witness, glaring at me the whole time she was speaking. Fortunately, she didn't help his case; her whole testimony focused solely on discrediting me, but she also threw him under the bus by saying he wasn't careful enough with his habits.

One day in August of 2014, when I hoped the trial would soon come to an end, I woke up with little Ziggy by my side and made a vow to reinvent myself. Someone whose name would not ring any bells. Someone who could make a fresh, clean start. The damaged-goods girl would be no more. I had applied to legally change my name and received my certificate of that change just before the final few weeks of the trial in the fall of 2014. I made a commitment to myself that I would become a person who dedicated service to others by helping other girls and young women recapture their lost confidence and offering them a health-and-wellness model to succeed. After being at the very bottom-dregs of destroyed self-esteem, subjected to almost two years of torture and being held hostage, trafficked and drugged, I could be an example to others that my recovery meant there was hope for them too. I could do this! As my spirits lifted, I began jotting down my life plan going forward.

When I shared my ideas with Mom and my counselors, I received nothing but encouragement. I could see the hope and relief in their eyes, and it helped spur me on. Mom wasn't thrilled with my name change but when I explained it would help keep me hidden in the future from revenge-seekers, she relented. At that time, I truly believed a new name would mean a new me.

Finally, when the trial was over in November 2014 and D.H.'s sentence was set, with the sixteen years reduced by time already served plus time for the guilty-plea agreement, it amounted to a total of six years to still be incarcerated. Even though it seemed so unfair to have it reduced to just another six years, I could begin to envision my future. I saw myself in six years, when he would first become eligible for parole, and believed I would be strong enough to cope if he was granted that parole. My step was lighter, my walk more confident, my focus more lasered on my goals, and my health was improving. Life was going to be good. It was the nightmares that I just couldn't seem to escape and going to sleep became a place of terror for me.

As the year 2015 began, I was working on my recovery program diligently and had a new name for my online wellness consulting. I called my business Honey Consulting and Wellness. Victims under interrogation by their abusers' defense counsel are often left feeling extremely bad about themselves—sour, ruined, not worthy, and doubting that anyone would ever want them as a friend or partner. I believed that the word "honey" brought an air of sweetness to that scenario, erasing the bitterness. I had been told that I was a "sweet little girl" when I was young and maybe this was subconsciously also a way for me to recapture that essence. I was already gathering interest from young women looking at what I had to offer through my business, so I was looking forward to a life-fulfilling future, turning my horrible experience into a tool for changing lives for the better.

That future was looking bright except for the demon on my back. No amount of work or sacrifice I made would get it off. But I had become an expert at manipulation and control. No one knew to what level I was struggling with addiction. Just because the nightmare of the trial and sentencing was over, I was naïve to think the constant, aching need would fade into nothingness. In fact, my secret illness got worse with my shame over what I thought was weakness. Addiction was still not recognized for what it was—a disease of the brain. The stigma and shaming kept me in the shadows, defeated and unable to fight the deep and undeniable physical and mental craving of that soft blanket of comfort. Getting high and dumbing down, depending on how I felt and what I had access to. Most of the time, my goal was to completely numb the emotional pain I was living with, despite the work I had done to manage and live with it.

There is nothing harder than leading a double life. On the outside, I appeared to be recovering nicely. On the inside, I was in constant subterfuge. I found myself withdrawing more and more from the public and then slowly from my new business. It was all just too much and, once again, I began to feel like I was failing. Ashamed, desperate, I was unable to find any workable option to cope with the ongoing trauma and pain from my childhood and my victim status of being taken hostage, sex trafficked, and physically and mentally tortured. I was doing everything right—why wasn't I able to cope?

Mom, now a veteran observer of the signs of relapse, begged me to accept some help. The problem was that there was no right place for me. Addiction was being treated as a crime. There didn't seem to be a process in place to help substance users to not only get clean and stay clean but also treat the reason behind the addiction in the first place. It was an assembly line: detox for ten days, kicked back out into the world or, if you were lucky enough to be able to afford a private treatment center, you could do another thirty days as a building block to learn how to live with your addiction.

It doesn't just go away. Addiction is a part of life that must be integrated into every day by working so very hard to stay clean and sober. It's a battle with a traumatized and changed brain that few can win. I had done my research and, God knows, Mom had turned over every stone, looking for some place I could go for an extended time to truly treat the trauma *and* the addiction because both were dependent on the other. Cost was the issue now. I dealt with more humility, guilt, and shame because I knew what it had already cost my family to have me in rehab. Mom constantly assured me that money was not something I should worry about—it was an investment in making me well and nothing was more important to her.

It was so hard not to resent the people who were just trying to help. It may not make any sense, but the harder Mom tried, the more guilty and resentful I began to feel. I knew she was reaching a point of giving up as she watched me withdraw from her again, give up my business, stop coming for dinner, and even refuse to come home for Christmas. She had begun to call me less frequently, had stopped hounding me daily, and she even began setting boundaries. "No drugs in the house. No calling and asking me for money." But she always made sure I knew that when I was ready to ask for actual help—not money or favors—she would be there in a heartbeat. She was drawing a line in the sand, like recovering codependents learn to do. I couldn't go home anymore. I didn't want her to see me like this, a failure, an addict, a manipulator. If only I knew then that she never saw me that way, not for one moment.

CHAPTER FIFTY: MOM

LAST CHANCE (SPRING 2016)

I knew by this time, through experience and through learning all I could about substance use and living and loving someone in addiction, that the breakup of our relationship as mother and daughter was almost par for the course. After the trial, things had really started to look up. We'd been through one end of hell and back and lived to try and make it a part of our past. Erin's dedication to her recovery work, her new business to help traumatized girls and young women, and her own dedication to facing life head on again, had filled my heart with joy. I felt I could relax my hyper-vigilance over her and begin sewing my own life back together. I had no reason to believe the future was anything but bright.

The first time I noticed that a bright future was in jeopardy was Erin's gradual distancing. She began avoiding my weekly calls and always refused dinner invitations. Her dad said her FaceTime calls with him were strained and she seemed bundled up in too many clothes for the warm weather. That alarmed me as I knew she was hiding a wasting body from him. I hadn't seen her for weeks by that time and found myself projected right back to the time when I was in full-alert mode, stressed and anxious around the clock. She stopped returning my calls and would not answer the door in the apartment where I last knew she was living.

My days turned dark once more. Every morning when I woke up, the first thing I did was open the front door, hoping she'd be curled up on the step in a blanket, alive and sound asleep, and ready for help. Each day that I didn't see her there etched the pain deeper into my body, mind, and soul. But I held hope every day that she would call me, and I'd hear the words I longed for.

It was April of 2016, sixteen months since the end of the trial and four months since the last conversation I'd had with Erin. The past Christmas in 2015, she hadn't come home to spend it with us, but I had convinced her to come over and pick up her gifts. She agreed but was clear that she did not want to come into the house. She asked me to leave them on the step and not open the door when I saw her picking them up. If I didn't think my heart could break any more, it did with those words. Why did she hate me so much? But I believed she must want some sort of connection because she agreed to pick up her Christmas gifts. They were just small things, as I had told her, so I saw her openness to getting them as a barely-there thread linking us. There was hope.

The gifts sat out on the step over the weekend. Even though I thought she had probably forgotten or decided against getting them, I left the gifts there when I went back to work the following Monday. When I got home after work that day, they were gone. I'd missed her. Much later in this story, I came across a video she had recorded of herself in the car with the gifts on the passenger-side floor. She simply said into the camera, "This is my Christmas." She had felt so alone, so sad. But she could find no other way to be.

I was living the best I could, going to work every day, checking voicemail on my breaks, and still opening the front door every morning, hoping she'd be there waiting. And then one day, my prayed-for miracle happened. I was just driving out of the parking lot at work when my cell phone rang. I pulled back into a parking spot, intuition telling me I needed to answer this call.

"Hello?" I spoke into the phone. I didn't recognize the number, but I did know that sound, that voice. I listened to her crying softly.

"I'm sick of being sick, Mom. I'll go back into treatment." Her voice was resigned but her words were what I needed to hear.

I'll never forget those few moments as I let the tears flow and thanked God for bringing her to this place of acceptance. Someone in the throes of a hard addiction must come to terms with needing help on their own. Those TV shows depicting involuntary rehabs are made for drama only and are completely misleading. I was so grateful to hear her say she needed help and was finally ready.

I had stayed in touch with the first treatment center she had gone to where I felt she had received the most help. They knew the situation and kindly agreed, with almost no notice, to allow her to come back. I drove up with her again that afternoon, so happy to be in the car with her, although her appearance was shocking. She was so gaunt, so pale, and so quiet. She was welcomed back into full-time treatment, and the head of the intake staff agreed to give me a few days to figure out how to manage the costs. However, he did caution both Erin and me that an exception had been made. She would need to really pull herself together over the next few days.

Fourteen days after taking her to the center, I received a call from them to come and get her. She was being referred to a women-only rehab facility in Vancouver as she wasn't doing well on this round of treatment. She needed more specialized therapy, and they felt she would do better in the hospital-based center for physical rehabilitation as well. I picked her up and we caught the next ferry to Vancouver, heading to the recommended place of treatment where they were waiting for her.

It was a dismal place, a former hospital ward that had had no upgrades and smelled like mold and old furniture. I had a terrible time leaving her there as she stood in the window, her hands on the glass like it was a prison. My heart sank like a stone. A mother's intuition is strong but mine had become so hypervigilant over the past few years, I wasn't sure if it was my own distaste for that place or if I truly believed she would fail again.

I think I unconsciously breathed shallowly for the next few days, waiting for the facility in Vancouver to call me to come and get her because she wasn't participating. But the call came from Erin herself. She was coming home and asked if I could get her, otherwise she could go downtown to catch a bus and then the ferry to make her way back to the island on her own. I had visions of her getting lost forever in the tragic area of the Downtown East Side of Vancouver.

I knew that stubborn streak. Erin would try to find her way home and I didn't really have the heart to convince her to stay. Something was telling me that I couldn't really blame her as I had spoken to the nursing staff, as well as Erin a couple of times, and things just did not seem to be adding up. Again. I felt that this last try at finding the right treatment facility wasn't going to be the right one. It was more a place for abused women with street-worker history and less about addressing the core trauma behind the addiction. It felt like it might have been a "quick fix, release, repeat" program, which wasn't the type of in-depth, long-term treatment she needed. I'm not sure why the first rehab center recommended a stay at this place in Vancouver unless they had given up on her. I was, in no way, ready to do that too. I told her to stay put and I was on the next ferry, bringing her home once again.

We were all out of chances and the only thing we could do was monitor her symptoms and watch for relapse, praying it wouldn't happen again. She had been clean for almost four weeks by then and clearer about what she needed to do to keep going. But there was still no place for her to go. At least not in this province or even in this country that I could find. Any places with proven rates of success in treating highly traumatized patients with "hard" addiction issues were completely unaffordable—upwards of hundreds of thousands of dollars. These places that popped up in my research were where celebrities go and I knew it was out of reach for people like us. But I remained hopeful because I knew that deep down my daughter was a fighter. But she needed dedicated wraparound support to help her move forward.

CHAPTER FIFTY-ONE: ERIN

THE SOBER ARTIST AND POET (SUMMER 2016)

Being four weeks sober wasn't new for me but this time, as I settled into my new apartment after Mom brought me home from my last failed attempt at recovery at the hospital center in Vancouver, I had a revitalized sense of hope. And creativity. Summer was in full bloom in 2016, and I was inspired by all the colors and the energy of the city.

I began to paint earnestly. I had taken part in the art therapy program in treatment and again while I was working on my recovery at home and it reminded me of just how fulfilling it was. I was a frequent visitor to the art-supply store and even bought a proper easel and drawing table. Mom had given me a small easel and a few simple paints earlier in one of my recovery phases and I expanded my supply while also beginning some online research, finding artists whom I admired.

Within a couple of weeks, I was cranking out brightly colored paintings of fish as I had also found a passion for betta, a Siamese fighting fish. They were loners and, at the time, I didn't realize that I really identified with their aloneness. And their aggressive, fear-based behavior. I loved watching them explore their aquarium and used them as a form of quiet meditation. Then I would go back to my easel.

Following my first, almost-fatal overdose at home, while I was in art therapy at the treatment center, I had painted what I saw that night. I called it "The Demon." This was the creature that had been coming out of the wall, trying to stop Mom from doing CPR. When I began painting again this time, I wondered where my brush and palette might take me. I no longer feared the demon I saw that night, but I worried he might still be lurking somewhere, ready to reveal himself again if I began to slide. I focused on the positive and the bright colors and tried to forget him.

The funny girl in me also started to make an appearance and, at first, I felt almost out-of-body as I painted gifts for family and friends. Whimsical and humorous works of art began to flow. A pink fish on a large blue background for Mom for Christmas. She called it "Lonely Fish" and told me later that it appeared to be adrift in an ocean of loneliness. Sometimes how we feel leaks out onto the canvas, but I didn't realize it at the time.

I did another, smaller painting of Mom's favorite TV characters, the Borg from the Star Trek world, in a unique collaboration with her least-favorite cartoon character, Tweety Bird. I called it "Tweety-Borg." I'll never forget her exuberance over that silly painting or the big hug I got from her. She was thrilled with the idea of combining the two but I think she was even more delighted to see me smiling and enjoying life again. There were a few paintings a little more on the dark or somber side but, for the most part, I felt that I was doing pretty good with the bright colors and light that flowed from my brushes.

Pull Yourself
Together Man!!!

More paintings followed: a partial skull on black canvas for Al to go with his motorcycle motif in his workshop, sushi characters (there I went again with the fish!), and Day of the Dead characters because I found them beautiful.

And then I found myself diving a little deeper into self-portraits, trying to see the real me as I no longer knew who I was after everything that had happened—if I ever did know myself. Not since I was six years old. I felt a touch of darkness and put down my paintbrush, reaching instead for pen and paper. Poetry and black-and-white sketches came to life again. I alternated back and forth between the two mediums for a few months but, as time went by, the loneliness settled back in and

I began rehashing my past. The present became cloudy and the future looked bleak. It was happening again.

One day, I drew something that just poured out of me onto my sketch pad. Without thought, I saw who I was unfolding under my pencil. Torn.

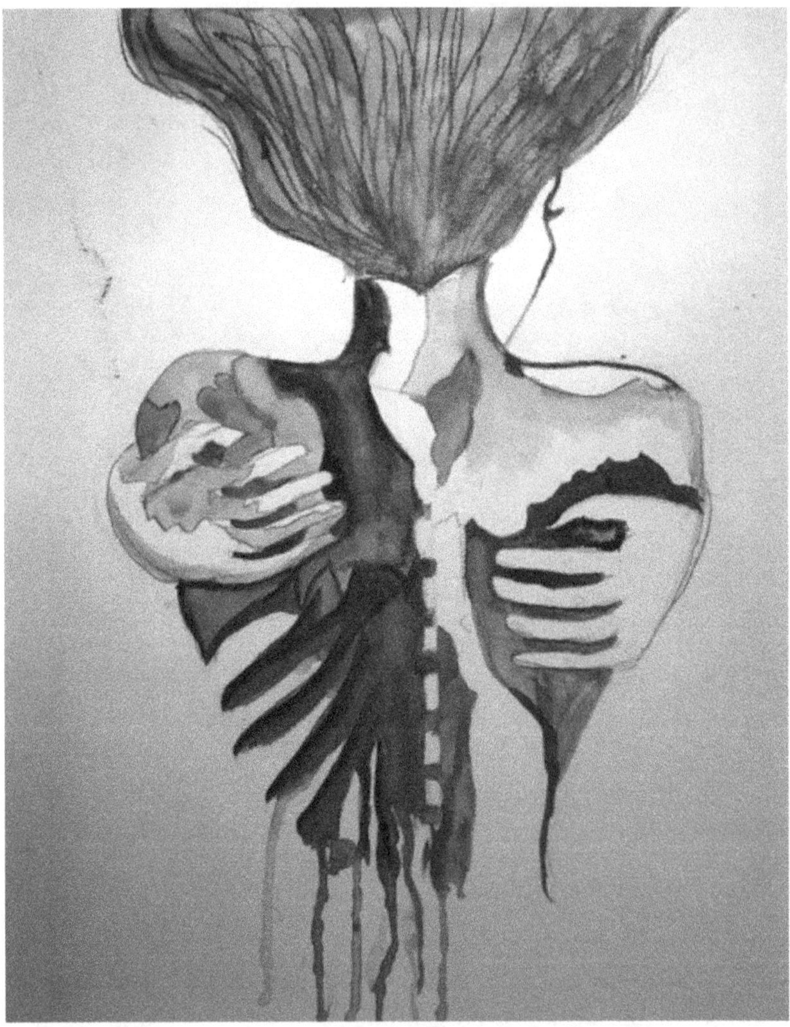

I probably could have rallied one more time. I knew the steps I needed to take but when I was down, I seemed to attract friends who weren't really friends. The paints dried up, the poetry hid under the couch cushions, and nightly partying became my only escape from dark memories. As I came to terms with what I felt was my failure yet again, I began to come up with a plan. Mom was hovering again; even Bruce had come back into my life, trying to help me, yet not understanding or realizing that what he was doing was likely making things worse.

I just wanted to "get gone." Me and Ziggy. A new adventure in a new place. I began to make my plans to move to Edmonton. I knew a couple of guys there I had been in treatment with and, as far as I knew, they had stayed clean and would be good influences. They would understand how I was feeling and what I needed to begin again. I'd had almost eighteen months of mostly successful sobriety, with only a couple of slips, but I was well aware that staying in this same place, Victoria, where it all happened, would only bring me down. When the demon jumped back on, my thinking became the polar opposite of the truth but I was already too far down and desperate to see it.

CHAPTER FIFTY-TWO: MOM

A BAD CHOICE (LATE SPRING 2018)

"You're not ready!" I heard myself say, much too loudly. Instant panic set in when Erin told me of her secret plan to get away. She didn't want me to tell Bruce as he would "freak out." Yes, he would. As I was. And so would many of her friends in recovery, but I was woefully unaware of who her actual friends were these days. I only knew she was relapsing, and she was in no condition to move to a strange place, away from her only resources for help. She'd been doing so well this past year, but I'd lost touch for a few months, living in that space of abject terror, recognizing the signs of her absence that told me a relapse was on the horizon.

"Well, I'm going anyway," she replied. "I feel like I'm ready and you know I need a fresh, clean start. I need to be someplace where I feel safe, and I don't feel that way here in Victoria. It's too easy for D.H. or any of his crazy siblings to find me here. It's a small city and everybody knows everybody else. In Edmonton, I have my new name, and no one would know anything about my past. Here, everyone knows and I'm sick of the questions, the sideways looks, and the constant pull back into that world of nothing but drugs and parties."

How I longed to believe her. I could understand her motivation and knew that she had the best of intentions, but it was also very clear to me that she was hovering on the brink of destruction.

"What happens if you get into trouble?" I asked her. "It's a fifteen-hour drive or a wait for a flight for me to get there and help if you wind up in a dangerous situation. I really can't support you in this decision. I really feel it's a bad move for you."

"Mom, I don't need you to rescue me. I need to learn to figure out things for myself and I have a couple of clean and sober friends I was in treatment with who have offered to help me get settled."

"How do you know they are going to be helpful rather than harmful?" I countered.

"I just know," she replied. "They are friends and wouldn't lie to me. This is a good thing, and you might as well know that if you won't help me, I'm going anyway."

"What about Ziggy?" I asked. "You know Bruce has a new puppy and it's bonding with Zig. And I know how pissed off you are with Bruce because he's been trying to control your daily life. I don't agree or support his actions, but I also get that he likely feels that because he rescued you once from D.H., he has some kind of responsibility to make sure you stay safe. It's fear of losing you, Erin. I have that same fear. You know that!"

"I need to get away from everyone who is trying to control me. Including you, Mom. Only I can save myself and this move to Edmonton is what I need to do. Of course I'm taking Ziggy with me. I already bought an approved airline carrier so he can ride in the plane with me under the seat." Her words were resolute, and I could see there was no dissuading her from leaving.

I tried one last time to change her mind. "I understand how you want to be away from what feels like micro-management and control. Try to understand where it is coming from though. You can't fix relationships by running away and we can all do better by giving you some space. But you've been missing from my life again for the past few months so you can't accuse me of trying to control you. If it's Bruce you are trying to escape from, just tell him you need time and come and stay here again. I just need to know that you are going to keep working on your recovery program and that you'll ask for help if you are relapsing."

Wrong thing to say, I know that now. I put a condition on my help, trying to be a good reformed codependent, drawing my line in the sand. But the timing was wrong. I saw her face turn to stone, then she turned away from me and reached for the door to leave.

"Wait," I said. "I'll help you sort out your travel arrangements. I don't want you to feel I've abandoned you. I know you already harbor feelings like that, and I also know you are stubborn and you'll go on your own, leaving us both feeling wretched. What can I do? When are you thinking about going?"

As she turned back to me, I briefly saw the little girl I had raised. She was relieved and happy to have my help even as I was breaking up inside. Something about this whole situation had landed a black bomb in the bottom of my gut. What could I do? She was my daughter. Mentally and emotionally a train wreck but with a stubborn streak a mile wide and no clear vision of what the consequences of this move away could mean.

"I'm going to move this summer and I'm already looking at flights and movers to get my apartment packed up. I'll just need your help to pick up the last bits I'm taking with me, grab Ziggy, and get me to the airport." Every one of her words landed on me like a sharp blade. I reluctantly nodded. We were already at the end of June, her thirty-first birthday was in a couple of days, and I was grateful that we still had time for things to change. Hopefully.

"I just need one thing from you Erin," I said. "I want you to promise me that we'll talk every day, even if it's just by text, until you are settled and have found work and reconnected with good, influential people."

"For sure, Mama Bear," she happily replied. "I'll be a little scared there by myself for a while so it would be great if we could talk once a day. Things will get better with a little distance between us, but I appreciate the fact that we can stay in touch. Once I'm all settled, you can come for a visit!"

"I'd love that honey." I was somewhat relieved to hear that she would want me to visit her. There was some hope and I reached for it, unsuccessfully trying to ignore the ache in my heart and the overwhelming sense of foreboding. We talked about the final details, and I spent the next few days wondering what miracle we needed to happen to stop this runaway train. Her detachment from me over the past few months (and every time she had relapsed) was painful, but at least she was nearby and I knew I could get to her quickly if she really needed me. Knowing she would now be more than a thousand kilometers away scared me to my core. The thought of me on the island and her a full province away felt like an entire continent.

I would not be able to throw her a lifeline. And then, just when I thought things couldn't get any worse, another blow.

CHAPTER FIFTY-THREE: ERIN

BROKEN BONES (SUMMER 2018)

It all happened so fast. I wasn't even high at the time. I stepped out of the tub after taking a shower and suddenly I was on the floor with my leg wedged behind the toilet and my foot at an unnatural angle. What the hell?

The pain was excruciating. My world warbled in and out as I gasped for breath, reaching for my towel on the floor and calling for Bruce. How embarrassing. I was using his shower and didn't want him to see me naked on his floor, writhing in pain, every inch of me exposed. I managed to get the towel wrapped around me and pulled my contorted foot out from behind the toilet. And the world threatened to go black. I heard myself calling him and the next thing I knew, I was being carried out to an ambulance and heading for the hospital. Oh God, please give me something for this pain.

"I broke several bones in my foot and ankle. I had to have surgery to put some pins in," I spoke into the phone. I had phoned Mom to answer her multiple missed calls after I was out of surgery. "I'll be spending my birthday, foot up in the air, and doing absolutely nothing!" I joked into the phone. *This tramadol is great stuff,* I thought to myself. A really effective pain med plus my benzos (benzodiazepines for anxiety) seemed to be just the right combination to right my world again. I couldn't feel anything in my broken foot and ankle and, actually… I couldn't feel anything at all! I was lighthearted, feeling alright, and assuring Mom everything was fine. I hadn't felt this good in a long time, even with the fat cast on my foot.

"Are you listening?" I heard her ask. "You'll cancel your plans to move to Edmonton now, right? It takes a very long time for broken bones to heal so uprooting yourself now isn't an option."

"I already found an apartment on the west end and have to move in on August 1st. I booked the movers and gave my notice at my apartment a long time ago. So, I have to be out and, yeah, I'll delay it a couple of weeks but I'm still going. I can probably wear an air cast by then, so it'll all be good. Don't worry, Mom."

I could hear the disappointment in her voice but right now, nothing mattered. My plans were in place, all was a go, and the prescription for tramadol would help keep moving me in the right direction. Minor setback, really. I just needed to see my doctor once more to convince her to prescribe enough tramadol to get me through a month or so, then I could find a clinic or doctor in Edmonton to renew it. If I still needed it in a few weeks. Right. I was so excited for my new life to start!

CHAPTER FIFTY-FOUR: MOM

THE LAST GLIMPSE (SUMMER 2018)

We were standing in the Victoria airport, checking the status of Erin's flight, when I was overcome again with such a debilitating sense of foreboding. I was holding Ziggy's travel carrier while she had him on his lead, her giant purse slung over one shoulder and her hair piled high on her head in a fetching yet unruly knot. She always had such a creative and beautiful way with hair. I briefly regretted selling the salon as maybe, just maybe, we wouldn't be standing here now.

As I studied her excited features, it struck me how ethereal she really was. When other travelers walked past, I noticed how they hesitated and looked at her with full attention. This wasn't the usual behavior of people in an airport where we all tend to just glance and look away, not noticing, never remembering the face we just saw. Her very essence was one of love, kindness, and compassion and she just unwittingly drew attention—not just with her beauty but even more so with her aura.

For a moment, I felt like a stranger. Who was this very young girl in a grown woman's body? Was she really my daughter? We had drifted apart and come back together so many times over the past six years that I felt the mother-daughter tether had become brittle with the tension. But it had hung in there with intense maternal love. I knew she was still struggling inside and trying to put on a brave front. The physical, emotional, and mental trauma were still ruling her thoughts, actions, and very existence.

How would she survive? After everything she'd been through, Erin amazed me with her strength, resilience, and determination and excitement to begin her new life. But my foreboding wasn't imaginary. I knew deep down in my gut that she was not stable, and the slightest upset could trigger yet another relapse. And I wouldn't be there to catch her this time.

I walked with her all the way through the queue leading to security where I knew I'd have to let her go. She limped along beside me on her cast and picked Ziggy up off the floor to pop his flight sedative into his mouth, disguised in a tiny morsel of chicken she had ready in her purse. She was so concerned he'd be stressed even though he would be tucked safely under the seat ahead of her. And I was so concerned for both of them, heading off into what I considered to be an unknown place of new terrors and trials.

As we stood hugging once more, I waved at a few people to please go ahead as I wasn't ready to let go of her. Finally, she said, "Mom, I gotta go. I love you. I'll call you as soon as I land in Edmonton and again when I get to the hotel." She had a few days to spend in a hotel until she could get the keys for the apartment she had arranged online.

"I love you too, sweetheart," I whispered through my restricted throat, tears running down my cheeks. I could sense people around us glancing sympathetically as they saw two women, one young and hauntingly beautiful and one obviously a little worse for wear, having a very difficult goodbye moment.

I watched as she hobbled along with the line leading to security. She had Ziggy held up high on her shoulder as she struggled to get her purse and the pet carrier onto the belt leading to the X-ray unit. I very badly wanted to launch myself through the doorway and help her, but she finally got everything under control and made it through the scanner. Ziggy was looking directly at me over her shoulder, obviously confused but always happy when he was with her. I just had to trust that they would be okay.

Just before leaving the security area, she turned and gave me a little wave. I waved back and blew her a kiss, but she had already turned and was limping determinedly toward her gate with her little dog, pet carrier, purse, and carry-on bag balanced precariously. The rock settled further into the pit of my stomach, and I turned to walk out of the airport, back to my car where I could cry loudly and in private. It was the last time I saw her—my last glimpse of her blonde head bobbing through the throngs on her way to what she expected to be her new, happy life.

CHAPTER FIFTY-FIVE: ERIN

A NEW LIFE (LATE SUMMER 2018)

I hadn't felt hope like this for what seemed like a very long time. I was excited to start my new life, Ziggy in tow, as the plane landed in Edmonton. We took a short cab ride to the hotel where I'd be staying for a few days until I could get into my apartment. The front desk people were so ecstatic to make a fuss over my very cute dog, of course. And the bellhop was falling over himself to help me with my bags. I figured a girl in a cast with a little dog was likely to get a little more attention and a lot more help than your average "new girl to town."

By the time I got settled into our room, my ankle and foot were throbbing like a drumbeat. I had made solid efforts to limit the amount of tramadol I was taking but now that I had several hours to just lie on the bed, relax, and recuperate, one or two more out of the prescription cycle couldn't possibly hurt.

I woke up several hours later, feeling so groggy. Lifting my head off the pillow took way too much effort. Where was Ziggy? I felt around beside me where he had been lying and there was nothing. As I painfully sat up, I saw him in the corner, tail between his legs, looking imploringly at me. I knew that look and I also knew he'd been holding it for a long time, so I managed to get my one shoe on, attach his leash, and take him out for a much-needed pee and walk.

This would be the routine for the next couple of days. Tramadol, sleep, eat, take Ziggy out for his walks. Rinse and repeat. I'd be seeing my apartment in person once my possession date arrived and even though I had seen pictures of it on the internet, I still had no idea of what the neighborhood was like. I didn't know Edmonton at all for that matter, I just knew I had to head west from the hotel to find the address. I was excited but also feeling a lot of fear of the unknown.

It had been hard in Victoria, surrounded by people and things that reminded me of what had happened to me. Knowing I would now be surrounded by people who didn't know me or my past, I felt freer than I had for years. A new start, a new place, new people, new work (I had to start doing something as soon as I could get the cast off) and, above all, my faith in myself and in God would prove I could get off and stay off the opioids. Mom would see a whole new daughter next time we got together.

The day I checked out of the hotel and took the cab to my new apartment was what I really felt was the start of my new life. I couldn't disguise my shock at seeing the apartment building up close. The inside just *had* to be better. Outside was a peeling facade, dirty windows, garbage in the front yard, and some rather shady looking characters shuffling down the street. I knew this area of town wasn't upscale, but it was all I could afford and obviously the ad had been misleading. All I could hope for is that the apartment itself would live up to the promise of being "newly renovated."

The landlady was waiting for me at the side door and gave an appropriate scratch underneath Ziggy's chin. She was alright in my books as she was obviously smitten with my furry best friend. That made it more difficult for me to express delighted surprise when she opened my new apartment door. It had obviously been cleaned but there was no disguising the smell of past rotting garbage, old doors and windows, and a general sadness in the kitchen from older appliances chugging along with effort.

"What part was renovated?" I asked my landlady.

"There is a brand-new tub and shower in the bathroom. You'll love it," she said as she walked ahead of me down the hallway. As I peered around the doorframe into the bathroom, I wanted to say it out loud but in my head I asked, *Since when does a blue bathtub constitute "new"?* It appeared to be in relatively good shape, but I wondered where she got it from because I was sure blue bathtubs hadn't been around for decades.

But I was grateful she accepted my application as a stranger from out of town with a dog and no references. I was lucky to get a place, so I would have to just work at brightening the place up to make it mine and Ziggy's nest.

I heard myself thanking her profusely as she handed me the keys. I had paid for the first month and damage deposit up front, so all I had to do now was wait for the moving truck to arrive that afternoon. Then I could have all my own things around me, hang my paintings, and, once I was settled, get in touch with my two friends from the treatment days. The two guys I knew were solid people, clean and sober, with jobs and a network they could introduce me to as I really needed to make some new friends. Life was good.

But first, I needed to find a walk-in clinic and doctor to renew my subscription for tramadol. All this stress of moving and being on my feet was taking a toll on my poor broken ankle and foot. I must have gone through the limited number of pills my own doctor back home had prescribed for me. I was sticking to my prescribed dosage of benzodiazepines for my continuing anxiety, but I was finding that tramadol was giving me the warm, fuzzy blanket I really craved to dull my senses, dull the pain in my ankle, and dull the world in general. I didn't need to think or worry or be afraid.

Mom was calling again. I quickly texted her back to let her know I was okay. I was feeling so tired and didn't want to talk. She always had so many questions! How are you? How is Ziggy? Are you settling in? Have you met your neighbors? I could answer that one truthfully. I'd met Trudy across the hall. She was so nice and welcoming, and it turned out we had a lot in common. A past saturated in hard memories of abuse, trauma, and lots of dope to muffle the noise of our thoughts. She was still into cocaine, which I had left behind months ago. I didn't need that stimulant or its high anymore to keep going. D.H. had forced me to use "white" when he needed me to perform like a circus animal. Now I just wanted things to be slow and quiet, so my benzos and the tramadol were doing what I needed.

When I finally reconnected with my two guy friends from rehab, I soon figured out that maybe they weren't quite as clean and sober as I had understood them to be. However, I was in no position to judge. Meth was the new game in town and even though I was around it when I was hanging out with some new people I met through my friends, I didn't feel the need to try it. Not right away, anyway.

Over the next couple of weeks after moving into my apartment, I had seen two doctors who were more than happy to renew my tramadol prescription, just by looking at my foot and hearing my explanation of how much pain I was in. I was waiting for surgery to replace the pins that had been put in and it was easy to explain how I needed some kind of strong painkiller to keep me going until that happened. I also found a nearby pharmacist who, without question, replaced my "lost" prescription. Twice. It wasn't this easy back home.

Despite my reluctant dependence on my medications, I was holding it together pretty good. I either talked or texted with Mom every day, I regularly walked Ziggy, and I was eating pretty healthy. The groceries were thanks to Mom calling a local store to deliver bags of food that I couldn't possibly go through. I was appreciative; grocery shopping was a pain in the foot and I couldn't take Ziggy into stores and hated leaving him alone in that dreary (and scary) apartment alone.

I had gone through the money I saved so fast, buying a few things for my apartment, paying for prescriptions and, if I'm honest with myself, other "helpful" substances. I didn't consider the dangers of who or where I was buying such small quantities from, as fentanyl was just becoming a huge topic as a contaminated street drug.

I was on a roller coaster of feeling I needed something to pull myself out of my subdued and sedated state whenever I wanted to leave the apartment, and then back into that quiet place where my fear and anxiety could take a rest. I began to imagine that D.H. had somehow been released from jail and was coming for me. The nightmares had returned in earnest, and I was terrified of being kicked out of my new apartment already. Rent would be due soon and I was broke.

Mom kept insisting she'd come and visit me, but I wasn't ready for that. I needed more time to get settled and on top of what I now recognized as the beginning of a full slide into relapse if I didn't get my shit together very soon. I was no longer managing my prescriptions, and

I kept forgetting what I was taking and when. It was around the end of August, four weeks after my arrival in Edmonton, that I started to suspect someone was following me, watching me, and hanging around outside my door. I could no longer leave my apartment.

CHAPTER FIFTY-SIX: MOM

NOT LIKE THAT (LATE SUMMER 2018)

Things weren't going as Erin had hoped. Or as I had hoped. I could hear desperation in her voice and all the excuses as to why she was still taking tramadol. I had already learned how addictive that drug could become, especially to someone already reliant on substances. I also knew it was meant to be very short term for her broken foot and ankle. It had been two months since her fall, and she should not have still been on tramadol.

"I am in so much pain, Mom." she'd say when I questioned why she needed money for more prescriptions. "I don't have provincial health care yet so I'm paying full price. I just need to make it until I have the surgery on my ankle, then I'll be fine. The pins are wrong or something, I'm in agony all the time."

"Have you told the clinic doctor about your additional pain?" I asked.

"Yes, but he said I would have to wait for surgery, there was nothing he could do." Her words were muddled and her voice slow and syrupy. I recognized the signs of too much sedation.

"Also," she continued, "there are some really creepy, bad people around here. I'm afraid to leave my apartment. I'm going to send you some pictures I took of a body left in the garbage bin behind my apartment building."

"What!?" I shouted into the phone. "Have you called the police?"

"The police here don't care, Mom. There's so much crime, they've given up. I just have to make sure I only go outside in the daylight and that I have Ziggy with me at all times."

I couldn't believe what I was hearing. What kind of hellhole had my daughter moved to? There was a ding on my phone and a picture came up of a couple of garbage cans propped against a wall in a dingy parking lot.

"Do you see the body?" she asked. I looked hard but I couldn't see anything but garbage cans with tied black plastic bags poking out of the top of them.

"No, I don't see a body; you must have been dreaming," I told her.

Erin began whispering something into the phone and I couldn't hear her. Something about someone watching her and that she was in trouble. I was terrified.

"I'm coming to get you," I said. "And I'm going to call your dad to see if he can get there even sooner than I can. Please just wait where you are and one of us will be there soon."

"Okay, I gotta go, Mom. I'm super tired and need to lay down." Her voice was still just barely a whisper and then the call ended.

I called Ken, her dad, right away. He was at work but as we were both always on high alert and had been for several years by then, he quickly answered. I gave him a rundown of the conversation I had just had with Erin and shared my heightened sense of urgency about her safety. Safety from potentially bad street drugs and a relapse, and safety from what I believed was a dangerous place for her to be living.

Ken listened quietly and when I finally stopped gasping out my fears and asked him how fast he could get to Edmonton from Regina, I heard him hesitantly say, "I don't want to see her like that. We've done all we can and it's up to her to get herself straight now."

I was devastated and felt instantly alone to figure out what to do, but I also understood his resignation. The not-yet-healed codependent in me was screaming to rescue her again and all the counseling and well-meaning advice I'd been given was telling me to step back and let go, give her the space she needed to rescue herself. I was being torn in half.

"Not like that," I heard him say again. "It's too hard to see her relapsing; we can't help her anymore."

I was disappointed but ended the call with the assurance I'd let him know when I talked to her again. And I began the familiar pacing and worrying. It was a Thursday, late afternoon, and I made a few calls looking for some support, someone who would go to Edmonton with me. I didn't think I could do this on my own, but I was also leaning toward the advice from friends, family, and a couple of Erin's support workers: give her the weekend and if she still wasn't sounding any better by Monday, I'd get on the next flight and be there to pick up the pieces.

Waiting until the next day to call Erin was extremely difficult for me. I hardly slept a wink and my senses were fractured and raw. She didn't answer and I left a message. Then I called again a few hours later. The pattern continued well into Saturday when my last text message to her was that I was going to get in touch with the two guys she knew from rehab, to see if they had seen her. She had given me their phone numbers in case of an emergency, and I considered this a major emergency. She had never taken this long to call me back and not a day had gone by since she left for Edmonton that we didn't at least exchange a text, always with a heart emoji at the end. Something was terribly wrong.

It took until Sunday for both of her friends to get back to me, assuring me that she hadn't been in touch with either of them for at least a couple of weeks. I had one last option as I tortured myself with thoughts that if I'd left for Edmonton when my gut told me to, I'd be there by now.

"I'd like to request an emergency wellness check, please," I said into my phone. I had called the Edmonton Police Service and was put through to the appropriate department. "My daughter has complex PTSD and I think is relapsing from an addiction to prescription drugs. Maybe even street drugs. She hasn't missed a day being in touch with me since she moved there six weeks ago and now I haven't heard from her since Thursday night."

We were now getting into day four, late Monday, of no communication and I was barely running on steam. I had been frantically trying to get a last-minute flight to Edmonton but thought the police would be a quicker solution and could help if she was in trouble. The night inched by far too slowly as I slept in fits and starts. I called the same police contact again the next morning, only to be told they had an unusually high call load, but I was assured they would be contacting Erin's landlord and meeting her there to enter her apartment soon.

Finally, I received a call that the police had made contact with the landlady and they were on their way. The attending police officers would call me when they had something to report, even if it was late. The time was now past seven o'clock in the evening on Tuesday. The last few days had been agonizing, but despite the high state of anxiety I was living in, I was also relieved that help was on the way. I was fully expecting a call from them stating she was okay, albeit a bit of a mess. And then I'd hear her voice telling me her phone had died and she'd been too out of it to plug it in to charge.

Anticipating that call I imagined and the sense of relief at hearing her voice, I spent the rest of the evening trying to keep myself occupied. TV didn't distract me and reading was a waste of time as the words were impossible to absorb, so I spent the time looking at a flight for me to Edmonton and a return one for me, Erin, and Ziggy. This would be it. I wouldn't let her out of my sight again.

Close to midnight, I finally turned out the lights and sat up in bed as Al restlessly tossed and turned next to me. I was thinking to myself that the police must have been delayed again when the doorbell rang, followed immediately by knocking.

CHAPTER FIFTY-SEVEN: MOM

WORST FEAR (SEPTEMBER 25, 2018)

As I stumbled out of the bedroom, heading to the front door and pulling a sweatshirt over top of my pajamas, my thoughts were scattered in all directions. The first crazy thought was a question… did I even get dressed today? I had no recollection. It was half past twelve, early Wednesday, and suddenly the path leading from the hallway to the front door seemed interminably long, like it was narrowing into a point that I did not want to reach. My next thought was maybe it was Erin! She didn't have a key and perhaps she had been on her way home all this time we had been trying to get the police to her apartment.

I pulled the front door wide open, Al directly behind me, still struggling to pull a shirt over his head. On the doorstep were two police officers from our local municipality. I clasped my hands together and pressed them against my heart. I was already sensing the earth below my feet beginning to shift. A vision of overwhelming grief, tears, anger, revenge, and my own death all converged on a terrible shore that would define my life from this moment forward.

I shook my head slowly. I was so confused. I had called the Edmonton Police Service so why were two local cops standing there? They asked if I was Wanda. I nodded. "Are you Erin Gray's mother?" Again, I nodded but I was already beginning to pull back into the living room, shaking my head, and I heard Al invite them in. *No,* I was thinking, *please don't let them in because then this moment does not have to happen.*

"Perhaps you would like to sit down?" one of the officers asked me.

"No, I don't want to sit. Why are you here? What happened?" I asked.

When the hats come off, you instantly know from watching television that the police aren't there with good news. One of the officers continued, his eyes shifting from me to Al and back again. "You had called Edmonton city police, requesting a wellness check for your daughter Erin. They contacted us about an hour ago to ask that we regretfully tell you that your daughter was found deceased in her apartment this evening."

A muffling of whatever words followed, barely penetrating my consciousness. My ears were filled with a strange, rushing sound. I felt the growing horror in my mind and heart turn into a dark mass that would color my coming days and nights ahead. The earth I stood on, which I thought I knew so well, began to shift and evaporate. In its place, I stood on a strange, dark, and empty planet. I was cold, numb, and isolated in my shock and grief. Here I would wait out my days to die and hold my little girl in my arms again. That was the only hope that I had left.

Inside my body, my lungs no longer took in air and my heart was beating so loudly as it tried to keep my life force going. Not knowing how I got there, I realized I was sitting on the couch with my head in my hands and I was rocking, back and forth, back and forth, as a low keening sound came from my throat. I heard words being exchanged between the two police officers and Al. The coroner had been called, something about a detective assigned to the case, evidence of drug paraphernalia and perhaps someone else previously in the apartment, but gone when the landlord let the police in. The words were all a jumble, and I began to shake my head when I heard them say it appeared to be an accidental overdose. Everything that I knew, everything I was, and everything that could still be, came to a grinding halt. I felt so hot; every fiber of my being was on fire and my whole body was racked with pain.

I croaked out a few words. "It's a mistake, she wouldn't have done that. She has Ziggy with her, and she would not have done that with him there. It's someone else."

"There was a little dog in the apartment, and he was taken in by a neighbor who said she was a friend of your daughter's. Apparently, she told the Edmonton police that she would keep him until she heard from you. The detective in charge of your daughter's case will definitely be calling you first thing in the morning. In the meantime, is there anyone we can call for you?" he asked.

"Our son, Ryan, and his wife. Her brother. No, we'll call him. I have to call him. I have to call someone." I wasn't making sense, I knew that, but the buzzing in my ears was getting louder and suddenly I just needed them to leave. Al was thanking them and I never looked up, even after they expressed their condolences and left.

Al sat beside me on the couch; his hands were shaking and as I looked up I saw the abject pain in his eyes and the paleness of his face. He put his arm around me and I leaned over onto his lap, my hands still gripping my head. It felt like everything was pouring out of me onto the floor and soon I would be nothing. I heard a terrible sound. It was coming from me as I began to howl uncontrollably into his lap. He cried as I howled and life did a switchback turn; nothing would ever look familiar or bright again. Erin had asked me what I was so afraid of and it was here. My worst fear. Losing her.

CHAPTER FIFTY-EIGHT:
MOM

RENDERING (SEPTEMBER 25, 2018)

There is a physical rendering that happens when a mother loses her child. Every minute of every day in the ones that followed that terrible night, resulted in a slow shattering of the parts of me that were the parts of my daughter. We shared cells when I carried her in pregnancy and gave birth to her, and we were forever intermingled. Now she was gone, and our shared cells were adrift in a cloud of loss, pain, tears, denial, anger, and the deepest grief known to humankind. I physically felt from the moment I heard the words "your daughter was found deceased," that those integrated parts of what made her and me died with her. It's not only mentally and emotionally devastating, but the physical pain is also real. The healing would be a long time coming, if ever.

Once my screaming finally stopped that night, the tears flowed continuously, and I found myself mumbling incoherently. I had so many questions and I was sure in my mind that this was all a mistake. There was no chance of sleep. Even though it was the middle of the night, I believed we needed to call Ken, Erin's dad. He needed to be the first to know although I was concerned about telling him because we knew he was by himself, temporarily separated from his wife. But it was so hard to see past my own pain. I was on autopilot.

I could barely croak out the words. "Erin's gone, Ken. The police were just here and said she was found deceased in her apartment." Silence. Then I heard his voice, his own howl of "No!" into the phone. His shock and his grief were palpable and added to the pain I was in. No parent should ever have to hear they would be outliving their child.

I muttered into the phone. "There's a detective who will be calling in a few hours because they are investigating her death. Someone else may have been in her apartment. Ziggy is with a neighbor there at the apartment. We need to talk tomorrow about what to do." And then he was gone, having hung up to suffer in his own anguish.

I needed to be alone. I convinced Al to go back to bed for a while as I stayed on the couch, pillow clutched to my middle, staring out at the night sky. Praying, begging, offering everything I had left to make this night all go away. I'd wake up in the morning, Erin would be sitting outside on the patio with a coffee, and I'd tell her about my horrible nightmare. I'd go over and wrap my arms around her and tell her how much I love her.

I must have dozed briefly or maybe my mind just couldn't take anymore and it shut down. When I opened my eyes, I felt that comforting vision of her in my arms begin to float away. My arms were empty, limp, and useless. She would never be in them again. Fresh pain flooded in, encasing my mind and my body as the sun began to come up over the horizon. My first day without her. The one before had held hope and today all the hope was gone and the rendering was done.

CHAPTER FIFTY-NINE: MOM

THE DAYS AFTER (SEPTEMBER 26, 2018)

All my emotions were laid out on the table. We were making phone calls to family and closest friends. Ryan and his wife Britney had arrived at first light. There were no words. Only hugs and barely concealed sobs. My sisters, brother, and cousins listened in stunned silence on the phone while I uttered those terrible words, altering our existence: Erin is dead.

My cousin was the first to arrive. Having lost a child himself to crib death, he was the closest to understanding just how much and how fast I was disintegrating into the deepest grief known to humans. A friend showed up at the door to be sent away gently—it's too soon. "She's not coping." Muffled conversations, the sun too bright, I closed my eyes and vowed never to open them again. There was too much color in the world and it didn't feel right because the one person who was the brightest, most colorful, and most loved was no longer on this earth. Didn't the color drain with her?

No food, no coffee, no tea. Please stop asking. It hurt to answer. Too many people to call, too many questions, too many heartfelt but unhelpful condolences. I just wanted to be alone. In the shower, my crying equaled the amount of water pouring down over my head. My skin was raw, felt like it was inside out, and every inch of me hurt. There was a heaviness in my bones that was foreign to me; I was being dragged down and could hardly put one foot in front of the other.

I sat at the makeup table and stared at the stranger in the mirror. Who was this pale, sad person with eyes too big for her face, her lower eyelids red and leaking? The blotched face, red nose, down-turned mouth made little mewling sounds. I would have to get acquainted with this stranger. This was my new identity—the mother of a dead child. I would never be who I was before those words were delivered and maybe, deep down, I had been mentally preparing myself for this. I never expected it to be such a horrific train wreck but then, it's impossible to imagine how it would be. Who would ever want to put themselves into that imaginary place? There was a deep sense of knowing that the rest of my life would be so different than what I imagined.

I pressed a tissue against my eyes, trying to dry the tears. Lifted a mascara wand to my eyelashes, thinking maybe a little color would inspire me to breathe fully again, stand up, and begin to make plans of what to do next. But the crying just wouldn't stop. The mascara ran down my cheeks and I gave up, putting my head down on my arms and howling once more into the top of the makeup table.

I managed to get dressed, dry my hair, and drag a brush through it. The parade of people had slowed and it was just us now, the quiet whispers welcome after the first onslaught of the ringing doorbell and phones. My life-long best friend Susan was going to be coming soon, bringing comfort, food, and help in terms of next steps. She had gone through this process after losing her husband suddenly and I felt some relief that someone would tell me what I needed to do. It would be complicated with us here in Victoria and Erin's belongings and apartment in Edmonton. And her remains. That thought brought on a fresh lot of helpless crying and tears. Your child should never have to become "remains."

Feeling adrift and aimless, I decided to go through text and Facebook messages, wondering if I'd hear from anyone in Edmonton who had seen her in the last couple of weeks. I came across one message that brought about my first sense of anger. A well-meaning person who probably thought I would find solace in her telling me that she understood what I was going through because she had lost her husband several years prior. I heard my own angry voice saying out loud, "You don't have a fucking clue how I feel! How dare you compare losing the husband you had for decades to me losing my daughter!"

I felt Al's arms around me as I raged into his shoulder. "You can get another husband, but you *cannot* get another daughter you gave birth to! How could she even say that!" Even in my rage and pain, I knew I wasn't being fair because everyone grieves in their own way, and I had no right to expect them to understand the uniqueness of a mother's deepest sense of loss. Only another mother would truly get the horror of it.

Susan had arrived and after we embraced and cried together, we decided the next best step would be some planning. She was efficient and knew exactly what calls we needed to make. Finding a funeral director and calling the coroner's office would need to be first. As we ran down the list of to-do's, I felt a strong sense of detachment coming over me. How could I be sitting here, planning what to do with my daughter's body when I wasn't even sure she was really dead? What if there was a mistake? Is it possible she was off partying somewhere and the young woman in her apartment wasn't even her? She was always offering a bed or couch to someone who needed a place to stay for the night. I needed to know for sure.

It was when I was starting to question the reality of whether Erin was truly gone that I got the call from the Edmonton police detective in charge of her case. He introduced himself as Detective Edson and expressed his condolences.

"How do we know it was Erin?" I asked him. "I understand there may have been someone else in her apartment so maybe the body you found isn't even her?"

"We are sure we have a positive ID but the coroner will confirm that with you. I have to ask you to call their office as soon as we are done talking. I'm sorry, this is a terrible time but there are a few things that need to be looked after as soon as possible."

I had a million questions and peppered him with them. His patient voice answered each one to the best of his ability. There were answers I didn't want to hear like, yes, it is definitely looking like a drug overdose. And the heartbreak of hearing she had likely been deceased for at least two days when she had been found. They would be looking into her phone and laptop to see if they could trace her last steps and locate anyone she might have been in touch with. The hope was to find the person or persons who had been in her apartment, likely around the time she had died.

"Did she suffer?" I heard myself asking the detective.

"No, we don't believe she did," he answered. "Again, the coroner will confirm but we believe she likely just stopped breathing on her own and passed away peacefully. There were no signs of a struggle."

"What about Ziggy? Is he okay?" I had momentarily forgotten about him but after hearing that Erin had died at least two days before being found, I wondered how he had survived. I vaguely remembered what the police officers who had come to the door had said about him being taken in by her neighbor.

"He was thirsty and very happy to see the police officers when they arrived," he said. "We didn't have to take him to the pound, which is usually what happens in these cases. Your daughter's neighbor across the hall offered to keep him until you can come and get him. He was playing with her dog and having a good lunch when we left Erin's apartment."

"Right. I remember now. I'm glad he's okay, thank you for checking on him and letting me know he's okay."

"You'll have to get in touch with Erin's landlord to access her apartment. I'll text you her phone number. Do you know what your plans are yet?" he asked.

I was on speaker phone and as I looked up at the faces around me—Al, Ryan, Britney, Susan all had their eyes on me—I suddenly realized this was really happening. I was making plans to bring Erin home and not in the way I had always imagined it to be. I felt my entire being collapse in on itself as I ended the call with the detective without a clue about what I was going to do next. Landlord, detective, coroner, funeral home, airplane tickets, car rental, Ziggy—how would I get him home? *Same way Erin took him to Edmonton,* I thought. But it was all too overwhelming. If there was a deep hole I could crawl my black, empty carcass of a soul into, I'd be there. Forever. And never come out to never have to deal with all this.

It had been almost forty-eight hours without sleep by this time and the shock and exhaustion were making me useless. All I knew at that moment was that Erin's family of origin—her dad, me, and Ryan—would be the ones going to Edmonton to pack up her apartment and bring my girl and her dog home. I don't know where that powerful assurance came from but there was not a doubt in my mind that this was the way it was going to have to be. Whatever or whoever was telling me this was now in charge until I could sleep, gather my broken self together the best I could, and put things in motion.

CHAPTER SIXTY: MOM

A TERRIBLE TASK (SEPTEMBER 27 – 30, 2018)

Last Thursday I had my unknowingly final conversation with Erin while she was having serious episodes of paranoia and incoherence. By Saturday I had begun to fear the worst. And by Tuesday, the worst had been delivered. Now it was Thursday again. How did a whole week go by, and an entire lifetime collapse in on itself? Ryan and I were flying out early the next morning. Ken was meeting us at the airport so we would have time to meet with the funeral home and then go to Erin's apartment to meet her landlord. Everything seemed to be happening quickly, and I clung to the busyness of it to stop the constant desire to scream again and make myself disappear. Thoughts of Ziggy waiting and wondering where his beloved mistress had gone kept me putting one foot in front of the other. He was the last little soul to have seen her and I longed for that bond, that connection, and I wished on every star in the sky that he could talk and tell us what happened.

As our plane landed in Edmonton, I looked out over the city and blamed it for her death. In my irrational mind, I truly believed that if she had stayed home in Victoria this would never have happened. I saw this as a brief trip to hell to bring my girl home. This godforsaken city would not be allowed to keep what was left of her—ashes in a temporary box designed for air transport.

We had decided to have her cremated. Every moment, every decision, was based only on doubtful intuition and desperation to do the right thing. Everything had become "what Erin would have wanted."

After checking into our hotel, Ryan and Ken sharing a room next to mine, I wondered if this might have been the same room Erin had stayed in while she waited for access to her apartment. I don't know why I decided on the same hotel she had stayed in, perhaps a bleak desire to retrace her steps? The confines of the hotel-room walls were closing in and the well of uncontrollable grief pushed against the barrier I had placed around myself. I needed to keep moving. After a quick call to the funeral director to confirm we were meeting with him later that afternoon, we were soon using GPS to find Erin's apartment where her landlord would be waiting for us.

The decrepit condition of the area we were driving into further deepened my resolve to do what we needed and get home again. A woman pulled into the parking lot behind the apartment building we had just arrived at. I looked up at the gray façade. I knew Erin's apartment was on the second floor and I tried to imagine her gazing out the window at the garbage cans lined up alongside the wall by the parking area. Seeing dead bodies dumped into them. She must have been terrified, and I could not imagine how far her mental health must have deteriorated in such a short time to actually see terrible things that weren't there. I should have been there to lead her away from all this.

The landlady was very sweet and obviously completely devastated. She told us how much she had instantly liked Erin and how shocked she was that this happened. As we climbed the stairs to the second floor, I kept imagining the key going into the lock and Erin popping her ahead around the corner, surprise written all over her face. "What are you guys doing here?" she would say. Laughing and delighted to see us.

But the door opened into silence. As we slowly walked into the apartment, I was overcome again with that gut-wrenching sense of loss. Everything changed. Gone. Forever. Her things were everywhere but she was nowhere. Her couch, TV, paintings, dishes, ornaments—all staring back at me accusingly. Why weren't you here to stop this? I imagined their inanimate, angry thoughts coming at me from all directions.

I stood in the doorway to her bedroom while Ryan and Ken walked through the rest of the apartment. I saw where she had died at the end of her bed, lying there with Ziggy in her arms, crying, coming to terms with her loneliness, her trauma, her unending sense of hopelessness. And her final breath, of which she wasn't even aware. Her mind shutting down, the fear abating. Maybe there was a quiet peacefulness for her in those last few moments. Were her last thoughts of Ziggy? She'd be terrified for him, but she had also embraced a closeness with her higher power, with God, and she would have trusted that He would look after her beloved pet.

I wondered if she thought of me in those last few minutes too. And I wondered if she knew how much I was crumbling and descending into a place of devastation that felt it had no place for me to ever climb out of again. And what was left of my shattered heart gave way to yet another agonizing thought of her aloneness at the end. I learned later in my grief recovery that the majority of drug-overdose victims die alone. That is the most incredibly sad and wrong thing to exist in this harsh, unforgiving world.

I felt a stickiness on the floor beneath my shoes and realized it was likely dog pee. Poor Ziggy had likely felt terrible about peeing on the floor, but he wouldn't have had a choice after a few hours. It reminded me that I needed to see him sooner than later, so I left Erin's apartment, walked across the hall, and knocked on the neighbor's door. Immediate yapping that I recognized as Pomeranian Ziggy's high-pitched excitement continued as the door was slowly opened. A young woman about Erin's age stood there warily but as soon as I made eye contact with her, she exclaimed, "You are obviously Erin's mom—she looks just like you! I mean … looked just like you. I'm so sorry." Ziggy wiggled past her and jumped his two little front paws as high as he could reach on my legs. I picked him up and held him, smelling his sweet fur and wetting his coat with fresh tears.

"Thank you for looking after him," I said gratefully. "I'll take him back to the hotel with me this evening, but can I ask that you keep him just a little while longer tomorrow while we go through Erin's apartment? We have to pack up things to send home and I think he'll be stressed wondering where she is."

"Absolutely, but I think he probably knows she has left us," she said. "Dogs are smart that way and they get on with things." After gathering up Ziggy's leash and handing it to me with a bit of food to tide him over, she gave him a goodbye pet and said, "I'll see you tomorrow, I'm home all day."

We spent a couple of hours looking for Erin's apartment keys but they were nowhere to be found. I was even more convinced that someone had been there with her when she was overdosing and the coward fled, taking her keys and locking the door when he left. Leaving her to die alone. I was sickened by the thought.

The landlady had left us a spare key and as we closed and locked the door for the night, I dreaded the thought of coming back in the morning to what would be a fresh hell of heartbreak. But we still had things to take care of. It was Friday by then and we had to meet with the funeral director before the weekend and make arrangements to pick up her ashes, along with the multitude of other tasks that come with dealing with the loss of someone you love.

The funeral director was stereotypical in his kindness and compassion, and I was grateful he allowed us to keep Ziggy with us while we went over the details. Erin had not yet been cremated as they were waiting for final documentation from the coroner, and they always ask the bereaved family members if they would like to see their loved one. At first, my thought had been an adamant yes, but it was gently suggested that I may not want to as a drug overdose can have an alarming effect on the deceased. I didn't know if my fragile mental health could withstand seeing her like that. We reluctantly declined the viewing and there are many times to this day that I wonder if I should have seen Erin. But in those moments, only days after her death, I wanted to remember Erin the way I had last seen her at the airport. Head held high, optimism written all over her beautiful face, beaming with that big smile. Seeing her after death may have taken away that ethereal image I had of her.

After a sleepless night with Ziggy tucked in bed beside me, softly snoring, we awoke to a sunny day in Edmonton. But the sun didn't chase away the dark clouds around us as we made our way back into Erin's apartment to begin the terrible task of packing up her life. Depositing Ziggy back with Erin's friend Trudy across the hall, I was relieved to see him happily run to play with her dog. He seemed none the worse for wear, despite his ordeal. We unlocked Erin's door and walked in again, only pausing briefly before we began sorting out the rooms.

Erin had never really finished unpacking as she had only been in Edmonton six weeks, so all of her boxes were still stacked in the spare bedroom. We had made arrangements with a local charity to pick up all the things we knew we couldn't bring back with us. Again, it was a case of "what Erin would have wanted" as she had spent her whole life giving to others. She would have been happy knowing her furniture, dishes, clothes, and personal effects we weren't able to keep would go to someone who needed them. But it was still hard and I was reluctant. There were so many things we couldn't pack up to have sent back to Victoria for me or Regina for Ken that we had to be brutal with our decisions of what stayed and went.

I looked after the bedroom first, packing up Erin's clothes and asking Trudy next door if she would like to go through them as they appeared to be similar in size. She was thrilled to have them and what she didn't or couldn't take went into boxes for the charity truck. Opened food, broken items, and things we knew the charity wouldn't take went into a large bin on the other side of the street behind the apartment. Every last little thing that went in there made me feel terrible for throwing it out.

A couple of hours after we took it all to the bin, a shocking sight rocked us to the core. The container was crawling with desperate people. *Scavengers*, I thought, and I wanted to run out and chase them off. *You can't be fighting over my daughter's stuff like that!* Ken made me see reason, citing that Erin would be okay with homeless people taking her things like that. I guess that was "what Erin would have wanted," but it was just more proof of the state of the world, seeing that kind of poverty, desperation, and greed.

I was on my knees in the living room, going through a box of photos and paperwork. Ryan and Ken were sorting through books on the TV stand and the couch. There was paper everywhere, notes, poems, reminders of appointments long past… organized chaos. I reached into the box I was going through to bring up another handful when the world collapsed on me.

"I can't. I can't do this. She's gone. It's impossible, she *can't* be gone. I can't do this. I can't do this. I can't do this." I was shaking uncontrollably, repeating the words over and over. I felt Ken and Ryan's arms around me, and we all cried together. This was all that was left of our daughter and Ryan's sister. I never felt so empty, so bereft, so lost and confused. What was the point?

Empty of tears once again, even if only temporarily, I gathered myself and took some deep breaths to get myself under control. My entire body was shaking, but I resolved to carry on. After all, what were the other options? None. It had to be done, and we had to do it. There was no one else I would trust her things with.

CHAPTER SIXTY-ONE: MOM

THE LAST WORDS—A MESSAGE (SEPTEMBER 29, 2018)

The rest of that first day felt more like I was a witness to a stranger, hired to clean out the apartment of someone I didn't know. Disassociation. A way to distance oneself from what is happening. Autopilot had kicked in for me as the only way I could get through that terrible task and come out the other end with a sane thought. As we were boxing the remaining things, Ken found a notebook lying partly tucked into the back of the couch, hidden under a pile of blankets that had already been folded to be taken to the charity truck.

As Ken handed it to me and I opened it to the first page, I saw a strange, bewildered look on his face that overshadowed the mask of grief we were each wearing. I read the words in the four short lines:

I remember the sand on the beach in Saskatchewan where I last saw my cousin Gary.

I remember the nights in our haunted theater where I'd wake up to the sound of a hundred people at a dinner party.

I remember visiting Chad's grave in the middle of a field in the middle of nowhere and promising I'd be buried beside him.

I remember the smell of the storms in Edmonton where I would sit and watch and kill to smell that forever.

In stunned silence, I sat back on my heels and reread her notes, her last written words. The third line of her writing where she made a promise to Chad settled on me like a stone. Did she know she was dying? The suspected cause of death was accidental overdose but perhaps she had some inner knowledge that she was on a path from which there would be no way back. And no way out. My poor girl. Alone. A last message for us. A last hug for Ziggy as she took her final breath. The agonizing pain was so physical that I couldn't take a breath.

I looked at Ken and said, "I was wondering what to do with Erin's ashes. I thought we should keep them, but I didn't know if that is what she would have wanted. It's not like we ever had a discussion about what to do with our child's remains. It's too surreal and something we never would have even thought about—us burying one of our children."

Ken was shaking his head, his gaze on the floor as he tried to process what her words meant. His own words were lost in his tortured thoughts.

"It's not right," I cried out loud. "It's out of the order of life, this terrible thing we have to do. We should have gone first. You know, you kind of expect your parents to die and maybe even a spouse. That's normal. But never a child. I can't grasp how very wrong this all is."

"I know," he said quietly. "I was wondering the same thing about her ashes. I guess she has told us where she wants to be laid to rest. But I agree, we've both lost parents and grandparents and we know friends who have lost a spouse but this … this is unbearable."

Ken was never a man of many words, and I was surprised at this. It showed the level of his suffering. There was no way to make any sense of this and no way that we could understand and absorb the depth of pain and wrongness. Never should we have lost our daughter and been left to suffer like this. At that moment, I didn't believe that time would help. We were too broken, too raw, and too eternally wounded.

The roles were reversed. I felt like a child, and I longed for my daughter to console me in my grief. It didn't matter how many loving people surrounded and supported me, there was a deep sense of utter loneliness. A sense of something so terribly missing, so lost, that I didn't know if it'd ever be found. I wondered then, where the lost things go.

Sitting there on Erin's apartment's floor, surrounded by what was left of her, I prayed for something—anything—that would ease this pain. And I experienced a moment of thankfulness to Erin. For letting us know with her final written words in the notebook where she wanted to be. Laid to rest beside her cousin Chad whom she had adored so much. And at the foot of her grandparents, my mom and dad. Her beloved grandpa. She had always been extra close to him but among the eleven grandchildren that he and her grandma loved equally, he had a special place in his heart for Erin. And she had that special place in her heart for him. Later on, I would learn that he was waiting for her. He'd had an inner knowledge that she was not long for this world.

Of course, it made sense that she went home to her roots. Where everything had been so innocent at the very start of her farm-girl life. Maybe that was when she had been the happiest, and don't we all want to go home in the end?

As the day drew to a close and we carefully combed Erin's apartment again for anything we may have missed, a knock sounded on the door we had left ajar. A man in faded jeans and a brown sweater over a dress shirt stood in the entrance.

"Hello, Mrs. Gray?" He was middle-aged with a slightly receding hairline and eyebrows that seemed permanently in a perplexed shape. He looked as tired as I felt. I recognized his voice.

"You must be Detective Edson. Yes, I'm Wanda. Please come in." I introduced him to Ken and Ryan then asked him if he'd found who was in the apartment at the time of Erin's death.

"I'm afraid not," he replied. "It's like looking for a needle in a haystack but we are looking into her laptop and phone, hoping to get a clue as to where she had been and who she had been communicating with. And please call me Dan."

"Thank you, Dan. We want to know who would leave her like that, take her keys and lock the door behind them. They could have called an ambulance and saved her life." I was desperate to get across to him how important it was to find out who I could put the blame onto for where we were right now.

"I'd like to ask you some questions and I'm wondering if we can go somewhere quiet for the interview?" he asked, looking around at the chaos of stacked boxes and furniture awaiting pick-up the next day. "We can sit in my car, if you don't mind," he said. "This neighborhood isn't all that conducive to having a discussion outside. And just you, for now. As you were likely the last family member she had been in touch with."

I looked at Ken and Ryan, reluctant to leave our little unit of bonded grief, but they both nodded and said they would keep sorting and packing what little was left by this time.

Sitting in the passenger seat of the detective's car, I was again in a surreal moment, wondering how I got here. The car smelled of old coffee and if there had been an essence to it, it was a hint of hopelessness. I wondered how he could do this job every day.

"Can you please tell me about your last conversation with Erin, when it was, and when you started to suspect something was wrong?" he asked. His voice was compassionate, but his eyes were distant. A practiced way of dealing with grieving parents, I supposed.

As I detailed the last conversations I'd had with Erin, he took notes the old-fashioned way in a small notebook, and I was reminded of the book we had just discovered with our daughter's wishes for her burial. I told him about it and he nodded, perhaps just a little more interest showing in his eyes now.

"Can you also please describe, to the best of your knowledge, what Erin's lifestyle was the last few months and if you know whom she might have been friends with here in Edmonton?" he asked.

"I can give you the names and phone numbers of the two guys she had been hanging out with. They had been in rehab together on the island. I'm going to call them both myself once I'm home again. I don't think I want to see them here." I was really struggling now, trying not to cry my way through the interview.

As I began to talk to him about Erin, I found myself going all the way back to her childhood. Her love of animals and farm life. And her desire to make the world a better place for everyone she met. I described her experience as a Miss Teen beauty-pageant contestant and her legacy of being a peer counselor in almost every treatment center. And then

I told him about D.H. and what he had done to her as well as the other victims.

A seasoned detective can typically be stone-faced, hardened to the daily onslaught of horrible things that human beings can do to each other. But when I told him how Erin was lured, physically and mentally abused, sex and drug trafficked, and held hostage through the whole ordeal, I saw a change in his demeanor. I was taken aback by the tears in his eyes. It broke my resolve and I, too, dissolved into fresh tears.

"I had no idea," he said quietly. "This is far more complex and Erin was not, what I don't like to say, 'your typical drug overdose victim.' I'm so very sorry for everything you've gone through, sorry for the loss of a life that could have been so much. Rest assured I will be working hard on this, to get you some much-needed answers."

With that, he ended the interview. I climbed out of the car, feeling like I had someone in my corner. To Detective Dan Edson, and hopefully to others, Erin would not disappear in memory as just another lost drug addict. Every single person who has lost their life to drugs deserves respect, compassion, and a deeper understanding of what got them to that point. But Erin was special and I finally felt it wasn't just because I was her mother. It was important that others know her story, what an impact she had on people in her life, and how devastating her loss was. I watched him drive away and then slowly walked back into the building where Ken and Ryan were sealing the last of the boxes.

CHAPTER SIXTY-TWO:
MOM

LIFE ON HOLD (SEPTEMBER 30, 2018)

On the last day of cleaning out Erin's apartment and carefully packaging her paintings to be shipped home, I took one last look around and thought to myself again, *What a terrible place to die, my poor sweet girl. I'm so sorry. I will never fully understand what brought you here and I will always regret not coming back sooner and bringing you home.* This was just the beginning of the shoulda, woulda, couldas. I had a long road ahead of me and everything I thought the future was would now be on hold. Waiting for the healing.

On our last day at Erin's apartment, the charity truck we had requested to come for the donations was soon loaded and gone again, her belongings gratefully received. The drivers were kind, respectful, and so gracious. Erin had good taste and she had some nice things. It hurt my heart to give some of them up but logistically we couldn't possibly send everything back to the island. It gave me some comfort knowing Erin would have easily given everything she had to charity. That was just who she was and it made it doubly hard to understand how something so awful could happen to someone so beautiful, inside and out.

After doing a final walk-through with the landlady and giving her the keys, I headed across the hallway to talk to Trudy, who had been so kind to care for Ziggy.

"I need to ask you something. The police and coroner think Erin died about two days before she was found," I said. "Did you see her on that weekend? Or see or hear anyone else in her apartment?"

"She died on the weekend?" she said, her eyes wide with shock. "Oh my God, I feel awful. On Saturday, I had just got home, and she knocked on my door. I'd had a terrible day and didn't want to talk to anyone. I looked through the peephole and she was standing there, looking all strung out, and I pretended I wasn't home. The two guys who live down the hall told me she had been knocking on their door too, but they didn't want her to come in."

"She obviously needed someone," I said. "She was reaching out for help!" I was devastated and struggled not to reach out and shake Trudy.

"Oh my God, I'm so sorry! I had no idea." She was crying now and instead of shaking her, I reached out to give her a hug.

"You didn't know. Thank you for being a friend to her when she first moved in. She told me how grateful she was that you were so welcoming. And thank you for looking after Ziggy." I was reassuring her because maybe I understood in some way. I had withdrawn at times when I didn't know what to do to help Erin.

Ken and Ryan were waiting outside and the three of us climbed into our rental car and drove away from the building. I turned in the seat and looked back. I knew I'd never forget the place where my daughter had left this earth.

The remainder of the day was spent checking out of the hotel and, finally, going to the funeral home to pick up Erin's ashes. I learned so much about bringing a loved one home. When cremated, ashes are placed in a special carrying case, approved for airline transport. I had imagined picking out a beautiful urn and holding her on my lap as we lifted off, away from Edmonton. But due to airline security, everything is done so specifically with strict regulations when it comes to transporting remains. Erin's ashes were in a black box and sealed with a letter of authorization attached. It seemed cold to me. I couldn't wait to get home.

Erin was not the only one in a specialized carrying case. Ziggy would also be in his airline-approved pet carrier, small enough to fit under the seat so he could stay with us as we flew back to Victoria. For now, he was on a leash in the airport, making friends with everyone and being the star of the show with all who stopped to give him some attention. During the flight, he enjoyed a restful snooze from the mild sedative we got from Erin's Edmonton vet. Being Pomeranian, he was naturally highly active and could be anxious. I had often wondered at how amazingly capable he had been at keeping Erin calm when she was having panic attacks.

A few days after we had first learned about Erin's death, one of the people in her life that I called was Bruce. That phone call broke him. He had rescued her from D.H. and they had remained close. At one point, when Erin was at her lowest, she had said to me, "Mom, if anything ever happens to me, please promise me that you'll let Bruce have Ziggy. He lives alone and loves him. I've already dumped all my cats on you." I remember both of us laughing about the cats but, at the time, I had dismissed her wishes and said nothing was going to happen to her. We wouldn't need to give Ziggy to Bruce because he would be with her until he was a very old dog. And she would be a very old lady. Anything different was something I could not and would not imagine.

As we all hugged goodbye at the airport, Ken gave Ziggy another little ruffle of his fur and we parted ways. I watched him walk away and was reminded how thankful I was that we had an easy-going relationship. Some couples, after divorce, never speak again or do so through arguing about unresolved issues. Somehow, we had remained respectful of each other, always in dialogue about our two kids, and we had grown sadly closer over the trauma of the last two years with Erin. I wondered if he would be okay once he got back to his home. I doubted that any of us would ever be okay again.

As Ryan and I settled in our seats on the airplane, I realized that I actually had both of my adult children with me, traveling back home together. Ryan beside me, sitting so silently. And Erin in the transport case at my feet, now silent forever. My memory drifted back to when the three of us came back after our trip to Hawaii so many years ago. Things were so different then. We had a joy-filled vacation together, building memories, showing off our tans, and looking forward to every day that followed. How did life take such an ugly turn?

We had made arrangements for Bruce to meet us at the airport in Victoria. He was thrilled to have Ziggy, but I was struggling with the agreement. I wanted to fulfill Erin's wishes, and I knew Bruce would take good care of him, but that little dog was a part of my daughter and it was going to be very hard for me to let him go. But a promise was a promise, and I had no fight left in me anyway. It is what it is, my dad would always say.

Al was waiting at the airport for us, Bruce was outside for the handover of Ziggy, and after many hugs and tears, we all went on our way home. I had no idea what the next steps would be. Everything I knew had been taken away from me. The death of a child. The loss of a future.

PART FOUR:
EVERYTHING AFTER

CHAPTER SIXTY-THREE: MOM

A DIFFERENT ME

There was no normal anymore. I was never coming back; there would have to be a new me assembled out of the old me but with parts missing. I had been dismembered; too much trauma had happened over the past few years. Physical loss and emotional loss had ripped the fabric of our lives. A horrible rendering through death. I felt the pain of our cells dividing and believed it to be forever, leaving an empty carcass and hollow soul. Reaching those depths of despair reveals "indicators": thoughts of self-harm, suicide, depression. A mother's job is to look after her child, whether that child is six months or sixty years. The child will always be the child. The first thoughts when a child dies are that you, as a mother, must follow her. Because that is your job—to be with and protect your child. Even if you know her soul is safe and perhaps, just perhaps, finally at peace and happy. It takes a very long time for that feeling of "I must follow" to begin to fade.

I had no idea what to do next and the days began to bleed into each other, quiet murmurs around me, friends hovering, and a heaviness to the very air I was struggling to breathe. The burden of accepting Erin's death weighed on me like a heavy cloak—soon I would collapse into a pile of uselessness underneath it. I felt my face grow longer, my grief-worn features deepen, and the black lump I saw in the mirror instead of me took a deep bite and expanded. It fed on my sadness and it grew, taking up space. Yet oddly, I felt emptier. How could that be?

Melancholy by Albert Gyorgy

For the past nine years, I had been fully occupied with Erin's disappearance, rescue, trauma, and addiction. What I had was battle fatigue. This was what combat trauma looked like except it wasn't one enemy but multiple. The enemy of killer drugs and addiction plus the hidden enemy of unresolved mental trauma. There were no tanks or guns but triggers of a different kind: hunger, loneliness, isolation, shame. And there was the ever-present horror movie that Erin had playing in her head when she was still alive. Sometimes the house lights would come on unexpectedly and the visions would become real again. I had a better understanding now of those times. Of how reliving the nightmare over and over was her constant companion and she was unable to put those images and the pain away forever.

In the weeks following her death, I would find myself going through notes, witness statements, victim-impact statements, trying to piece together random parts of this nightmare and make sense of it. Even after I had put all the documents away in a tote, sealed forever, the horrific experience of what I read would suddenly appear in my mind, uninvited and at the most random times. Then I would feel and understand those moments of torture for her. I could be fully focused on something else and suddenly the horror, the pain, and the reliving was playing across my mind. Everything else would disappear and I saw it all happening. Her written words were the pages of the script to a true-crime film, and I would suddenly find myself in her body, seeing through her eyes the atrocities done to her. And then I would replay the night she overdosed at home where I was in my own body, desperately trying to bring her back to life. Why would our graphic, Technicolor memories not leave us alone?

I recalled times, after her rescue while she was working on her recovery, when she and I would be talking about something totally unrelated to the trial or her addiction work and suddenly she'd stop and become still and so quiet. I'd see a shattered look in her eyes, like she was breaking inside. She was being transported back into that nightmare world. Now I understood how life-altering and intrusive that psychological trauma could be. It was consuming and debilitating. So what could I do about my own recovery from trauma and child-loss grief? I was becoming very aware of the state of my own mental health and how it had come to be. I was terrified of the deep hole I had fallen into. I could no longer see any light at the top.

From 2010 to 2018, I had spent my time trying to "fix" everything that had gone wrong and I developed my own case of PTSD. But I was still experiencing the trauma in trying to come to terms with my daughter not surviving the disease of addiction. So, I didn't feel "post traumatic," I felt "present traumatic." And I believe now that in the unrelenting, raw grip of early grief, I had decided that I would not survive this pain.

There are three realms: physical, spiritual, and what I believed was hell on earth—I was living in the hell realm. I had two choices: let it consume me, pray for a terminal disease or a horrific accident, or I could begin to try to understand how to recover. Countless others before me had somehow survived similar losses and, sadly, there would be many more. How could I make myself useful and help other mothers struggling under the dead weight of a grief too heavy to bear?

I began to read everything I could get my hands on about trauma and addiction, including first-person accounts from survivors of sex trafficking. Sex crimes are the worst for a victim to recover from and horrific for the parent to know what their child had gone through. I learned that loss of self is the very essence of trauma, and I began to understand how Erin had become so lost, unable to find herself again after being held hostage, drugged, and forcibly stripped of her self-esteem and control. Physically, during her captive months, she had become addicted to the drugs she was fed. Mentally, she had collapsed inward and lived a life of pain, even after regaining her freedom. The traumatic memories were the always-open gateway to her active addiction and I began to slowly realize that, as many times as I had grown frustrated with her relapses, she had been coping the best she could. The scars were so deeply ingrained that the "light touch" of counseling she had received while in addictions treatment centers had barely scratched the surface.

At the start of this descent into such a fragile state of mental health for her was an adverse childhood experience (ACE). I had been devouring everything written by Dr. Gabor Mate to try and fully understand how Erin could have been so vulnerable to the attentions of a serial predator. My strong, beautiful daughter had her outward appearance perfected as well-adjusted, determined, funny, driven, and in charge of herself. But internally, now that I was aware of how she'd been hurt as a child, I could see what a brave front she had put on. But I still asked myself why I hadn't seen through it. And how did D.H. recognize her vulnerability and chip away at that exterior, revealing the cracks in the foundation of her true self? Was I that distracted or in denial that something was terribly wrong? Was he that good at portraying himself as her saviour? In fact, he was her destroyer. Her childhood trauma that could have been helped, had we known, opened her up to someone who would damage her to the point of no return. Wrong person, wrong place, wrong time. And now there would be no more time for her.

I was determined to learn more and cursed every day I had lost while floundering in the chaos of trying to save my daughter from the effects of addiction. The addiction was the symptom of something much deeper, much more sinister, and much more difficult to treat. I truly felt that was the key that had been missing. I was conflicted, feeling that the thirty-day faith-and-abstinence program could not possibly have worked on its own. I now knew in my soul that the only help that might have made a difference was a complex system of mental health treatment and a carefully balanced and monitored prescription-drug regimen. And it all had to be available without long waiting lists and unaffordable costs.

People who were loved and supported were dying while on waiting lists or disappearing into the cracks because they did not have the deep pockets of Hollywood and professional-sports celebrities. I was beginning to get a clear and concise picture of the state of Erin's mental health that had not been addressed through any of the traditional methodologies like rehab. I could see how ass-backwards the whole mental health and addictions system was. We can send our loved ones to rehab, praying for each time to be the magic bullet that would "fix" the addiction. But where Erin *really* needed the help was in-depth, focused, and limitless mental health treatment for her years of trauma.

When I looked back at the last few years, I could see that, for Erin, detox and rehabilitation treatment centers were a Band-Aid. The wound under the bandage would continue to fester until someone peeled it back and applied the healing she so desperately needed. Only then could she face her addiction to opioids, after she had reconnected with herself, her body, and her emotions. Given the proper course of treatment, she could have been the full and amazing young woman that she deserved to be.

Being at this still-raw stage of grief, only a couple of months after her death, I was able to see the facts more clearly, but it did not make me feel any better. And I still did not like this new me. Slow, sluggish, mind always in a fog, aimless, hopeless, gripped so soundly in my grief that I was slowly becoming cocooned forever. It was time to reach out. To grasp at something to pull me out of the mire, take what I was learning about PTSD, childhood trauma, addiction, and loss and put it to use. Give myself a reason to live and a purpose again. Become a new me I could live with. I knew the grieving years ahead of me stretched out relentlessly long and I was paralyzed by the thought that I'd never see the end of this road where the pavement was always thick and black without any sunny days to lift the pall that hung over me. The help I needed to begin to extricate myself from this terrible journey came from unexpected sources and my first encounter with Erin's spirit.

CHAPTER SIXTY-FOUR: MOM

HEALING TOUCH

An incredibly caring and loving friend was determined to help as she watched me destructively collapse into myself. She offered to set up an appointment for me with her "aunty," who was a healing-touch practitioner and she explained what would take place. The practitioner would come to my home and administer a therapy that would hopefully help heal my body and mind through what is often called "the laying on of hands." But there is no actual contact with the body during the treatment; it's more of a hovering of hands in a healing manner, targeting my natural but stuck energy of grief. Healing-touch therapy is based on the theory that the body, mind, and emotions form a very complex and integrated field of energy. Aunty would be helping me balance or realign my disrupted and pain-filled energy field. I was more than ready for help.

As I settled onto my back atop the portable bed she brought with her, I tried to relax under her calm and peaceful demeanor. She was a lovely woman with a peaceful and loving energy. I was a little nervous, not knowing what to expect, but open to the experience and also doubtful that anything could chip away successfully at this wall of sadness I had in and around me. Aunty didn't speak much and gently murmured calm assurances that all would be well. I began to drift. I felt tears running slowly out of the corners of my eyes, down my temples to my ears, and onto the bed. Inside my head and body I could hear and feel little mewling sounds, like a lost kitten. Was that me? I had no idea what Aunty was doing but I sensed her warmth and began to let go and embrace what was happening, even if I didn't know what would come of this treatment.

I must have drifted to sleep. Or was I wide awake with my eyes closed tightly? I heard a voice.

"Mom? Mom? Are you there?" It was Erin's voice. I could hear a sliding sound like something brushing against an object. Suddenly, I was there. Standing in front of a never-ending, gray-colored wall, reaching upward forever with no windows, no light, no kind of opening at all. I pressed both of my hands tightly against the wall.

"Erin?" I cried loudly. "Are you there? Where are you?"

"Mom? Mom? Where am I?" her voice echoed from the other side. I could hear the sliding sounds again and somehow knew it was her hands against the other side of the wall, directly in front of where I stood. I pressed harder with my hands, running them back and forth.

"I'm here," I shouted. "Right in front of you. What is this wall? Can you get through somewhere?" I was in full panic mode. Erin was right here with me, and I couldn't see or reach her through that impenetrable wall of gray.

"What's happened?" Erin asked. "Why am I here, I can't see anything!"

I was crying, calling her name and repeatedly banging my hands against the wall. And then an incredible calm washed over me, my ragged breathing slowed, and I knew what I had to do. My daughter was terrified, and I needed to pull myself together to help her.

CHAPTER SIXTY-FIVE: ERIN AND MOM

TERRIFIED

ERIN

I didn't know where I was. There was no essence of time, and I felt so alone. The last thing I remembered was my friend Toby's birthday and we were partying. Did I fall asleep? Where was Ziggy? He had been nestled up against my stomach when I laid down on the bed. What was in that stuff Toby gave me? I felt like I'd been out for ages.

I was drifting and alternating between absolute wonder and absolute terror. Wherever I was, I had an inner sense that I would need time to adjust to my new surroundings. My new world. One minute I felt clear, loved, energized. And the next I was trying to turn around and go back the way I came, only to be overcome with terror. I was not ready to go forward yet. I had to go back to get Ziggy, say good-bye, and tell my mom I was so sorry. Tell my family how much I loved them.

That's when I felt her presence. Mom. So close but somehow not within reach. I stretched out my arms and felt a solidness beneath my hands. I thought I was standing in front of a wall, and it reached upwards and outwards with no end. And I became scared again.

"Mom?" I heard my own voice echoing in the void that surrounded me. "Mom? Are you there?"

"Erin?" *Yes, it's Mom's voice!* "I'm here, where are you?" I heard her shouting.

"I'm here, I'm so scared. I can't find the way out." I slid my hands along the wall and pounded frequently to see if I could locate where Mom was standing on the other side.

Suddenly I knew she was right there. She sounded as scared as I felt. We both leaned into the wall and it was almost as if I could hear her breathing and feel her safe warmth. I missed my mother so much. What happened to our time?

"Sweetheart." Mom's voice changed from scared to calm assurance. "You are going to be okay," she said. "I think this wall is the veil that separates us right now. I want to be with you, but you've moved on before me."

I leaned my forehead against the wall and felt her tears as if they were my own. We couldn't get through and she would have to let me go.

"Will I really be okay?" I asked her. "What happens now? I don't remember anything, and I don't know where to go. I love you, Mom."

"I love you too, sweetie," I heard her answer in a sad, calm voice. "You are definitely going to be okay. Just look forward, don't try to go back. It will be easier there than it was here for you. And I'll always, always be holding you in my heart."

And suddenly, I knew where I was and what had happened. I was transitioning and even though the wall stood resolute between us, we could reach through with our love at any time. I stepped back, turned, and began to drift again but with less fear, more acceptance, and more understanding. This was the most peaceful I had felt in years. Someone I loved was waiting for me and I was going to be with them soon.

MOM

It was quiet. Erin was gone and I no longer stood at the wall. As I slowly opened my eyes, I saw Aunty, my healing-touch angel, standing at the side of the bed and lovingly asking me how I felt. I didn't know if I was ready to share the moment I had with Erin's spirit and I just nodded my head, slowly sat up, and prepared to face the rest of my life.

CHAPTER SIXTY-SIX: MOM

A PLACE OF COMFORT AND THE ASHES OF LIFE

Even though I'd had that beautiful yet excruciating experience of being with Erin during my healing-touch session, I was still in the deepest throes of loss. I had now come to accept that she was truly gone and took comfort in knowing she would be okay. But would I be okay? The thing I needed to pull me out of this deep mire of grief came in the form of a public film screening that depicted addiction in a new way.

A friend had invited me to the local university to watch the film and the room was filled with people from many walks of life: grieving parents, industry leaders in addiction and homelessness, and facilitators of healing. I was introduced to one of the industry leaders who suggested I look into an organization called Moms Stop The Harm (MSTH). He believed they would be a good resource for me as they had an additional arm of service called Healing Hearts, a place to join other parents and family members who had lost a loved one to overdose. I had already looked into grief counseling at that point and talked to a couple of therapists, but there was something missing for me—a lack of true understanding, I thought. Grieving the loss of a child is a darkly unique and exhausting type of emotion, but even more so when it is under the stigma of death due to illegal and/or prescription drugs. It's like we have to come in apologetically in order to be accepted and cover up the fact that we lost our precious child to such an abhorred subject of misunderstanding and ignorance.

A week later, I entered my first Healing Hearts meeting with trepidation, not knowing what to expect and scared of becoming a mess in front of strangers. I wore my grief on the outside whereas others kept it in. What would it be like for me to enter the conversation as someone who had been skinned alive and then had their skin turned inside out and put back on? I was terrified about how I would be accepted in this raw state as a pulsating entity of hopelessness, bleeding, and loss.

An hour and a half later, I knew I had finally found my "home" for depositing some of my pain. But it wasn't a dumping ground where I was leaving my pain for others to deal with; it was a place of utter and complete comfort. I told Erin's story as I cried uncontrollably and there were no sideways glances or any fake utterances of condolences. These were my people, drawn together like no one should ever have to be, but united in true understanding of what empty, wrung-out shells we were. The stories leading up to our children's deaths were all similar but different at the same time—with one underlying commonality.

Our children had been subject to some kind of debilitating trauma in their lives and, in some cases, undiscovered trauma that became a mental health issue of no known origin. It was just there from birth. Regardless, we were all in the same horrible boat, traveling a raging sea of all the stages of grief. None of these stages were linear, and different emotions reared their ugly heads at the most inopportune times. While the rest of the world was moving on from our loved one's death, we were left on the shore of a deserted island with no rescue in sight.

But we had each other and with time, we would each find a reason for hope and a purpose to carry on. For us, there would be no "moving on" or "getting through." We would be learning to "live with" an eternal grief that would always be a part of us. But time would take that unbearable pain and mold it into something we could work with and make use of, even if it was just being there for somebody who needed a place to deposit their own heartache for a while.

I was even more grateful for the support of my Healing Hearts group when I had to face the task of what to do with Erin's ashes. Her wishes with her last written words in her journal had been to be buried beside her cousin Chad in our family plot at the tiny cemetery in Saskatchewan. I still had her ashes in the nondescript air-transport case we had brought back with us from Edmonton. I had been avoiding the painful job of putting her ashes into the urn we had bought for her. It was a beautiful blue container, imprinted with butterflies, her signature image that we saw in almost all her paintings and doodles in her journals. We had set a date for the memorial service in Saskatchewan for the following April, so I felt in no rush to switch her ashes from transport to permanent place in the urn. But every time I saw that black box, it took me back to the city of Edmonton, my feelings about that place and what it had taken from me. And it didn't suit my bright, beautiful Erin. She was light, sunshine, warmth, and love and she didn't deserve to be left in that black symbol of all that had gone wrong.

I picked a day when I knew no one would be around for several hours. I had no idea how hard opening the box and putting her ashes into the urn would be. It's not something people do every day, especially when the remains are of their child. I picked the kitchen island to take care of this thing that was so important to get done. The sun was shining in the windows and the moment I'd started was surreal. I had set the urn on the counter with the black box beside it, wondering how I was going to manage the emotions that would pour out of me in sync with her ashes pouring from one container into the next. As I lifted the bag out of the box, I saw it was securely closed with a metal tag and an ID number. Is that all Erin was to the crematorium? A number? It was amazing how the little things had become such big offenses to me. It was so impersonal.

A sudden rush of doubt flooded me. What if these weren't her ashes? What if they had got mixed up and these were the remains of a stranger? And what if Erin was still alive and these ashes were a case of mistaken identity? Was she was living on the streets of Edmonton, fully messed-up but fully alive? All these doubts and questions swirled around me as I carefully cut the tag off the bag and began pouring the ashes into the urn. I poured slowly, more slowly than the tears that were rolling down my cheeks yet again. A glint of silver popped out of the ashes and I stopped pouring to sift through them with my fingers, looking for what had caught my eye. And there they were. Tiny little titanium screws, the ones that would surely have been used to put her broken ankle back together. She had complained about them, swearing they were causing her pain and that she could feel them in there. And now I had them in the palm of my hand.

I sank to my knees at the counter, clutching the screws in my hand. I turned my back to the wall of the kitchen island, drew my knees up to my chest, held my clenched fists to my heart, and wailed. Here was the truth and the proof. I could no longer fool myself into thinking that maybe there had been a mistake and she was still alive. These tiny bits of evidence, tightly held in my hand, sealed the case. There was no mistake. She was gone.

"Is this all that is left of her?" I asked the still, quiet air in the kitchen. "Ashes, bits of metal? This can't be. How can someone so full of life, with so much to give and so much to live for, be rendered into mere dust like this?" My questions echoed back and I received no answer. My faith had been sorely tested and, like my grief, my desire to believe in a higher power wavered back and forth with my anger at such an unjust and undeserved death of a light brighter than the sun.

As I pulled myself back up to stand at the counter, I tipped the screws out of my hand into the urn and picked up the bag with her remaining ashes. As I slowly poured the remaining ashes into her urn, I heard myself whispering apologies to Erin, over and over. "I'm so sorry sweetheart, I'm so sorry it has come to this. I should have done better. I should not be standing here doing this. I would give my soul to put these ashes back into form and bring you home again, so you could live the full, happy life you deserved. I'm so sorry."

The last of the ashes drifted down into the urn. I secured the lid, hugged the container to my heart, and placed a kiss on the butterfly etched into the urn. As I set it on the mantle above the fireplace in the living room, I again resolved to do better. To honor her memory in a peaceful rather than raging way. To remember her light. If I could only talk to her one more time.

CHAPTER SIXTY-SEVEN: MOM

THE MEDIUM

The weeks following Erin's death were going by, sometimes in a dissociative fog, sometimes with a sense of calm clarity as I struggled to maintain my resolve to do better. At the same time, I was learning through my Healing Hearts group that I had to be less hard on myself. Not just for all the regrets of what I thought I should have done to save Erin but to also allow myself to wallow in my grief when I needed to. I sometimes found myself lingering in a cloud of loss and hopelessness, unable to move forward into daily living. Instead of fighting that cloud, I was learning to let it in—with conditions. Grieve, cry, scream if I needed to. That's the only way I could get it out. But I was beginning to recognize that there were still some things to look forward to, even for brief moments in time.

Birthdays, an action-packed movie sitting beside my husband, lunch with friends, time with my son and daughter-in-law, sitting on the grass watching the deer and geese meander through the valley. All those things were soothing balms to my raw, open wound and I craved them. At times, I wanted to be at the lowest point, to stay where it was familiar, but I was also becoming aware of brief times where I embraced the things that distracted me and showed that life could be appreciated again.

The saying that time heals all wounds is only partially true, depending on the depth of the injury. The rawness of the early days following Erin's death was softening, though I knew in my heart that this was a wound that went so deep, it would never fully heal. But it would scab over, creating a pain-dampening barrier between that acute rawness and moments of peace and even an emerging but cautious happiness.

The first time I heard myself laugh out loud, I felt guilty. Laughter and happiness had become strange emotions, and they felt inappropriate after so much time not being able to feel that way. But I knew it was a step in the right direction and I allowed myself the extra space to accept that I would laugh again. And the next laugh would come quicker, until it no longer felt inappropriate or insulting to Erin's memory. She was born full of love and laughter, and I know she would want me to feel joy again and carry on her ability to laugh out loud at the silliest of things. But God, it was so hard. I felt like I needed her verbal permission and once again, I would give anything to talk to her one more time.

It was at our next month's Healing Hearts meeting that the subject of talking to our loved ones in the spirit realm came about. I listened with deep interest to the stories from a couple of moms who had reached out to their child's spirit through a medium. I had been to psychic fairs, just for fun with friends, but I had never actually had a session with a medium. I believed the other moms' experiences, but I also doubted the ability to actually speak with someone who had died. Even so, I had a strong feeling I needed to try it. What I was missing in letting Erin's spirit move on was the assurance that she was okay, that she no longer needed me to hold her hand and tell her what to do next. I believed wholeheartedly that Erin and I had had a spirit realm/physical realm experience when we met on either side of the gray wall in my healing-touch session, but I didn't know if she had actually found her way to where she needed to go. It bothered me day and night whether she was still lost, scared, floundering in the unknown, on the other side of the veil. I'd do anything to see if there was a way to know for certain that she was settled and okay. I went home after the meeting and immediately made an appointment with the recommended medium, Debby, for the following week. She was very popular but had a cancellation, so I took it as a sign that I was meant to try this.

The following weekend, before I met with the medium, I was out cutting grass on the tractor and thinking about how much I needed to talk to Erin, how much I was hoping for a connection to her during the upcoming session. And what I would give to see her again for just one more lingering hug. A movement out of the corner of my eye caught my attention. I looked up toward the house where the wrap-around flagstone patio was and saw Erin standing there. She had her hands on her hips, her blonde hair blowing across her neck, and she was laughing. Her head was thrown back and, even though I couldn't hear anything, in my mind I heard her infectious, loud, and unapologetic belly laugh. I knew she was laughing at me, hunched over the lawn tractor that was always belching smoke, backfiring, and giving me nothing but trouble. I put the clutch in and shut the tractor off. I don't think I took my eyes off her for one second, but I must have blinked because she was gone. I'm not sure how long I sat there, staring at the spot where I had seen her. Was I so desperate that I had conjured up her image? Or did she, somehow, briefly transcend that mystic divide between the living and the dead, to show me that I needed to believe, accept, and understand that her spirit was not gone to me forever? I was filled with wonder and gratitude and looking forward even more to meeting with the medium in a few days.

When I first walked into Debby's office, I was rather surprised at the normalcy of it. She worked out of her home and the room she welcomed me into was just below ground level, so it was a bit dark yet it was cozy and inviting. I settled onto the loveseat with my back to the wall and a softly lit lamp glowed warmly beside me on a small table. There was the expected slight scent of incense in the air and as I looked around, I could see no evidence of collectibles. It was rather simplistic, which I assumed was meant to create a place of focus without the distractions. Debby wasted no time in getting down to business.

"I'm so happy to meet you, Wanda," she said. "I'd like to explain how I work with you and get a better understanding of what brings you here today."

I nodded, staying silent because, for some reason, I was perhaps testing her. To see if she was truly gifted or would pick up on what I was saying to give her enough information to create an experience I would fall into, believe, and walk away from amazed at her incredibly talented gift of speaking to angels. Debby looked directly into my eyes and I felt relaxed, letting go of my fears. She asked no more questions and simply began to speak.

As she drifted through images and sensations, describing what she was seeing, hearing, and feeling, she would often pause and ask me, "Do you know what I mean?" "Do you know whose spirit is showing itself to me?" Sometimes I would whisper "yes" or just nod as the descriptions were so close to people I knew who had passed. One person in particular, right at the beginning, shocked me the most.

"Does the Okanagan mean anything to you?" she asked.

"No, I don't think so," I replied.

"Someone who was close to you died with pain in their chest," she continued. "Maybe a heart attack? But there is pain in the back, too. This person was female. She cared a lot about you. But I'm still getting the Okanagan message. Were you there with someone recently? Someone who is no longer with us in body?"

"I can't think of anyone," I replied. "At least not recently. My friend Sandy lived in Summerland in the Okanagan, but she died over two years ago." Suddenly I felt a light go on in my thoughts.

"It may be her," Debby said. "Time is not a factor in the spirit realm. But she has a message for you. She said to tell you that she was there for her when she first arrived. She was the first one. Do you know who she is talking about? Who is she telling me that she was there for?"

As the light I felt dawning increased in strength, I knew Debby was communicating with Sandy. One of my closest friends for decades. She had died two years ago from lung cancer. And I remembered how she told me she had been ignoring the pain she had in her back because she thought it was a muscle strain. By the time she pressed her doctor for further tests, it was too late. I had gone to see her just a few weeks before her death and we had hugged hard on her front porch during a sunny day in the Okanagan.

I began to cry. Why would Sandy have been the first to greet Erin when she arrived in the spirit world? Why wouldn't it have been a family member? I had thought Chad or my mom and dad would have been the first spirits to take her hand and help her over the threshold.

Debby spoke again. "Why wouldn't I be the first? You were always there for me." As her gaze drifted back to me from looking just past my shoulder, she told me that was the message she had for me from Sandy.

All my skeptical thoughts disappeared with this first experience in our session. I felt Sandy's presence and my heart filled with love, missing my dear friend. I thanked Sandy out loud and told Debby about her. What a kind soul she was and maybe it wasn't so surprising she'd be the first on the scene. But I still hadn't told Debby about my real reason for being there. I hadn't mentioned Erin's death or my desperate need to hear from her.

Debby suddenly jumped up, mumbling to herself that she didn't know where she'd put it. "I know, I know," she was saying. "I'll find it, you want her to have it. Wait. Wait. I think I know where it might be." And she quickly left the room. I could hear her rummaging in the hallway and she came back to her chair quickly, dumping the contents of a large purse out onto the table in front of her. As she rifled through the assorted items, she was still mumbling about "it" being there somewhere.

Suddenly, "A-ha! Here it is," she announced, handing me a small rock. Painted on one side of the rock was a tiny butterfly.

"I didn't get the sense that it was your friend who wanted me to give this to you," she said. "I was in a group session last week and one of the people there gave me the rock. He didn't know why he was giving it to me. He just said he had a strong feeling that I was to have this rock and it would end up going to someone who needed it. What does it mean to you?"

I knew the connection had been made and this was Erin's subtle way of telling me she could hear my heartfelt desire to know if she was okay. I began to tell Debby of Erin's passing and how I was so scared that she hadn't transitioned well and was still in limbo, scared, lost, and confused. I ended by telling Debby that I had come here believing Erin was alone and I wanted to know if she was okay. It was Erin I was seeking a message from, so I was surprised to be touched by Sandy's spirit.

I learned so much that day during our session. When I told Debby I thought I had seen Erin standing on our patio a few days before, she didn't seem at all doubtful or surprised. But she did say it takes immense energy for loved ones to make themselves visible to us and that's why they never stay long. I should feel so blessed Erin was able to manage that for me. The fact that she was laughing at watching me fight with the lawnmower, even if I couldn't hear her, was the way I wanted to remember her. Not stuck in terrible addiction and wasting away, but in the light and laughter that was her true nature.

As I was absorbing Debby's explanation of the apparition, she suddenly stopped, put her hand on her chest, and said in awe: "Oh, I am in the presence of a wonderful spirit guide. His strength is almost overpowering."

I could see Debby's face turning red and sweat began to bead on her forehead. She had her eyes closed and she kept patting her chest with her hand. She was gently rocking back and forth, her eyes closed and a strange look of amazement on her face.

"This man is immense in spirit. I can barely harness the energy he has," she said. "In all my years as a conduit between the living and the spirit world, I have only encountered this kind of beautiful energy once or twice before. He is someone close to you and wants you to know something." She stopped talking, her breath came in short gasps, and suddenly her eyes opened wide.

"He said to tell you, 'I've got her.'" Debby moved to wipe the sweat from her forehead and asked me, "Do you know who this was who gave me the message?"

I began to cry in great, gulping sobs. The two people so close in life were now together again in death. I knew it was my dad. And a wash of relief flooded through me. Erin was safe and her grandpa had her in his arms. I gathered my thoughts and my crying slowed as Debby kindly gave me the space and time to recover.

"That would be my dad," I told her. "He loved Erin, and they were very close, closer than I think he was to the rest of his grandchildren. He was very spiritual, and I remember when we were in our final vigil with him, as he was taking his last breaths before he died, the minister who came to see him said she had never met anyone so deeply spiritual and accepting of the end of his life on earth. She called him a spirit larger than life."

Debby nodded. "That makes sense. I won't forget this session and the conviction I felt from his spirit that he is a very powerful guide for others. He is the one who is taking care of your daughter, helping her transition into the spirit realm. It's not easy for some people to move through the veil and settle on the other side and I have a sense that Erin struggled. It can take time. But know he is there and holding her close, helping her achieve spiritual peace and happiness."

It had been four months since Erin died when I had that session with a spiritual medium. We recorded the session and I listened to it many times over afterward. A couple of weeks later, Debby emailed me and said Erin's spirit had briefly come to her while she was in another session with someone else. She had a message for me.

"Life there was really hard there for me, Mom. But it's so much easier here."

And I breathed a sigh of relief. A gentle sense of letting go came over me. She was there, loved, supported, at peace, and happy. That's all I wanted for her. Now I just needed to seek that for myself in a life without her. I had a long road ahead of me but finally I could take the next step forward, knowing she was okay.

CHAPTER SIXTY-EIGHT: MOM

UNREMARKABLE

In the midst of finding my new family at Healing Hearts and meeting with the spiritual medium, I had received the autopsy results from the coroner's office in Edmonton. They arrived one day in the mail, and I knew instantly what that thick envelope held. As I sat with it on my lap, I deliberately examined the reasons for my hesitation. People close to me had asked me why I wanted to put myself through reading the coroner results of the death of my child. And kindly advised me not to. I knew this was a task no parent should ever have to do, but in my heart I truly needed confirmation of the physical cause of Erin's death. I needed answers and to put that part of my questioning sadness to rest.

The report had taken such a long time to arrive. The wheels of documenting death turn slowly in this busy world of people dying. It had taken almost six months to arrive and had then another two days of the envelope staring up at me from the top of my desk before I slid the letter opener under the flap to reveal the contents. My hands were shaking and the papers shifted.

I was still shocked to see her name at the top of the report. I had come to accept that Erin was no longer physically with us, but I still had moments of surety that perhaps there would be a miracle and it wasn't her. The surgical screws in the ashes had been more evidence for me but perhaps I still held some vague hope. After all, other people had surgeries involving screws so, as vague as it was, it allowed me a place for doubt. And hope.

My doubts and hope were gone when I read the description of her appearance. The coroner had my daughter on his table when he was doing his report, and the clinical tone of the results was disheartening. I know the coroner was just doing his job and the very description of that type of work would require a clear and defined detachment from the subject in front of him. The word "unremarkable" in these reports means there is no obvious indicator that could be remarked upon when examining each part of the anatomy. But I was still affronted that this particular term should pertain to my daughter. There was no one more remarkable in her existence than Erin and I raged against a world that lumped the loss of a beautiful life into a category of work that didn't warrant a few words of kindness, compassion, and acknowledgement. Every minute of every day, I had been wearing my nerves on the outside of the body, so everything was extremely over-sensitized. Everything hurt so much more deeply. Even a sad, cold word like "unremarkable" cut to the core.

I would later write an article for the online magazine *Life As A Human*, for which I was a contributor. I would call it "Grieving Mothers on a Mission—My Personal Story". I know there was, and still is, a growing number of shattered mothers reading the autopsy reports for their children crying and cringing over that word. Unremarkable. What a heart-wrenching and terrible dismissal.

What composing that article *did* do was get me back to the only thing I loved doing more than teaching yoga and meditation: writing. There was a long absence between my last piece (written in 2013 in Erin's first year of hopeful recovery) and the next one written and published seven years later, almost to the day. I was reminded of the troubled life I had been leading and its effect on my energy.

Beyond my dismay at the autopsy's wording, I searched for other clues to Erin's death. Finally, I reached the page where the toxicology report was laid out. This would either tell me what I suspected—that she had overdosed on prescription drugs for her anxiety—or from street drugs, possibly poisoned with fentanyl. I still held on to a debilitating anger at whoever else had been in her apartment and left her there to die alone. Or, even worse, this person may have knowingly given her a poisoned supply and just didn't care and wanted to make an escape.

And there it was. Erin had died of fentanyl poisoning but there was a host of other drugs that culminated in what is often referred to as a "cocktail." One of the leading amounts was tramadol, which she had been over-prescribed for her broken ankle, and all of the now-familiar anti-anxiety drugs for her PTSD were also in large quantities in the autopsy toxicology. I zeroed in on the tramadol as I knew it was an opioid that, if used over an extended period of time, would cause mental and physical dependence. I'd also read that tramadol can cause hallucinations, which would explain her seeing things that weren't there. Like the bodies she saw in the trash behind her building. That was just a day or two before her death.

I asked myself how much more my heart could break. But it was happening again. It was almost in slow motion that I felt a slow shattering in the place that once held my life force. Reading the report was the final blow. My poor, sweet girl had been in so much pain and so addicted that she felt she needed these terrible things to make her feel less terrible. I was sickened, broken, and unconsolable as I laid my head on the papers on the desk and let my tears blur the printing. Now I knew for sure. And it was no balm for my soul.

CHAPTER SIXTY-NINE: MOM

CHANGES

It was early in 2019, four months after losing Erin. I still felt hollowed out, a shell of who I used to be, but after the session I'd had with the medium, a deeper acceptance began to grow in me. I had come to terms with the fact that the police in Edmonton never did learn who had her keys when they locked the apartment, and we would also never know who had been with her the night she died. There would always be those unanswered questions, a mystery I would have to accept as unsolved. I knew I had to close the door on that one forever.

I had been through many doors: Erin's initial disappearance, the horrific discovery she had been held prisoner and abused beyond comprehension, her subsequent battle with addiction, her death, the process of "closing down" all the things that proved she existed—her bank account, government reports, notifications to everyone and every place that she had touched in her life—and even her ashes as the final proof that her material person was no longer here. All of these were doors that opened to show me new and sometimes terrible things and then closed. At first, I felt each door closing with a hard slam, reverberating loudly. But now, as each door closed, I sensed a quietness and gentleness that was not there before. I wouldn't wish this raw, altered existence on anyone, but I was coming to understand that it was thankfully getting less jarring and there would be fewer doors that needed to be closed.

Prior to and following Erin's death, I had been suffering from what can be described as extreme trauma (sometimes referred to in modern terms as combat trauma)—caused from a consistent and prolonged flooding of cortisol, the stress hormone, through my entire being every day. I had been trying to win the war but defeat was the outcome. I had lost the battle so I began to search for what the experience had taught me and how I could fashion the new me into someone with a purpose again. I likened it to losing the most important job of my life, protecting my child. I had been terminated from the position because of what I still saw as mistakes I had made on the job, but I had also been battling a double-sided and formidable enemy determined to make sure I'd lose the fight. This dual enemy was trauma and addiction. The pain from that battle would be my lifelong companion now.

My grandfather on my mother's side was wounded in the battle of Vimy Ridge, coming home with shrapnel still lodged in his knee and also suffering the devastating effects of being gassed at Ypres. I was just a baby when he died, but the story of his bravery and determination to live the rest of his life the best he could was carried on in the family. That shrapnel stayed a physical part of him to the end. I couldn't begin to compare my experience with his on the field of bloody battle, but I could relate to a simile of the shrapnel. Grief is broken pieces of heart, soul, love, and hope. Even though the wound eventually begins to heal, the parts of what hurt so badly at the beginning remain forever as an invisible presence that sometimes moves and comes to the surface, reminding you of the agony of loss. It's profoundly isolating, and those moments are wrapped in loneliness.

Accepting the loss of Erin was one thing, recognizing my expanding empathy for others through the resulting grief was another. It was a huge step forward for me and now that I was able to move away from the anxiety of wondering if Erin was truly gone and whether her spirit was at peace, I could take some quiet moments to reflect on what was happening in the world around me. I felt as if I'd been absent for a long time, lost in my own world of raw, unending, and debilitating mental, emotional, and physical pain. I'd been sure I would never see the other side of this terrible place. There were things that changed in me and for the better, which was a dawning and welcome surprise as I examined these new thoughts, feelings, and reactions.

Yes, a part of me died with Erin. I was sad for that lost part of myself but I was also now more peaceful, less judgemental, and no longer continually worried. That lost part of me transcended with Erin after I had a glimpse of death, grief, and the ensuing touch with the spirit world. I have become more intuitive and trusting of my gut and have a better developed sense of awareness and caution around judgemental people. My fear of death is gone, my wish for death is gone, and I know I still need to work on lessening the burden of guilt and regrets.

I can now clearly see that when someone criticizes another person, particularly around the stigma of drug use, there is a void within that judgmental person. The place where they could carry compassion and a yearning to understand is taken up by self-centeredness and a deep insensitivity that speaks of weakness and unwitting cruelty. They are busy with their own preoccupations. But this is because they have not been initiated into this terrible club. And I pray that they never have to be, for there is nothing more life-altering than the loss of a child.

Even though grief is not linear and can move from manageable to unmanageable, I had begun to reach the stage of hanging on. I was learning to integrate the loss and not fall victim to the usual buzz words around grief like "getting over it" or "moving forward." I was beginning to acknowledge, accept, and even agree that I must and can move through the pain and grief. It's very dark inside that grief but the darkness is where the healing begins. Grief was a part of who I was, acknowledged and understood but no longer leading the way. This was who I had become. I had lost a part of me but also gained a deeper inner knowledge of who I was and what my life meant. Had I really made it? Yes, I had "hung on" until I did.

CHAPTER SEVENTY: MOM

GOING HOME

Everything had been arranged for Erin's memorial in my hometown where she had been born and raised for the first years of her young life. She would be going home again, as was her wish in her journal. We hoped for good weather at the end of April in 2019 as the climate in the prairies can be temperamental—it would either cooperate or hit us hard with a late winter blast.

I will never forget and be forever grateful for the massive turnout at her graveside service in that little prairie cemetery. Every cousin, aunt, and uncle—some traveling thousands of miles—stood in solidarity and sadness with us as we let our little girl go. Erin's spirit was fully with us that day and Mother Nature was her companion. The weather had been cold and miserable, but for that one day the sun came out and warmed the earth where we laid her to rest and kept us company throughout the rest of our time there.

At her grave, as we lowered her blue butterfly urn into the ground, I remember whispering that "this is wrong, something is so terribly wrong" as a fresh wave of grief overtook me again. Many tears were shed and as we stood from kneeling to place all of our hands on her one last time, a gentle breeze washed over us and I felt her equally gentle presence. It was very hard to leave the cemetery; I had to be reminded that she wasn't truly there, it was only her ashes, and we had her spirit and memories to take with us on that beautiful sun-filled day.

Later, I found another poem Erin had written, possibly years before any of this happened, and I wondered, once more, at her intuition that perhaps she'd meet an untimely end.

WHISPER by Erin Gray

Broken hearted whisper
Into the dreary night,
Is all that I will leave behind
To prove I lost the fight.
The pain and anger beat me,
Even though I tried.
But I never really wanted life,
I never said it nor implied.
So why should I continue
To just vaguely pretend?
When I can just as easily
Come to my own end.
So do not shed a single tear
Over my helpless soul
For in the calm and black of death,
I will for once be whole.
Listen keenly to this whisper,
My final lost farewell.
I have taken off life's blindfold,
To be broken of this spell.

We had a gathering in the Legion hall in our hometown, where we shared memories and watched a wonderful video put together by Ryan, entitled "For Erin." His final gift for her. From birth to her last few years, pictures of happier times flowed across the screen accompanied by a couple of pieces of music I had chosen that just seemed to fit her so well. "Beam Me Up" by Pink and Emily Blunt singing, "Where The Lost Things Go" from the more recent *Mary Poppins* movie. We laughed at some of the images of her hilarious antics and cried again at others. My friends from high school showed up to give me a hug, which was so special and reminded me how a small-town/farm upbringing forged forever friendships. We ate, we visited, and Jim, a good family friend and relative of Ken's wife Kim, gave the most compelling and compassionate speech about what a beautiful person Erin was. He had grown to know her through her years of addiction struggle and reminded friends and family that she was not defined by her addiction and remained the amazing, talented, and beautiful young woman they all remembered. Gratitude to Jim forever.

As we prepared to come back to our lives on the island, I vowed to return for regular visits and tend to Erin's gravesite, as well as those of my beloved family surrounding her. My great-grandparents, grandparents, mom and dad, and Chad's mom and my sister-in-law Irene, who died much too young following his death. She would know and understand my loss and I always thought the depths of her grief played a part in her tragic and final illness. And, of course, Chad, Erin's favorite cousin. Now they were resting close to one another as she had wanted. I pictured them together in horseplay and telling terrible jokes in Heaven, like they did when they were young.

It's those of us left behind who still struggle under the weight of suffering, yet we survive and learn to keep putting one foot in front of the other.

CHAPTER SEVENTY-ONE: ERIN

IT'S ALL OKAY

There is no way to convey what things are like for me now. Being human and in the physical realm can be wonderful but it can also be very hard—for some, it can be unbearable. I had done my best to send a message to Mom, through Debby, that my life on Earth was predominantly painful, interspersed with times of absolute joy and happiness in the early years. But those hard times were not Mom's fault. I had been dealt a rough hand at the outset and set on a path along a rutted road with so many switchbacks. That was just the way it was.

My transition from the physical to the spiritual realm was not easy to start with either, but now the tethers that bound my soul to my body and the earth have been released. I had always believed in God and often I had prayed hard to be lifted from my addiction. I had felt abandoned so many times and thought it was my fault. Here, in the spirit realm, I finally feel that I am no longer always looking up and begging for rescue. I am a part of it all and there is nothing to ask for anymore. This is truly the epitome of enlightenment, knowing, being. I can no longer form the words, only the feelings, and it is beautiful. Here in the spirit realm, I am finally at peace, and everything is so much easier.

Mom was struggling so much when I died, and for years before that as well when I had been so sick with my disease of addiction. At the cemetery, I sensed everyone's pain and knew what it was like for the ones left behind. But the feeling I had was a curious empathy, a detachment with a deep knowing that this was a part of life. A forever meaning of death, the after-existence. And it was all going to be okay.

The choices I had made and the things I had done… none of it mattered as those were the things of life in the physical realm. The people who had hurt me and were now in the spirit world too, pass by me and through me. And it no longer matters. It no longer frightens or hurts me. Their path on earth had been a rough road as well but we are now all joined as one everlasting stream of pure, unsullied, conscious energy. It is truly lovely.

For a brief time at the beginning of my adjustment into this place of light and energy, I felt a deep sorrow for Mom. I knew how much she was struggling to find out who and what had started the events leading to where I am now. But in the end, it truly does not matter. Mom will come here to this place someday and the angst to know will be over. There is only limitless, unending happiness and serenity here. We are each other, in life and in death.

If you believe in a higher power, whether it be God, Allah, the source or whatever name you dedicate to your HP, we are all a part of, attached to, and exuberant in our spiritual world.

Would I come back to a different body than I had been given (or, as some believe, chosen)? Would I live again in the physical realm? Would my history be forgotten as a new person in a new life? Would it be a hard life like before or would it be smooth like we all wish for? It doesn't matter. Time is not a "thing" here. I would or I wouldn't. I only have my sensations and they are all-encompassing goodness. What will be, will be and even though there is no "now" here, I remain happy in this collective place of spiritual calm and happiness. I hope you know that in your soul, Mom. I believe it is slowly becoming your awareness, your knowledge, and your acceptance. We are all love and I will always be a part of you, as you are forever a part of me. It's all okay, I am okay.

CHAPTER SEVENTY-TWO: MOM

GETTING INVOLVED, GETTING EDUCATED

Grief is a fickle thing. You never know if the tide is going to come in or go out. But I was now able to go for longer times between the waves crashing my shore, re-opening wounds, and tumbling me back into the depths of my loss to drown. But something had shifted for me. I no longer passively treaded water, waiting for the undertow to pull me down into the murky depths forever. Now I found myself swimming stronger against the current and looking toward the shore with purpose. I felt a burning need to listen more fully, read more information on trauma and addiction, and, above all, learn fully what had happened in my daughter's life for it to end the way it did.

I was unfortunately already a leading expert in child loss to substance use. I'd been on the frontlines of that battle, had witnessed the war being lost, and had been left on the ground, bleeding, wounded to the core but surviving my injuries. I leaned fully into learning everything I could about the whole sad, sordid process and quickly came to the understanding that I would only be scratching the surface. There were true leading experts like Dr. Gabor Mate, author of *In the Realm of Hungry Ghosts: Close Encounters with Addiction,* and Professor Bruce Alexander, author of *The Globalization of Addiction.* Both were highly qualified to deeply explore the origins of drug use and connect the dots to trauma and the loss of family ties. These resources and more are listed at the back of this book. I had the trauma, addiction, and loss experience but I had also been flayed open by it and could only refer to the effects it had on my own psyche and how I lived the rest of my life.

There is a belief that drugs alienate love. If you look at a potentially killer drug as an entity (and I often had flashbacks of the demon that both Erin and I saw with the same visual description), it is easier to separate that drug from your loved one. Because the person you love, whether passed or still fighting, is not the substance that is going into their body. I never stopped loving Erin for one millisecond through our whole time of living with her addiction. Even when she was shouting at me, swearing, fighting with me, and refusing help. I knew that what I was witnessing was not my girl. And that is something we absolutely *must* never forget! The addiction is not the person.

I decided, in my desire to contribute and learn more, that I would begin to get more involved in events to raise awareness of this global epidemic of addiction. The stigma against people who used drugs grated at me and I was deeply offended by terms like "druggies" and "junkies." But even more hurtful was hearing comments such as, "A sign of good parenting is raising a child who doesn't do drugs." As if there isn't enough guilt to carry when we fail to protect our children from death. I was a far-from-perfect parent, but I did raise my children with love that they never had to question. And I know from experience that even children who have been over-protected—to the point of being smothered in parental bubble wrap—can grow up incapable of living like functioning adults with goals and ambitions. And that floundering, directionless persona can lead to medicating anxiety and depression. I don't know if there is a perfect balance of protection and over-protection but I do know that addiction can land on anyone, at any time. So, pointing the finger of blame is only a step backward to finding answers.

I joined a rally in downtown Victoria one day, about nine months after losing Erin, holding a sign with a montage of her images and the tagline from the book *Gone Too Soon*, published by the BC Centre on Substance Use. I had been fully expecting a sad funeral parade of weeping mothers, but it was a rally with participants from so many different walks of life. It became very clear to me that this growing epidemic of death by poisoned street drugs and prescription-drug overdoses was a malady that had a vast ripple effect. It wasn't just mothers, fathers, and siblings who were broken by their grief—it was an entire society. I was empowered by and amazed at the incredible reaction from the general public. People shouted their support, joined in the walk, and asked how they could help. And there was the other side too, of course. The looks of disgust, revving engines, and honking horns were angry rather than supportive. Car horns seemed to take on the emotions of the person behind them; it was obvious if the honker was a supporter or a hater. The hater is ignorance.

As we walked and ended at the Ministry of Health, pleading for changes to how addiction is viewed and those using drugs are treated, I had a good look around at who had been walking far in front and far behind me, where I was with a couple of other moms I knew from Healing Hearts. And I saw people actively smoking pot and ducking around corners to use their drug of choice with others. This was the first time I had been in the physical presence of someone high since losing Erin, and I was triggered into a state of anxiety. On the spot, I realized I wasn't ready for this. I had joined my first rally for raising awareness too soon after Erin's death.

Everyone progresses at a different pace through grief, but we don't know where we're at until we've tested the waters. I was filled with fear, sick with dread for those people I saw using, and as I looked around and saw other mothers bravely holding up their signs with their children's faces and dates of death, I saw the link between what I could see happening in the streets with people using drugs and the outcome of the grief left behind when it all goes wrong. I cried all the way home that day with the stark realization that this was the toughest battle ahead for society as a whole, and I vowed to try and use my experience and lessons to nail home a way to wake up as many people as I could to what had happened and would continue to happen. This gap in compassion and healthcare was snowballing, a runaway train, people were being mowed down in front, and those with the ability to slow the devastation were looking the other way.

CHAPTER SEVENTY-THREE:
MOM

EDUCATION AND UNDERSTANDING: KEYS TO COMPASSION AND DEFINING THE DISEASE

I wish I knew then what I know now. We've all said that many times throughout our lives. During what I call the "chaos times"—when Erin had been missing, then rescued, then catapulted down into addiction—I spent my time and energy floating above the meaning of it all. Instead of learning about what addiction truly was, how it came about, and, most importantly, how to live with a loved one who was stricken with the disease, I focused on treating the symptoms rather than getting to the root of the problem. I wish I could go back and with deeper knowledge and a practical strategy of what I needed to be doing, rather than hovering and trying to control the situation. Would the outcome have been the same? Maybe, but perhaps I'd have fewer regrets because my eyes would have been wide open for more of those painful years.

What is addiction? According to the British Columbia Centre on Substance Use website: "Addiction is a treatable medical condition that affects the brain and involves compulsive and continuous use despite negative impacts to a person, their family, friends and others."

Let's examine the word "treatable." It's not a simple matter of checking into a rehab facility and after thirty days of treatment you're released, cured, never to use a substance again. It's far more complex than that. It takes time, it takes money, and it takes a thorough approach—all depending on the circumstances of the person who is living in active addiction.

People in active addiction are not just the individuals living on the streets we see every day. They are family, friends, neighbors, coworkers, and sometimes we are shocked to discover someone we would never have believed was using any type of drug, legal or illegal, is struggling with addiction. Our legal system is still punishing the addict rather than providing support in the form of a solution. Instead, this form of persecution is pushing people who are using drugs into the shadows. And into shame. Loneliness and isolation are direct contributors to leading the addict further down that dark path of no recovery. It has become a vicious cycle.

Johann Hari's book *Chasing the Scream: The First and Last Days of the War on Drugs* (Bloomsbury Publishing, 2015) was a great resource for me. At the beginning of Erin's addiction days, I too thought she should just be able to quit. She was loved, surrounded by family and friends supporting her, plus a network of mental-health professionals, and I just couldn't understand why she was so stuck. Hari clears away the cobwebs of lack of knowledge and understanding, explaining how "everything we think we know about addiction is wrong." (TEDGlobalLondon, 2015). In his book *Chasing the Scream*, Hari also delves into the history of the war on drugs and goes on to describe what Dr. Gabor Mate questions: "What if the discovery of drugs wasn't the earthquake in their life but only one of the aftershocks?" (Hari, *Chasing the Scream*, 2015).

That statement was a true awakening for me. I had begun to understand that the drugs weren't the leading problem; it was the underlying childhood trauma and her experience of being held hostage and sex trafficked. Just because she was out of that situation and getting help for the addiction, didn't mean she was going to just be able to quit and be better, able to live the rest of her life in a healthy way. Not without a much deeper method of treatment involving a step-by-step approach to peeling away the multiple layers of her trauma disorder.

To this day, we still do not have a thorough approach in place and people are dying by the hundreds every month and it is ever-escalating due to the poisoned drug supply on the streets. Drug-related overdoses and deaths prompted the government of British Columbia to declare a public health emergency (gov.bc.ca/health website) in April 2016. Eight years later, at the time of this writing, we are still taking one step forward and two steps back. There doesn't seem to be a strong-enough appetite for change and looking at what policies and solutions are working in other parts of the world. This is a global, not just local, epidemic of addiction illness and we are all held hostage by this toxic drug and overdose crisis. Society as a whole needs to step up to the plate, take responsibility, and change the narrative around substance use. Yet the stigma remains and is drowning out any constructive approaches to a system that works for all.

In 2001, the country of Portugal took a forward-thinking approach to establishing a national strategy involving a health-based, integrated, and patient-centered model. They stopped punishing their citizens who needed help and instead of prison, offered a system of recovery, prevention, and education. Medical assistance was implemented in the form of safe supply of substances, and they even developed a program of employment, offering potential employers tax breaks if they offered jobs to those in recovery.

This program has been wildly successful. Billions of dollars have been saved due to the elimination of criminal prosecution and thousands of lives have been saved. (Drug Policy Alliance: Drug Decriminalization in Portugal www.drugpolicy.org). Lives of contributing, healthy and grateful citizens. What was the trick and why isn't it being implemented in other parts of the world? Bureaucracy. The political parties in Portugal all agreed to step out of the way and let the leading experts in addiction and recovery take the helm. We, as citizens of our own country, need to keep the heat on and push our political parties to stop the archaic thinking, let go of the bureaucratic control and take the same approach as Portugal.

This is where I became more familiar with the work of Moms Stop The Harm (MSTH). I had been attending the Healing Hearts grief meetings regularly for several months and knew that MSTH had begun offering the grief support component to families, but I had only skated on the surface of who and what they really were and still are—a force driven by love and need for change.

The MSTH is a network of Canadian families impacted by substance-use-related harms and deaths. Their mission statement is to advocate for the change of failed drug policies, provide peer support to grieving families, assist those with loved ones who use or have used substances, and end substance-use-related stigma, harms, and death.(Our Mission. Our Vision. Our Values. momsstoptheharm.com/mission-vision-values).

Coming together in 2015 as broken-hearted and deeply grieving mothers who had lost their children to substance-use-related deaths, MSTH cofounders Lorna Thomas, Petra Schulz, and Leslie McBain took their pain and channeled it into a mission for change. Since then, the organization has grown from coast to coast and the fight continues to save lives and lobby the federal government to wake up to the potential of addressing this medical emergency in a progressive and proven way.

Not everyone agrees with the model of safe supply to help substance users navigate toward successful, long-term recovery. The stigma rears its ugly head again for many when they hear about supplying those in active addiction with free drugs. Often there is kickback and statements are made about why taxpayers should be paying for free drugs to addicts. Here is where the problem lies. There is a lack of education around the process and how effective it is in treating addiction. It provides a safe product that helps individuals not only deal with managing the demands of the body's dependence on drugs due to the illness, but the supply is also accessed through dedicated resources that also provide much needed physical and mental health treatment through multi-tiered systems of support. And the bottom line? *It saves lives.* If my daughter had had access to those systems of support, she would not have turned to a street source and died alone and abandoned by a society that still treats people with opioid addictions as criminals.

I stand by Moms Stop The Harm. I truly believe in the MSTH mission, and their heartfelt act of providing love and support in the Healing Hearts sessions saved my life. Love, loss, and pain drive these dedicated and still-grieving mothers with an energetic force that is unrelenting, and I am so proud of their continued efforts. They provided a place of empowerment and support for me when I was at my most broken and vulnerable and for that I will be forever grateful.

CHAPTER SEVENTY-FOUR: ERIN

FOR ALL THE YOUNG WOMEN: PORTRAYAL OF A PREDATOR

These are words I would have said to other girls and young women had I survived. It is my cautionary tale as told through my mother and is based on my first-person experience, court documents in evidence, and what I conveyed to Mom as she sat silently and patiently listened in our talks together, and then later through the wind chimes, for what I wanted her to know and share.

When I was in recovery during my battle with addiction and trauma, I became very clear on how I was lured, trapped, and victimized: a hostage to a serial sex trafficker. I decided to take my experience and turn it into a tool to help carry a message to as many vulnerable young women as I could. Because this can happen to anyone. I saw myself visiting high schools, colleges, and speaking at sexual-assault centers. I wanted my story to empower women so that they would have their eyes opened and avoid this terrible ordeal that I had only heard of or seen on the fringes of my earlier life. Before it happened to me.

I had as many shoulda, woulda, couldas as Mom did, and can say from experience that we all wear blinders sometimes, operating from a filtered instinct because we think we're safe and know all the facts. I had been fooled by a master at his craft because he knew how to appeal to what I needed and wanted, not because he cared about me or wanted me to be happy, but because he needed me to fulfill his sick fantasies and provide an income for him.

What is a predator? In the wild animal world, it is a creature that tracks, kills, and eats its prey. In the human world, the outcome can be the same but it is not based on pure instinct and the need for survival. It is a sick mind camouflaged as caring, kind, and charismatic. "… a person who looks for other people in order to use, control, or harm them in some way. *a sexual predator [=a person who commits sexual crimes against other people]." *Britannica.com*, s.v "predator", accessed January 4, 2025, www.britannica.com/dictionary/predator.

First, a predator selects a victim by determining if she could be a potential candidate for his game of torture and control. Then the predator/trafficker begins to prey on a new victim, through a five-stage approach to "train" the victim. "The five-stages of human trafficking are luring, grooming and gaming, coercion and manipulation, exploitation, and lastly, recruitment." (Crime Stoppers, HTinWC-5-Stages-of-Human-Trafficking.pdf.1).

When I randomly met D.H. through a friend who was thinking about buying a puppy from him, I had no idea how my life was going to be taken on a roller coaster ride that would leave the rails and eventually crash. My physical and psychological injuries would be life-altering and then life-ending. The luring began almost immediately. Looking back, he appealed to everything that I cared about: animals (especially dogs), my desire to travel and explore the world, and my love for friends and family. He told me about his family living in a foreign country and how wealthy they were, with acres of wilderness and a plethora of animals they supposedly rescued and cared for. It was a dream world for me.

He began to entice me with offers to take me traveling and meet his wonderful family, and by sharing his passion for animals. I fell hook, line, and sinker. And as the weeks and then months went by, I found myself falling into what, at the time, I believed was love, but I was also starting to question when all of these things he had been promising would actually happen. My questions were always met with continued assurances of his caring for me and that he had a "plan" to make sure we would have all the adventures he had enticed me with.

He gradually became a little less gentle with me when being affectionate. When I told him he was hurting me, he apologized at first and then began telling me I was "weak," a "baby," and that I needed to "toughen up." I told Mom I felt he was getting a little weird, and she insisted I get away from him. I was a bit torn when she said that because I knew something wasn't quite right, but I had already been reeled in by his charisma, charm, and good looks. My biggest mistake was telling him how Mom felt and asking him if I had anything to be concerned about.

That's when the chipping away began as he told me my family didn't care about me. I had shared a little bit of my childhood trauma with him, and he blamed my parents for not doing anything about it, even when I insisted that they knew nothing about it. He told me they lied, and he was the only one I could trust. It was just enough to plant doubt.

But he was already on alert that I wasn't going to be as compliant as he had thought I would be. One evening, he brought home my favorite take-out meal and a bottle of red wine. He was extra attentive and insisted on bringing me a glass of the wine to the living room while he reheated dinner. I hadn't been much of a drinker before, but I was in the glow of his attention and feeling very pampered. I sipped at the wine and waited for what the rest of the evening would bring.

I don't recall much from that night other than seeing his face hanging over me as he told me I was a little "piggy" and had drunk all the wine. I knew I hadn't, I'd only had one glass, but I just couldn't seem to get my thoughts straight and I could hear myself slurring as the room spun around me. The next morning, I woke up with the worst hangover. And bruises all over my body. D.H. told me I'd gotten really drunk and kept falling. I felt like such an idiot, and he reinforced that with his name calling.

The weeks and months that followed became a slow but steady indoctrination into his scheme of power, control, and abuse. It was carefully planned and methodical, and I didn't even see it happening. And then it didn't matter what I said, what I tried, the physical, mental, emotional, and sexual abuse was relentless. I was slowly drawn in through his use of GHB, the date rape drug, and then he moved on to stronger, more lethal and debilitating drugs. Cocaine became a daily dose for me when he needed me to be alert but the crash from it kept me from finding the energy to fight back. It was a constant see-saw from "downers" to "uppers" and most of the time I had no idea what he was giving me. I was his puppet, and he was the master.

What is a hostage? :a person who is captured by someone who demands that certain things be done before the captured person is freed. *Britannica.com*, s.v. "hostage" accessed January 4, 2025, www.britannica.com/dictionary/hostage. By this time, I was being held as security, so he could fulfil his conditions of personal torture and as a tool to make money by selling me to others.

What exactly is a sex trafficker? "Sex trafficking is a form of human trafficking that involves recruiting, moving, or holding victims for sexual exploitation purposes. Sex traffickers can coerce victims into providing sexual services by force or through threats, including mental and emotional abuse and manipulation." Public Safety Canada, accessed January 4, 2025, canada.ca/en/public-safety-canada/campaigns/human-trafficking/sextrafficking.html.

I honestly don't know at what point I had given up my soul to this monster, but I was so totally under his control that I saw no way out. And eventually I did not even seek escape. I was drugged, prostituted, forced to dance for men, and beaten and raped by D.H. regularly. In my drugged state, I was the witness to my own downfall, seeing what was happening from the peripheral images in my mind. I had become his ragdoll: used, played with, and then put back on the shelf until the next time I was needed.

What would I have done differently, given hindsight and another chance? I would have asked more questions instead of naively believing everything he said without proof. I would have confided more details of our relationship to a close friend instead of constantly covering up for him. I would have stepped back when Mom told me to get away from him and given deeper consideration to her maternal intuition.

D.H. was so good at creating the chasm between me and my former life that I didn't see it happening—nor anyone who loved me. It was that subtle. I lost all my friends during those months of being a hostage. He pushed everyone away and scripted every mean and horrible thing I ever said to friends and family. He told me how stupid I was and that I was nothing without him. In a gruesome combination of constantly being in a heavily drugged state and being emotionally whipped, I had become nothing and nobody in my mind. I believed that he was the only one who would ever want anything to do with me.

In your own life: ask questions, step back, demand proof. Confide in your friends and family. Don't allow anyone to beat you into submission, physically, mentally, or emotionally. If it sounds too good to be true, then it's a lie. Do all these things—it may be your only chance.

CHAPTER SEVENTY-FIVE: MOM AND ERIN

A CONVERSATION ABOUT TREATMENT, RECOVERY, RELAPSE

There is a wide range of definitions when it comes to determining exactly what the word "recovery" means. It is typically a time when someone has gone through a system of support or a variety of treatments to help with abstaining from harmful substances. The addict seeks a way to achieve continued growth and improvement in their well-being and health and, very importantly, manage setbacks. Relapse is a setback. It's when the individual begins using substances again and it can occur once or numerous times during the recovery phase.

There are various systems of treatment when it comes to recovery from substance use. There are medications to help "wean" off opioids, faith-based programs, peer and family support, self-care methods, and other approaches. It is an ever-changing landscape, and success can be elusive as every person being treated is different. It's a matter of finding what works for each unique individual and their physical and mental health situation. What is still missing, as I and many others believe, is a wrap-around program that delves deeply into the two-pronged approach of trauma treatment *and* drug rehabilitation treatment. Not one or the other. Both. At the same time. For a prolonged intense period with lifelong follow ups.

MOM

Recovery. Relapse. Nothing made me happier than to see Erin healthy when she was in recovery. And it shattered me when she relapsed. I soon learned it was common but each time I held hope that this time it would "stick." In those days, I still believed that she just needed to "beat" the call of substance use and then everything else would fall into place. I knew how much trauma she was dealing with, but I naively believed that once Erin had her addiction recovery nailed down and in place, she could begin working on her mental health. That's not how it works. What she needed then—and what everyone currently struggling with rehabilitation and recovery needs—is a multi-tiered system of treatment because it is not a case of what came first, the chicken or the egg. The trauma depends on the drug to numb the pain, and the drug depends on the trauma to justify the use.

ERIN

Creativity. Relapse. The strangest and most wonderful things happened to me during my recovery times. I was constantly amazed at my clarity of thought and my excitement to thrive and live a full, meaningful life. When my painting muse leaped to the surface, some said it was the unresolved child in me coming out on canvas. I didn't care what was lying at the bottom of it, I just rejoiced in how expressive and fun my painting became. When those whimsical, ethereal, and vibrant creatures leaped out of my watercolors and planted themselves defiantly under the brushes, I experienced a deep sense of gratitude and was filled with lighthearted joy for my clarity.

It was when I put the bright colors to bed and closed my eyes to sleep that the movie reel would play in my head again. Torture, fear, pain. I began to dread going to sleep and also began to lose ground in my recovery due to exhaustion from fear of sleep, and the recurring nightmares when I did. Small things would trigger me into a state of panic. D.H. was in jail yet I was terrified he'd find me, show up on my doorstep and put his hands around my neck, choking my newly found joyous life out of me. The pain and the anxiety would resurface, throwing me back into my ragdoll days. And I'd find myself wrapped in my comfy cloak of protection, whether it was painkillers, anti-anxiety meds or, eventually, anything I could get my hands on by whatever means I could to rest and sleep in peace again.

This was a relapse and I could see it coming but felt powerless to stop the descent. I still sketched and even painted when I was falling, at least until I hit rock bottom and could barely form a coherent thought or get out of bed. Everything I created during my descents came out black and white and full of pain. I was never sure if that was a good thing or not, maybe I was getting it out, but I was filled with incredible sadness when I looked at those dark pieces. I also knew, in brief moments of clarity, that I was playing Russian roulette. Each relapse took me further down. It was the draw, the pull, the need—whatever you want to call it—that was stronger than I was, and the risk seemed worth the place I could go where nothing and no one could hurt me. I missed out on my life.

CHAPTER SEVENTY-SIX:
MOM

GRIEF IS PART OF LIFE

Six years later, when I look back at what my life became after Erin died, I realized that my grief started before we lost her. The traumatic mental health and addiction slowly chipped away at my little girl, and I was losing her in pieces while she lived. There was always hope of recapturing the true nature of Erin—daughter, granddaughter, sister, friend—and as a believer in miracles, I prayed, hoped, and wished for it every day. But on every one of those days, I felt those pieces slipping away from me. I desperately tried to hold onto them and did my best to remind Erin of happier times—because it helped me remember who she really was too. I remember saying to her once: "I don't even know who you are anymore." Such hurtful words but I was speaking the truth.

Oxford Languages defines grief as "deep sorrow, especially that caused by someone's death." Simplistic and all-encompassing, but so broad in meaning. I see grief as unique to every individual who experiences it. It's like a fingerprint. No two people can have the same one. I also like the saying, "Grief is love with no place to go." (Jamie Anderson, author, *Doctor Who*). At the beginning of my deepest sorrow when Erin left the physical world, I hung onto that saying with all my might. I was stuck and had no place to put my love anymore. This weighed so heavily on me that it almost took my life too, drowning me in the sheer enormity of something I could not let go of.

I'm not drowning anymore. I found things and people in my life in which to put the love that had no place to go. Humans are an unusual and exact species. We like tangible things that we can connect to with our five senses: sight, sound, taste, smell, touch. When we lose someone we love, we can no longer see them, hear their voice, taste the essence of their skin when kissed, smell their unique scent or favorite fragrance, and we cannot touch them. We are cast adrift, scrambling in the dark, eyes open, hands grasping, even sniffing the air to seek for the one we lost. Yet we know that person is gone. No wonder we go through so many stages of grief as we shed all those things one at a time and accept the reality of losing not just the person but our ability to connect our own needs to them. We become very vulnerable.

I experienced every stage of grief deeply: denial, anger, bargaining, depression, and acceptance. Some days I would go through all the emotions and it would leave me beaten and exhausted. Other times I would enter one of the stages and stay there for what felt like forever. Denial and anger were in capital letters for me as I had a convicted criminal to blame and could not come to terms with the fact that someone else's actions had resulted in my daughter's life ending like it did. I wavered in the incredulity of it all: this *cannot* have happened, and I hate you D.H. for doing what you did to my daughter. What I found over time is that I not only had love with no place to go, I also had denial and anger blocking my attempts to get through to acceptance—the final stage of grief. Looking back, it was all a non-linear, volatile, and complete mess. What got me through?

The cliche "learn to forgive and you will be free" was not something I chose to do. It still isn't. I won't forgive D.H. as he doesn't deserve any kind of absolution and when I tried (because that's what I was told I should do), it brought me no peace. But the beauty of this is that I no longer carry the anger. The decision to not forgive—and I certainly won't forget—actually brought me a certain sense of finality, a closure to my phase of anger. I now make it a practice to go to my gut, my intuition, to know if a decision is the right or wrong one. I'm okay with my decision to not forgive. I don't seek retribution and doubt that I will ever see or hear his name again in my life. I know who he is, I know what he did, and if he ever reads this story he'll also know who he is. I guess a small part of me hopes he feels guilty but with some sociopaths and all psychopaths that emotion was left out of the recipe when they were brought into this world. Or maybe they lost it due to some horrible circumstance in their life. If that was what brought D.H. to become the monster and predator he was, it was not Erin's fault but she paid the price for his evil and perverted lifestyle.

The tools I used to help me come to terms with Erin's death, and all the terrible things leading up to it, are things I already had in my life. I just needed to take them out of the toolbox, clean them up, look at them, and ask, "Okay, now what do I use you for?" And the answers came, sometimes right away, but other times it took a situation or an opportunity for the solution to be revealed.

My family and friends. They were always there but I had insulated myself so much from their love and caring because I was just too much of an open wound, raw and full of anger, sorrow, grief. There was no room to let anything else in. Eventually, time helped that insulation slowly dissolve, and I was able to think about who had shown up, who brought hugs, tears, and food, and who kept calling me to check in. Most of my friends and family had moved on with their lives within a few months of Erin's death and I stood alone, wondering how I got left behind. How could they possibly be so normal when my world was still in shattered pieces of disconnection, sadness, and just stuck?

Moving on wasn't their fault, but Erin's memory was fading from other's minds and it didn't seem right. It would have been a terrifyingly lonely place, being left behind while others moved forward, but the one constant was my group at Healing Hearts, who let me continue to express my unique grief in ways that others could not understand. Because they were also still in that shattered place. It was all a process, with friends and family part of the healing at the beginning and my other "family" at Healing Hearts there until I reached a point where I felt I was going to be okay. It wasn't that I no longer needed the friends I made in the group but over time I was becoming stronger, more accepting, and more resilient. I also continue to have the comfort of knowing I can go back to my Healing Hearts family any time I need, because losing a child and the grief that goes with it is a part of me forever and I might need a little propping up now and then.

My work. As a long-time yoga instructor and creative writer, I was blessed with an outlet that I wish I could package and give to every grieving parent. Teaching yoga to a loyal and dedicated group of people who I consider friends more than students brought me a kind of solace that was exactly what I needed. On the yoga mat, you have three things to think about: your body, your mind, and your spirit. And it all begins with the breath. Returning to work not long after Erin's death was a difficult decision because, as a teacher, you need to be very present for your yogis and my emotional pain was front and center.

I arrived at the yoga room early on my first day back, settled on my mat, ready to bolt at any minute because I was terrified of breaking down. I remember choosing a kneeling position and I bowed forward, placing my hands on my eyes and my forehead on the mat. And one of those senses you dearly miss when you lose a loved one, blossomed up for me from the floor. I smelled Erin's perfume as clear as if she was right beside me. And the tears flowed. I had been sure I could not do this but she was there, telling me in the only way she could that I was going to be okay. My yogis filed into the room, I took a deep breath, then another, and dove back into doing the work I loved enough to help get me through this hard place.

Writing. This was another outlet that worked well for me. Journaling is a recommended tool for getting your pain out onto paper, but I took it just a step further. I wrote articles on recovery and grief, specifically around the stigma of losing a child to substance use. I submitted them to my editor and he enthusiastically gave me the reins, not changing a word and letting me write from what he said was "unfortunately but obviously an expert's point of view." This depth of grief was not something I ever imagined, in all my writing years, as something in which I would become an "expert." But here I was. As are all other grieving parents, reluctant in their new roles but arriving on the job with a level of experience that no one should ever have to achieve.

Outdoors. I love walking and hiking, especially if I can be in a place where nature is so much bigger than my emotions. In writing this book, I took what I called "decompression hikes" in our local park, which has steep hills and rough terrain. The effort to navigate the root-covered trails and climb the uphill parts forced me back into my body and my breath. And away from the exhaustive re-examination and reliving of my past and my pain. I actually hugged trees because it made me feel better. I always came back down from that little mountain, recharged and ready for the next session, knowing that Erin's spirit was with me every step of the way.

Read, read, read. Books on grief, books on recovery and, yes, even books on dying. They are enlightening and take away so much of the fear. And pop in a good murder mystery or comedy once in a while because the brain needs a break to just be entertained. Include those funny stories to remind you that there are still things to laugh about in this world. Maybe not right away, but eventually, pick up something that is a light read with funny bits. It's so hard, that first time you laugh, but it is healing. We were all born to laugh, and we need a little reprieve from the seemingly endless crying. The crying and the laughing are natural and needed but it is all about finding a balance, and that is what takes the most time to figure out.

Those are my main tools I use as I continue with my life. They may be entirely different for someone else but we all have a toolbox. We just need to dig it out of the closet and figure out which tools work for us. And be patient. Sometimes it takes a while to sort out and determine what we need to make it through. There are so many resources out there (I've listed a few at the back of this book) and there is no shame in reaching out to ask questions if you aren't sure what step to take first. But you do need to take a step. I almost didn't, preferring to stay mired in place because it had become familiar. And to be honest, I felt I deserved the pain because I thought I had failed. It's a human condition to think we have failed as a parent when bad things happen. But no one fails. We learn and that's what keeps the forward motion going.

CHAPTER SEVENTY-SEVEN: MOM

LEGACY AND MEMORIES

The greatest healing and the biggest acceptance came to me through some of Erin's friends she met while in rehab. I had briefly been introduced to a couple of people on our visits while Erin was in treatment, but I was so focused on her that I didn't really register their faces or remember their names. Her counselors and even some of the support staff told me she was a leader in offering exceptional peer support. The word of caution from her counselor was that she was giving so much of herself away that she had very little left to help herself. That was the epitome of my girl, generous to a fault and always looking after others before looking after herself. It was honorable but dangerous. All the advice given to her from staff, and from me, was met with kindness and polite listening but I could see that she was only biding her time until she could go and help someone else.

There are hard anniversaries when grieving for a loved one. I dreaded Christmas Day, Mother's Day, my birthday (because she always had a new, happy little painting for me... plus a huge hug) and I worked myself into a state of anxiety over her approaching birthday in June, nine months after her death. This would be the first one and I was at a loss for how to get through the day.

Erin had two Facebook accounts and I had successfully closed one because it was still under the name she had changed to in 2014. Her other account, under her original name, was proving to be a challenge to close. She had been in the process of changing back to her birth name again when she left for Edmonton, but I was unable to locate the legal documentation required by Facebook administration. It's not that I minded her original page still being up and accessible, as I treasured all her photos and posts, but it was the constant annual reminder that opened the hurt for me. "It's Erin Gray's birthday today! Help her celebrate!" I'd see that come up as a notification and I'd dissolve into tears of longing and loneliness. But I couldn't help myself; I'd go to her page and see birthday greetings from people who still did not know she was gone.

I had posted directly to her page a few weeks after her death, letting her online friends know about our loss and I received messages from a few people, expressing their shock and condolences. It was like balm for my ravaged soul to hear so many wonderful things said about how she had impacted their lives. To this day, usually on her birthday, I still receive messages from some of her friends who credit their lives to her help and support while they were in rehabilitation and recovery. For the first couple of years in grief, I would feel angry and resentful, wondering how this could possibly be. Someone who had saved lives by letting others lean on her solid support and made sure they were going to be safe—what kind of injustice was it that she should die? Why couldn't she have been one of the friends who had been saved rather than the friend who had saved others?

At the same time, I was so happy to hear the stories about how these friends of Erin's had gone on to stay clean and sober, establish successful careers, meet someone who loved them unconditionally, get married, and become mothers and fathers. These were all the things I had wanted for her. And all the things she had wanted for herself. But it wasn't meant to be. She was a vessel of hope, inspiration, and love that eventually became drained, and she was left empty with nothing remaining to take her into that life she had wished for.

It inspires me that her fan club is out there, thriving in their lives, and I am so proud of what my little girl did in her short life. With permission, the following are messages from two of the many people she had touched in her life.

Hayley F.

This was written to Erin as a post on Facebook while she was still alive:

Friends like Erin are one of the huge blessings that came out of my addiction. In the early days of recovery this girl was there for me and now over a year later she still is. I find such strength in friends like her. This made my day, going to the mailbox and finding a surprise gift box she had sent me. And along with all the amazing things in it, one of my favorite paintings of hers! What a talented girl! And as far as Reco (Hayley's dog) *goes, he loves his auntie more than ever right now. Thanks so much Erin for the love, strength, hope and friendship you show me time and time again. So thankful to call you a friend!*

And from Hayley to me, on learning that Erin had passed:

I have so many memories from that time that are still so fresh for me. One thing that will always stand out is how different your daughter was than so many other people I met during that time of my life. She had so much goodness and warmth and life in her still, despite all she had been through. She truly was a light to me during the darkest times of my life and she was such a beautiful soul. Erin's light will shine through, helping others in so many ways, the way she did while she was alive. Her friendship and presence in my life was huge during a time when I was so broken. When I think of her, I'll always think of the incredible light she had within her. Erin loved me and saw all the parts of me that weren't my addiction when I was actively trying to get out. Her friendship saw me through all the changes. Erin's story of what happened to her and what she endured was absolutely horrific, but that never stole the light she had and the compassion she had to come alongside other people suffering and love on them and help them see their worth and also see that they were not just the trauma that had happened to them. I'll forever be grateful for the time I had her beautiful friendship in my life.

Shawn K.

Erin was a passionate soul and had a flame in her spirit that I remember fondly. I remember her essence and her energy whenever she walked into a room. I would like to describe the energy that Erin had when she walked down the hallway, with her headphones on, her hood up, hands in her pockets and she walked with a swag [sic] *of confidence. It was a wonderful thing to see, I remember it fondly.*

There is a hope tree on the grounds of the treatment center where people place items in honor of loved ones who have passed away. I had a rock painted and placed under it in honor of Erin.

CHAPTER SEVENTY-EIGHT: MOM

THE ESSENCE OF ERIN

When Shawn wrote to me about the essence and energy that he saw in Erin, I held on to those words with my entire soul. This is what I had been trying to describe. The essence of Erin. There had been something about her from day one: her rapid and exuberant entrance into life; her high energy throughout her childhood; her desire to jump into absolutely everything with both feet; and how she gathered people, animals, flowers, and love to surround her and let all of it flow back, unfettered, unquestioned, limitless. She was, and still is in her spirit form, the very essence of love. Why she was dealt such harsh experiences in her younger years and again as a young woman, I'll never understand. But she left a grateful trail of vibrant, happy friends in her wake and that legacy will live on through generations that may never have been.

> Letter to Erin, My Sweet Child
>
> I still miss you, Erin, every minute of every day. I see the empty chair at the kitchen table and the empty space in the recent family photos that should have held your sunny, happy face. There is a piece missing in this world since you left, and I will always feel the absence of something incredible that was. I ache with the loneliness of not having you here. And sometimes it threatens to crush me under the weight of that profound absence. I dream of seeing you coming up the stairs, little ones in tow, and an adoring husband looking at you and your children with so much

love. I smile because I know you would keep him on his toes. Then I mourn what could have been again.

The fear, guilt, and regret for the loss of you and the loss of everything that could have been has left me feeling gutted and empty. My grief is a bottomless well and it is silent. The puzzle is complete but there is still a piece missing and it won't be found in this physical realm anymore. However, I can fill it with the bright colors you loved. These will be my happy memories of you. I am letting the world know of your existence, however short a time it was, and I am letting them know the incredible loving impact that you left on so many lives. You were amazingly talented, beautiful, kind, and loving. The essence of Erin will stay with everyone you encountered in your cut-short life.

Over and over again, I expect I'll have moments of utter devastation when certain words or images trigger me. But I commit to remembering all the good and, at the heart and soul of it, that is *you*, perhaps too good for this sometimes harsh and unforgiving world. I smile when I think of your complete, infectious joy of life. Your crazy belly laughs and sparkling blue eyes. I miss those parts so much.

I see you in your little green dress, ribbon in your silky blonde hair. I see you in your little jeans and white-with-red-stitching cowboy boots, your favorite footwear when you couldn't be barefoot. I see you jumping in the hay, leaping gleefully from the top of one huge round hay bale to another with no fear. I see your adoration for Grandpa and his for you. It's like he and Grandma knew your life would be short.

I need to be well—emotionally, mentally, and physically—to fulfill my promise to you and myself. I am letting go of that hard, dark lump of grief that has weighed me down so much. I am saying farewell to the pain, regret, guilt, and constant sadness. I need to keep embracing those good, happy memories and be what you epitomized: joy, energy, enthusiasm, zest for life, and limitless love. And then I can get it done in a way that honors you, saves me, and leaves a legacy.

Your strength inspires me. My butterfly, flitting contentedly from place to place without a care. And then someone and something broke your delicate wings. You fluttered and gained air again a few times, only to have the weight of life bring you down. But in the end, you found your own way to stay alight. Broken butterfly no more, you are once again flitting happily from flower to flower, energy to energy, spirit to spirit, landing gently on occasion where your light is needed.

I believe you would not want me to stay in this place of pain and unrelenting regret. That place of unforgiveness for my mistakes. So, I fight to do what is right in these moments, because I can't undo the past. I fight for you. For change. For knowledge and empowerment of others to give them hope for joy in life again, and maybe for ways to dull that agonizing pain of loss. Every day I will renew that fight to the surface, like a drowning victim who decides not to let go and sink into the watery grave below because it is too hard. And God knows, sometimes it feels too hard.

When you woke up from your coma in the hospital so many years ago now, you said "God has a plan for me." It didn't end like we thought it would, but this is where perhaps I pick up the reins you so gently placed down when you left this realm, and I will complete that plan for you. All I can do is commit to try.

So, I remember you with a full, open heart and lean on your spiritual guidance and strength. Then I can continue to work on my own trauma and grief recovery, living as fully as I can. The jagged edges of my grief have smoothed with time and with my tears. Like water slowly reshaping the stones, I have shifted, adjusted, and accepted my new course. At some point, this river of tears I have shed over the past dozen years will steer me toward the finish line at the ocean's edge. I'm not afraid. I understand this is part of life and I am grateful for even the hard things that will eventually lead me there. And I will revel in the sweet joy and love that was my girl. My once-broken butterfly. Whole again, and I will reach to wrap my arms around you.

I love you,
Mom

SHE DOES NOT LEAVE Celtic Poem by unknown author

She does not leave, she is not gone, she looks upon us still.
She walks among the valleys now; she strides upon the hill.
Her smile is in the summer sky, her grace is in the breeze.
Her light is in the winter snow, her tears are in the rain.
Her merriment runs in the brook, her laughter in the lane.
Her gentleness is in the flowers, her sigh in autumn leaves.
She does not leave, she is not gone, 'tis only we that grieve.

THE END

AFTERWORD

I learned more about trauma and addiction after Erin died than I did while she was still alive. You can't help but be thrown into a devouring need to learn how and why this happened, so once the obsession with treating the daily symptoms is gone, you only have your always-questioning grief to seek out the answers. My steep learning curve helped me realize that perhaps I could pass on my non-professional "pearls of wisdom" and it might change the course of things for someone I don't even know. Here is what I want to share:

Understand that addiction is pain. Telling your loved one to stop using drugs is like saying, "Stop being in pain." It is equivalent to telling the wind not to blow.

Use the line, "What can I do to help?" Even when I thought I was being supportive and loving, looking back now I may have come across more like Erin's judge and jury. If your loved one fights back, swears at you, or even tries to physically strike out, remember that addiction is pain. They are hearing that you want them to throw away the one thing that takes that pain away. This creates abject fear and fear equals anger.

Start by seeking help for your loved one's pain. And seek help and support for your own pain because watching them deconstruct before your very eyes creates its own unique and debilitating trauma. When your own fear for their life is turning into anger, remember this: no one wants to use drugs to decrease the mental and emotional pain they are in. Try to understand that they feel they have exhausted all options and there is no place to turn. Look again, try another option. Always be there even when they refuse. But, also, always make sure you are looking after your own mental and physical health. It's true that you can't fill a cup from an empty vessel.

Get involved with the fight to wake up health and government authorities. We all need to do better, and we absolutely have to push those that make decisions to do better too. Create a better understanding by telling people your story and enlisting their support. Trust me, lives depend on it.

And finally, let's pay attention and listen to the professionals who have actually lived the experience of trauma and addiction. As usual, life is the best teacher and if you haven't lived it, you don't understand or know it. We all have to start somewhere.

ACKNOWLEDGMENTS

I can't say enough about my closest friends and family who never wavered in their support—even when I was isolated and not wanting help. Thank you for your steadfast support in encouraging me to write about Erin's life. I needed all of that.

Al, you have been my rock. Pushing me to get this story written and doing everything you could to make space for me to do that.

Ryan, thank you for your insightful knowledge of the complicated twists and turns of writing a difficult story and getting it "out there." And for your steady, patient love to a mother who became absent when your sister left us. I'm back.

Erin, thank you for the chimes. For the gentle nudges during sleep and in the early morning hours. For the true nature of your goodness and kindness. You have definitely been my "cheerleader from the beyond" and I thank you from the bottom of my healing heart.

RESOURCES

Recommended reading and films:

Johann Hari. *Chasing the Scream. The First and Last Days of the War on Drugs.* Bloomsbury Publishing, 2015. **A history of the impact of drug criminalization.

Dr. Gabor Mate: "What is addiction?", https://www.filmsforaction.org/watch/what-is-addiction-gabor-mate. Films for Action, 2014. **A must-see short film.

Dr. Gabor Mate: *In The Realm of Hungry Ghosts: Close Encounters with Addiction.* Toronto: A.A. Knopf, 2008. **A book about real life addicts and the science behind why.

Dr. Gabor Mate: A film: https://thewisdomoftrauma.com. *The Wisdom of Trauma: Can Our Deepest Pain Be A Doorway to Healing?* SAND, Science And Nonduality, 2021.

Professor Bruce Alexander: *The Globalization of Addiction.* Oxford University Press, 2008. **A book about how globalization is leading to social dislocation and creating addiction as a substitute for what we are missing. Dr. Alexander is also the inventor of the well-known "Rat Park" experiment from the 1970s where he proved that isolation led to rats self-administering drugs in an effort to alleviate loneliness and detachment.

NEED SUPPORT?

Moms Stop The Harm: momsstoptheharm.com
Advocating for Change and Supporting Families Impacted by substance-use-related harms and deaths.

Holding Hope Canada: holdinghopecanada.org. *Support for individuals or families as they navigate helping a loved one who is using or have used substances.*

Healing Hearts Canada: healingheartscanada.org. *Free bereavement support for those grieving the loss of a loved one due to overdose or substance-use-related harms.*

ABOUT THE AUTHOR

Wanda Gray describes herself as an "unfortunate expert" in the world of trauma, addiction, and loss after being on the frontlines as a mother with a child who suffered from substance abuse caused by deep trauma. Gray belongs to *Moms Stop The Harm*, a network of Canadian families impacted by substance-use-related harms and deaths, and her writing has served as a form of cathartic therapy in short stories, articles, and now this book, *Broken Butterfly*.

Gray completed the creative writing program at the University of Saskatchewan and has been writing human interest articles for print and online publications for more than thirty years. She's a contributor to the online magazine *Life As A Human*, and teaches wellness and yoga. She lives in North Saanich, British Columbia, with her husband, where they share a two-family home with their son, daughter-in-law, and grandson, as well as three cats and a dog.

www.ingramcontent.com/pod-product-compliance
Lightning Source LLC
LaVergne TN
LVHW090752120625
813681LV00001B/60

* 9 7 8 1 0 3 8 3 3 2 0 4 2 *